The Decadent Dilemma

The Decadent Dilemma

R.K.R. Thornton

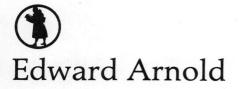

Edward Arnold

First published 1983 by
Edward Arnold (Publishers) Ltd
41 Bedford Square, London WC1B 3DQ

British Library Cataloguing in Publication Data

Thornton, R.K.R.
  The decadent dilemma.
  1. English literature——19th century——History and criticism
  2. Decadence (Literary movement)
  . I. Title
  820.9′008   PR469.D4

ISBN 0-7131-6372-0

Text set in 10/11 pt Paladium Compugraphic by Colset Private Limited, Singapore
Printed in Great Britain by Richard Clay (The Chaucer Press) Ltd, Bungay, Suffolk

The last time I saw Southey was on an evening at Taylor's, nobody there but myself; I think he meant to leave town next morning, and had wished to say farewell to me first. We sat on the sofa together; our talk was long and earnest; topic ultimately the usual one, steady approach of democracy, with revolution (probably explosive) and a finis incomputable to man; steady decay of all morality, political, social, individual; this once noble England getting more and more ignoble and untrue in every fibre of it, till the gold (Goethe's composite king) would all be eaten out, and noble England would have to collapse in shapeless ruin, whether for ever or not none of us could know. Our perfect consent on these matters gave an animation to the dialogue, which I remember as copious and pleasant. Southey's last word was in answer to some tirade of mine against universal mammon-worship, gradual accelerating decay of mutual humanity, of piety and fidelity to God or man, in all our relations and performances, the whole illustrated by examples, I suppose; to which he answered, not with levity, yet with a cheerful tone in his seriousness, 'It will not, and it cannot come to good!'

Reminiscences by Thomas Carlyle, ed. J.A. Froude (1881, written 1867), pp. 326–7

. . . works which minds drilled into conformity by repetitious university lectures lump together under the generic name of 'the Decadence'.

J.-K. Huysmans, *Against Nature*, trans. Robert Baldick (1959), p. 40

Contents

Preface

Many studies of the literature of the late nineteenth century in England have despaired of making sense of the term Decadence. Others have made attempts to define it, and yet others to extend its application either like Richard Gilman's *Decadence: the Strange Life of an Epithet* (1979) by seeing its use extending to modern problems. or by identifying elements which they choose to call Decadent and examining those features in literature and art of other periods.

My aim has been more modest: to catalogue what were the roots of the brief blossoming of Decadence as a movement in late-nineteenth-century England, letting the authors of the time speak for themselves where possible, and to examine the nature of the works of some of the writers central to that movement.

I have no expectation that this will be the last word on the subject, but I hope that the discussion of Decadence will be clearer for an account of how it grew, of what Decadence was for the 1890s, and what are the features of some literature and art called Decadent.

The publication of Jean Pierrot's *The Decadent Imagination: 1880–1900* came too late for me to do more than include it in the Bibliography; but I should say that it has much to add to my account and is essential reading for anyone wishing to understand the Decadence, particularly as it was seen in France.

1 The Climate of Decline

Aetas parentum peior avis tulit
nos nequiores, mox daturos
progeniem vitiosiorem.

(Horace's *Odes*, III, vi)

What goes up must come down.

Anyone who looks at the history of Decadence must soon be aware that an idea of decline is by no means confined to literature, and by no means confined to the nineteenth century. Decline is, after all, a necessary part of at least three major and distinctive types of theory about the nature of the universe and its history: first, that the world was created perfect, and subsequent variation is necessarily a decline; second, that the universe, or nation, or empire, or state (and so on) is an organism which has periods of infancy, growth, maturity and decline; and third, that the universe progresses in cycles which repeat either the decline from a repeatedly-made perfection, or the organic cycle of growth and decay.

There are numerous reviews of the prevalence and nature of such theories, often in conjunction with or as appendages to surveys of the idea of progress, as in J.B. Bury's *The Idea of Progress* (1920) or Arthur Lovejoy and George Boas's *Primitivism and Related Ideas in Antiquity* (1935, 1965). One of the most attractive surveys is in the early chapters of Koenraad W. Swart's study of *The Sense of Decadence in Nineteenth-Century France* (The Hague, 1964), which reminds us of ancient Indian beliefs in contemporary man's inferiority to his ancestors, before continuing through Mesopotamian, Mayan, Aztec, Greek, Roman, Jewish, Christian, medieval, Renaissance, Italian, Spanish, French, sixteenth- , seventeenth- , and eighteenth-century ideas of decline as a background to his examination of the sense of decline in nineteenth-century France. The subject is huge and not only would require but has required whole books to deal with it; and to embark on a full-scale history of the ideas of Decadence in general would change the nature of the book I wish to write. I do however wish to make it clear, as has not seemed clear to many writers on the late nineteenth century, that

Decadence in that period is a variant of a well-known theme and that its protean variety for the nineties may well be caused or intensified by its catching reflections from many times and many cultures. For this reason and to introduce some of the possible variations, let me glance at a selection of the more influential and intriguing expressions of the theme.

The Greeks and Romans stood firmly behind any Victorian's under-standing of his own society. 'It might seem ludicrous,' wrote Thomas Arnold in his *History of Rome* (4th edn 1845, I, p. x), 'to speak of impartiality in writing the history of remote times, did not those times really bear a nearer resemblance to our own than many imagine.' The glory that was Greece and the grandeur that was Rome suggested the increasing prosperity of the British Empire. Modern scholars and his-torians of ideas debate hotly whether the Greeks and Romans had any idea of progress at all (as is well summed up with useful bibliographical material in Ludwig Edelstein's *The Idea of Progress in Classical Antiquity*, Baltimore, 1967), but for the Victorian there was no such doubt. So convinced were the Victorians in fact that, as Edelstein rather too confidently says:

> other philosophies of history current among the Greeks and Romans were neglected until E. Rohde, in 1876, contrasted their progressive outlook to the theory of decay and insisted that the belief 'in a development *in peius*' had been more popular. Rohde wrote under the influence of that disillusionment with the progressivist creed which had begun to grip the *avant-garde* of European intellectuals, and he was strongly influenced by Nietzsche's discovery of the deep-seated pessimism of the Greeks – a pessimism Nietzsche extolled in contrast to the shallow optimism of his own century.   (p. xiii)

The idea of progress was, it is now generally agreed,

> missing from the oldest Greek literature. And when it did emerge it found the field already occupied by two great anti-progressive myths which threatened to strangle it at birth, the myth of the Lost Paradise – called by the Greeks 'the life under Kronos', by the Romans *Saturnia regna* or Golden Age – and the myth of Eternal Recurrence.
>
>   (E.R. Dodds, *The Ancient Concept of Progress*, 1973, p. 3)

Nobody has questioned, however, the ubiquity and antiquity of ideas of Decadence. Hesiod's gloomy view of the progressive decline through the ages of gold, silver, bronze and iron, with the age of Heroes inter-polated between the last two, set the tone and perhaps the terms of much nostalgic reference to a Golden Age, as H.C. Baldry suggests in 'Who· Invented the Golden Age?' (*Classical Quarterly* XLVI, 1952, pp. 83–92); Hesiod, it must be admitted, tended to confine himself to moral matters, and though degeneration might be accelerating, it was not uninterrupted. In his *Works and Days* the Old Testament tones ring out:

> Thereafter, would that I were not among the men of the fifth generation, but either had died before or been born afterwards. For now truly is a race of iron, and men never rest from labour and sorrow by day, and from perishing by night; and the gods shall lay sore trouble upon them.   (lines 174–8)

Homer equally, by depicting so powerfully a past heroic age, emphasized the associated idea of the decline of the present. Indeed the lines commonly held to be the first classical intimation of an idea of progress are by Xenophanes, a bitter opponent of Hesiod and Homer (see W.K.C. Guthrie's *In the Beginning*, 1957, p. 82; Dodds, p. 4; Edelstein, p. 1). Empedocles's view of the world saw the four primary substances brought together by Love or separated by Strife, and for him the force of Love was being displaced by Strife. Plato, claimed rather improbably by Edelstein as having a 'tragic optimism' which qualifies him as a believer in progress, seems on the contrary doomed by the theory of Forms to seeing mankind as always inadequately imitating a perfect model. Whatever view one takes as to who believed in, and with what details, the Great Year and its implications of decline – Plato, Aristotle, Heraclitus, the Stoics, the Pythagoreans – one can assent to J.B Bury's summary that 'the theory of world-cycles was so widely current that it may be described as the orthodox theory of cosmic time among the Greeks, and it passed from them to the Romans' (*The Idea of Progress*, p. 12). The most frequent adjunct to a theory of world-cycles was that the present age was towards the end.

Two simple reasons for the idea of decline among the Greeks being important to the Victorians were that the public school and Oxbridge system emphasized the Classics and that the Greek world could provide, as W.K.C. Guthrie remarks in his *In the Beginning* (1957, p. 13), 'a microcosm, a small-scale working model of human society in all its phases.' Richard Jenkyns in his lively and rewarding *The Victorians and Ancient Greece* (1980) explores more fully what the Greeks meant to the Victorians. None the less, the decline and fall of the Roman Empire is more central to the late-nineteenth-century's concerns, the very idea of Empire bringing it more strongly home to the ambitious and expansive age.

It is perhaps the Greek Polybius who first suggests the Decadence of Rome in the second century BC in the words of Scipio at the destruction of Carthage: 'I have a dread foreboding that some day the same doom will be pronounced upon my own country' (*Polybius the Histories*, trans. W.R. Paton, Loeb Classical Library, 1927, VI, p. 437). Cicero, though living in the period characterized by Florus as 'iuventus imperii et quasi robusta maturitas' – the manhood and, as it were, the robust maturity of the empire – picks up the thread for, although we may question his impartiality when in the first passage of his first speech against Catiline he rhetorically bewails 'O tempora, o mores!', he is elsewhere more soberly aware of Rome's decline. So too with Lucretius and, wherever one stands in the debate on whether he was primitivist or progressivist, it is simple to see where many Victorians stood with regard to Lucretius by looking at Matthew Arnold's verdict in his essay 'On the Modern Element in Literature'. There the features with which one becomes familiar in later discussions of Decadence are found in Lucretius:

> The predominance of thought, of reflection, in modern epochs is not without its penalties, in the unsound, in the over-tasked, in the over-sensitive, it has produced the most painful, the most lamentable results; it has produced a state of feeling unknown to less enlightened but perhaps healthier epochs – the feeling of depression, the feeling of *ennui*. Depression and *ennui*; these are the characteristics stamped on how many of the representative works of modern times! They are also the characteristics stamped on the poem of Lucretius.
> (*Complete Prose Works I*, 1960, ed. R.H Super, p. 32)

It is the morals as well as the spirit which Sallust describes in the first century BC. In his *The War with Catiline* (v. 9) he says that he must follow his account of the greatness of the institutions and the commonwealth of his forefathers with an account of 'how by gradual changes it has ceased to be the noblest and best, and has become the worst and most vicious.' Livy, anxious to point out the edifying lessons of history and in particular to praise morality and discipline, quickly tells the reader of his *Ab Urbe Condita*, which was to become a standard source book for later historians, that he should 'note how, with the gradual relaxation of discipline, morals first gave way, as it were, then sank lower and lower, and finally began the downward plunge which has brought us to the present time, when we can endure neither our vices nor their cure.' Seneca, too stoic to despair at adversity, assumes none the less that the world declines (as in *Ad Polybium; De Consolatione*). And Tacitus's *Annals* contain what Lovejoy and Boas call 'a typical expression of the three-phase theory of the general course of political history' (p. 97), which is a theory of decline. Florus in his *Epitome* (I, introduction) imitated the elder Seneca in dividing Roman history into four periods of organic development, namely childhood, adolescence, maturity and age, and there were frequent echoes of his interpretation since the work enjoyed a somewhat undeserved reputation until the seventeenth century. Marcus Aurelius, whose *Meditations* were so dear to Pater and through him well known to the late Victorians, writes of 'the periodic destructions and rebirths of the universe' (XI, p. 1). The decline and fall of the Roman Empire, assisted and defined (some would argue created) by Gibbon in particular, formed an example and a model against which many later historians would view their own empire in decline; and the corruptions of the declining Empire became a dreadful warning.

The lament at a decline from a golden age is of course a commonplace of literature, with the *ubi sunt* theme running strongly from Horace to Hardy with many a *'Gaudeamus Igitur'* or 'The Wanderer' between. In Teutonic mythology even the gods are subject to decline and Wagner, who was to become something of an enthusiasm for some late-nine-teenth-century writers, firmly grasped at the notions of the Twilight of the Gods and the Ring.

Christian thought shares the idea of catastrophe beyond which is a purified world, an idea strong in millenialist thinking but not only there. Norman Cohn, for example, opens his *The Pursuit of the Millenium* with the generalization that 'Christianity has always had an eschatology, in the sense of a doctrine concerning "the last times", or "the last days" or "the final state of the world"; and Christian millenarialism was simply one variant of Christian eschatology.' Certainly the literature of the medieval period is amply supplied with examples of gloomy views of the state of the world, and Archbishop Wulfstan's pessimistic forecasts find many a subsequent counterpart, right up to Billy Graham, evangelist, who repeats the old lie in the popular press: 'history conclusively teaches that the decay of a nation inevitably follows the decay of its sex standards' (*Reader's Digest*, August 1970).

In 1577 Louis Le Roy, a French classical scholar and in his arguments an ancestor of Désiré Nisard (for whom see the next chapter), wrote a book attempting to draw lessons from the past, *De la vicissitude ou variété des choses en l'univers*. Its fears of decline are typical:

> If the memory of the past is the instruction of the future, it is to be feared that having reached so great excellence, power, wisdom, studies, books, industries will decline, as has happened in the past, and disappear – confusion succeeding to the order and perfection of today, rudeness to civilization, ignorance to knowledge. I already foresee in imagination nations, strange in form, complexion and costume, overwhelming Europe – like the Goths, Huns, Vandals, Lombards, Saracens of old – destroying our cities and palaces, burning our libraries, devastating all that is beautiful. I foresee in all countries wars, domestic and foreign, factions and heresies that will profane all things human and divine; famine, plagues, and floods;

the universe approaching an end, world-wide confusion, and the
return of things to their original chaos.
(Quoted in *The Idea of Progress*, pp. 46–7)

The rhetorical flourish of the central part of this passage is the stock-in-
trade of the modern racist politician, but it also reminds us that
Shakespeare's plays, particularly the histories, are always conscious of
the last-day-like disintegration and chaos beneath the fragilely held
order. Le Roy claimed that, since Providence determines whether or not
an argument from the past is valid, these things need not happen; the
same argument was followed by Arthur Balfour in his *Decadence* which
was given as the Henry Sidgwick Memorial lecture at Newnham
College in 1908. Balfour suggested that the things which threatened
Rome might also be threatening the British Empire, but he was able to
hope that his time will be the exception and that 'we can escape the fate
to which other races have had to submit' (p. 42).

Francis Bacon believed that he lived in the old age of the world, so
retaining an idea of decline while asserting the value of his own period.
The idea is also present in Descartes, Malebranche, Arnauld, and
Nicole (see Bouillier's *Histoire de la philosophie cartésienne*), and
Pascal too compares man in general to a single man who is now in his
old age. Desmarets de Saint Sorlin, in J.B. Bury's words which remind
us of Yeats's autumnal image, maintained that 'Antiquity was not so
happy or so learned or so rich or so stately as the modern age, which is
really the mature old age, and as it were the autumn of the world'
(p. 82). Whichever side won the 'Battle of the Books' would have a
theory of decline, either having *declined from* a golden age, or man
having *reached* maturity or old age. Even when Charles Perrault took
over the championship of the Modern from Saint Sorlin, and congratu-
lated himself in his *Parallèle des anciens et des modernes* (1688–96) that
his age had arrived at perfection and that he need not envy future
generations because progress had slowed down as the days ceased to
lengthen near the solstice, the times may not have been degenerate, but
they were near the old age of the world.

Many French writers argued about the causes of Decadence in an
empire or a great country. Rousseau claimed that Decadence was the
result of an opposition to natural laws and of man's over-civilization.
Bossuet had explained, as many Victorians were to explain, that Decadence came from an enfeeblement of religious beliefs and a consequent
decline in moral standards, and was a direct punishment from God.
Montesquieu, whose *Considérations sur les causes de la grandeur des
Romains et de leur décadence* (1734) gave the word a wider currency in
scholarly circles in France and abroad, blamed political institutions and
material luxury for the Decadence. German theorists contended that

climate and racial characteristics were determining factors. By far the most widespread theory was simply that which assumed that Decadence is an inescapable part of the law of things, that whatever exists must grow, decline and die.

Of course, the nineteenth century saw a characteristic move in the opposite direction, seeing progress as its typical feature. Macaulay conveniently sums up the attitude in its most brassy form, as in the proud boasts of his review of Sir James Mackintosh's *History of the Revolution in England*:

> seeing that, by the confession of the most obstinate enemies of innovation, our race has hitherto been almost constantly advancing in knowledge, and not seeing any reason to believe that, precisely at the point of time at which we came into the world, a change took place in the faculties of the human mind, or in the mode of discovering truth, we are reformers: we are on the side of progress. From the great advances which European society has made, during the last four centuries, in every species of knowledge, we infer, not that there is no more room for improvement, but that, in every science which deserves the name, immense improvements may be confidently expected.

In a similar paragraph beginning with the confident assertion that 'The history of England is emphatically the history of progress', Macaulay notes the great strides from a 'wretched and degraded race' to 'the most highly civilised people the world ever saw', with vast empires and skills beyond the belief of the ancients. This race, he says,

> have carried the science of healing, the means of locomotion and correspondence, every mechanical art, every manufacture, every thing that promotes the convenience of life, to a perfection which our ancestors would have thought magical, have produced a literature which may boast of works not inferior to the noblest which Greece has bequeathed to us, have discovered the laws which regulate the motions of the heavenly bodies, have speculated with exquisite subtilty on the operations of the human mind, have been the acknowledged leaders of the human race in the career of political improvement. The history of England is the history of this great change in the moral, intellectual, and physical state of the inhabitants of our own island. There is much amusing and instructive episodical matter; but this is the main action.

Macaulay's exuberant optimism of 1835 was hard to dampen, but the erosion of the idea of progress in the nineteenth century can be epitomized in a footnote to Macaulay's hugely successful *The History of*

England (1848). Macaulay's footnote in the 1857 edition boasts that

> During the interval which has elapsed since this chapter was written
> England has continued to advance rapidly in material prosperity. I
> have left my text nearly as it originally stood; but I have added a few
> notes which may enable the reader to form some notion of the
> progress which has been made during the last nine years; and in
> general, I would desire him to remember that there is scarcely a
> district which is not more populous, or a source of wealth which is
> not more productive, at present than in 1848.

T.F. Henderson, the editor of the 1907 edition, added a note which
suggests the change in the second half of the nineteenth century, and the
despair at abandoning the hopes, or rather the confident expectations,
of the mid-century: 'England has almost doubled her population and
wealth since Macaulay wrote; but had Macaulay been now alive, he
would hardly have written so boastfully of England's superiority to
other nations, either morally or materially' (p. 74).

In 1918 Spengler's *Der Untergang des Abendlandes* massively denied
the progress of the present. Beginning, like Vico before him and Arnold
Toynbee after, by comparing modern western civilization with the
civilization of the Greco-Roman world, he asked

> Is it possible to find in life itself – for human history is the sum of
> mighty life-courses which already have had to be endowed with ego
> and personality, in customary thought and expression, by predicat-
> ing entities of a higher order like 'the Classical' or 'the Chinese
> Culture', 'Modern Civilization' – a series of stages which must be
> traversed, and traversed moreover in an ordered and obligatory
> sequence? For everything organic the notions of birth, death, youth,
> age, lifetime are fundamentals – may not these notions in this
> sphere also, possess a rigorous meaning which no one has as yet
> extracted? In short, is all history founded upon general biographic
> archetypes?   (*The Decline of the West*, 1961, p. 29)

For him it most emphatically was, and he applied his biographic arche-
types to history and came up with the gloomy forecast that the West
had passed through its period of 'culture' to a position where the future
could only be decline.

It is not through lack of example that I bring to an end this selection of
comments on theories of decline. Its purpose is merely to suggest the
background and to show that it is not in its philosophical basis that we
will understand the distinctness of the late-nineteenth-century
Decadence. Writers at the time recognized this point; even the
comically intense Max Nordau, whose *Degeneration* (English transla-

tion 1895) listed the characteristic features of the degenerate writers of his day in a way that seemed to demonstrate he was himself degenerate, pointed it out:

> In our days there have arisen in more highly-developed minds vague qualms of a Dusk of the Nations, in which all suns and all stars are gradually waning, and mankind with all its institutions and creations is perishing in the midst of a dying world.
>
> It is not for the first time in the course of history that the horror of world-annihilation has laid hold of men's minds. (p. 2)

The sources of the decline were of course different, and the irony of that decline when set against the conventional Victorican ideas of progress is an important feature. John A. Lester's notion of a *Journey Through Despair*, tracing the sense of frustration of the imagination by those very material developments which represented progress to Macaulay, highlights that clash, and he finds a clear expression of the note of the late nineteenth century in Grant Allen's summary of it: 'deep-questioning, mystic, uncertain, rudderless: faith gone; humanity left: heaven lost; earth realised as man's, the home and sole hope for the future' (p. 4). Max Nordau, with no sympathy at all for writers and one suspects precious little for literature, saw the *fin-de-siècle* mood as 'the impotent despair of a sick man, who sees himself dying by inches in the midst of an eternally living nature blooming insolently for ever' (p. 3). The situation may not have been new, but it was powerfully felt.

Theories of decline, then, are not confined to the late nineteenth century; nor are theories of Decadence solely literary notions. Indeed, the popularity of the term in the late nineteenth century in England may well be explained by the fact that it was felt to express something that was true of society as well as of literature. Like our own vogue words – 'permissive' or 'punk' for example – it crystallized an attitude and could refer to many aspects of society.

In the most superficial way, there was a sense of an ending in the approach to the end of the century, which combined with the sense of the ending of the reign of Queen Victoria. One does not need a Max Nordau to point out that the first is a mere convention of numbering and the second an accident of longevity, but Nordau recognized that there was in the popular mind a consciousness of the *fin-de-siècle*, however unreasonable it might be. The popularity of that term grew alongside the popularity of Decadence, so that *Punch* on 29 August 1891 was calling for a 'word-slayer' to kill off 'that pest-term' *fin-de-siècle*; from their subsequent use of it, one gathers they did not find one.

Nordau's views were not merely about literature. In a powerful piece of rhetoric which calls Yeats's 'The Second Coming' to mind, he wrote that

One epoch of history is unmistakably in its decline, and another is announcing its approach. There is a sound of rending in every tradition, and it is as though the morrow would not link itself with today. Things as they are totter and plunge, and they are suffered to reel and fall, because man is weary, and there is no faith that it is worth an effort to uphold them. Views that have hitherto governed minds are dead or driven hence like disenthroned kings, and for their inheritance they that hold the titles and they that would usurp are locked in struggle. Meanwhile interregnum in all its terrors prevails. (pp. 5–6)

Nordau merely popularized and extended in a less scientific way the views of Cesare Lombrose, but even Lombroso was willing to contribute an article on 'Atavism and Evolution' to the *Contemporary Review* in July 1895 in which he said that

It is a prevalent delusion of our times that we are always progressing. We picture progress to ourselves as an endless line leading straight up to heaven, without any turnings, and imagine our own white races at the top of the line, attaining by a continuous rise to immeasurable heights of civilisation. But a little calm observation quickly shows how great is the illusion of this view. Progress there certainly is in some nations, not so much in morality . . . nor even in religion. . . . All the same, an attentive consideration reveals the fact that, even among the most privileged peoples, the line of movement, far from being vertical, is always describing reactionary curves and winding ways; is varied by backward movements, just as in the case of individuals we meet with points of recurrence to atavism.   (p. 42)

He went on to explain his view that genius is a 'form of neurotic degeneration' and listed some of the signs of regressive atavism common to genius, of which the most interesting for this study are a 'callousness extending even to moral insanity, . . . in many cases an interchange of sexual characteristics (absence of beard, &c.), above all, very commonly perverse, degenerate, or ignorant children' (p. 46). Confusion of sexual characteristics or sexual roles is a mainstay of accusations of Decadence, whether in seventeenth-century Spain (see Swart, p. 26), nineteenth-century England, or today.

The nineteenth century had of course a new metaphor for progress in the Darwinian theory of evolution, and the tendency was to assume that evolution and progress were synonymous. This is not so, and popularizations of the opposite possibility meant that in the later nineteenth century there was not quite the same naïveté about ideas of evolution. Professor E. Ray Lankester, for example, published in 1880 a book in the Nature Series called *Degeneration. A Chapter in*

Darwinism. In it he described and gave examples of degenerative evolution, widening his discussion from zoological examples to examples of degenerate language and degenerate civilizations:

> With regard to ourselves, the white races of Europe, the possibility of degeneration seems to be worth some consideration. In accordance with a tacit assumption of universal progress – an unreasoning optimism – we are accustomed to regard ourselves as necessarily progressing, as necessarily having arrived at a higher and more elaborate condition than that which our ancestors reached, and as destined to progress still further. On the other hand, it is well to remember that we are as subject to the general laws of evolution, and are as likely to degenerate as to progress. As compared with the immediate forefathers of our civilisation – the ancient Greeks – we do not appear to have improved so far as our bodily structure is concerned, nor assuredly so far as some of our mental capacities are concerned. Our powers of perceiving and expressing beauty of form have certainly *not* increased since the days of the Parthenon and Aphrodite of Melos. In matters of the reason, in the development of the intellect, we may seriously inquire how the case stands. Does the reason of the average man in civilised Europe stand out clearly as an evidence of progress when compared with that of the men of bygone ages? Are all the inventions and figments of human superstition and folly, the self-inflicted torturing of mind, the reiterated substitution of wrong for right, and of falsehold for truth, which disfigure our modern civilisation – are these evidences of progress? In such respects we have at least reason to fear that we may be degenerate.
>
> (pp. 59–60)

Like many another writer who discovers degeneration, he had his formula for preventing it, in his case the full and earnest cultivation of Science.

Eugenicists too saw degeneration around them. Francis Galton, the most popular, the man who introduced the word eugenics in his *Inquiries into Human Faculty* (1883), had the explanation in the breed. In his *Hereditary Genius: An Inquiry into its Laws and Consequences* (1869), he recorded his belief that the rapid rise of the new colonies and the decay of old civilizations was 'due to their respective social agencies, which in the one case promote, and in the other case retard, the marriages of the most suitable breeds' (p. 361). The old fear of the barbarians at the gate become for Galton almost a hope:

> there is a constant tendency of the best men in the country to settle in the great cities, where marriages are less prolific and children are less likely to live. Owing to these several causes, there is a steady check in

an old civilization upon the fertility of the abler classes; the improv-
ident and unambitious are those who chiefly keep up the breed. So
the race gradually deteriorates, becoming in each successive
generation less fitted for a high civilization, although it retains the
external appearances of one, until the time comes when the whole
political and social fabric caves in, and a greater or less relapse to
barbarism takes place, during the reign of which the race is perhaps
able to recover its tone.   (p. 362)

Perversely, Galton's ideas about the 'disastrous institution' of the
peerage and its 'destructive effects on our valuable races' read rather
like material for *A Rebours*; his arguments are often sloppy and there
was a good deal of strong challenge to his views, but even a critic like
Francis Lloyd, who published *A Scientific View of Mr. Francis Galton's
Theories of Heredity* in 1876, bears witness to his popularity.

In the field of medical science there was concern at the increase of
insanity. That very phrase, 'The Increase of Insanity', was the title of an
article in the *Fortnightly Review*; and when Dr William Hirsch published his *Genius and Degeneration* (1896) in reply to Max Nordau's
book, C.L. Dana reviewed it in *Science* on 5 March 1897 with these
points:

The question at issue is in reality simply this: whether there are or are
not more neuropathic people per hundred of the population now
than a century or two centuries ago. We confess to the opinion that
there is now more of this neuropathic constitution. The statistics of
crime, alcoholism, insanity and nervous diseases; the fact that a
larger proportion of the population are brain workers living on a
higher mental plane than in former times; the diffusion of syphilis,
the stimulating influences of modern civilisation, the press, the tele-
graph, the railroad; the gradual increase of urban at the expense of
rural populations, all justify this position, which I believe only a
blind or sentimental optimism can deny.   (pp. 40–6)

It was, then, the scientific world as well as the literary which thought of
nerves as the modern malady. And Havelock Ellis, a man who provides
a link between science and literature in the late years of the century,
joined his fellow-scientists in seeing a change, though seeing it as a
move to the new as well as a losing of the old. He admitted in *The New
Spirit* (3rd edn 1892) that 'Certainly old things are passing away; not the
old ideals only, but even the regret they leave behind is dead, and we are
shaping instinctively our new ideals' (p. 33).

The rise of socialism also, to some a new force, was to others a suggestion of decline. In France in 1850, Ledru-Rollin published a book *De
la décadence de l'Angleterre*, which pointed to the growing discontent

among the workers with a system depending on uncertain world markets. The aristocracy was losing its control over the people, he argued, who would soon repeat the Decadent process by becoming the barbarians who would overrun the cultured but weak Empire. The strikes, riots, and the increasing strength of the workers in the later years of the century seemed to bear him out. Writers of the nineties, though predominantly middle class, were well aware of the socialist movements and were often associated with them, Shaw, Barlas, Ernest Radford, Davidson, for example.

There was unquestionably a decline in agriculture, a decline whose effect in literature can be seen most strongly in Hardy, who wrote specifically about the decline in Rider Haggard's *Rural England* (1902). The population in towns increased while the population in the country declined both in numbers and in wealth. Foreign competition, new inventions which made foreign products cheaper both to harvest and transport, an economic policy which refused to protect the British farmer, all combined to shake British agriculture.

It is probably too difficult to be precise about such a slippery concept as moral decline, although there were many who complained of immorality, not only that of the writers. But every age will find its Mrs Grundy or its Mrs Whitehouse and the late nineteenth century was no exception. More tangible and more significant, one can find those who combined moral with practical campaigns against what was undoubtedly a desperate situation. General William Booth of the Salvation Army saw England as in a very bad state. His analysis of the situation and his suggestions for its cure were published in 1890 as *In Darkest England and the Way Out*, where he asserted that one tenth of the population was destitute.

> Talk about Dante's Hell, and all the horrors and cruelties of the torture-chamber of the lost! The man who walks with open eyes and with bleeding heart through the shambles of our civilisation needs no such fantastic images of the poet to teach him horror.   (p. 13)

Not everyone liked Booth or his ways, but even his strongest opponents like T.H. Huxley did not disagree with his starting point. Huxley's reply to Booth, *Social Diseases and Worse Remedies* (1891), still sees the decay of civilization although he disagreed with Booth's remedies of establishing colonies at home and overseas:

> There are one or two points upon which I imagine all thinking men have arrived at the same convictions as those from which Mr. Booth starts. It is certain that there is an immense amount of remediable misery among us; that, in addition to the poverty, disease and degradation, which are the consequences of causes beyond human

control, there is a vast, probably a very much larger, quantity of misery which is the result of individual ignorance, or misconduct, and of faulty social arrangements. Further, I think it is not to be doubted that, unless this remediable misery is effectually dealt with, the hordes of vice and pauperism will destroy modern civilization as effectually as uncivilized tribes of another kind destroyed the great social organization which precede [*sic*] ours.   (p. 53)

A careful scientist like Lombroso, Huxley reminded his readers that evolution was not a 'constant tendency to increased perfection. . . . Retrogressive is as practicable as progressive metamorphosis' (p. 17).

In short, then, the idea of decline reached into many different areas of Victorian thought: general theories of population and the degeneration of races; socialism and the rise of the lower classes; the decline of British agriculture; the terrible condition of the poorest people in the country; evolutionary theories; theories of mental health; and the increasingly pressing question of belief, religion and morality. There was a ready situation into which to introduce a literature calling itself Decadent. The analogies were obviously ready, many of the criticisms already implicit, the basic ground of the debate set out, and the country prepared to respond eagerly to the idea of Decadence, which fuses together so many of the time's fears and anxieties.

2 The Idea of Decadence in France to 1900

It is seemingly perverse, but none the less accurate, to look for many of the roots of English Decadence in France. 'One had in the late eighties and early nineties,' said Victor Plarr in his book on *Ernest Dowson* (1914), 'to be preposterously French' (p. 22). British writers and artists of the time have particularly strong links with France. Charles Conder, William Rothenstein, Aubrey Beardsley, essentially different in character and technique, yet have this in common. Dowson spent much of his life in France, much of his education was there, and his equally irregular profession of translation kept him sharply aware of French literature. Wilde exiled himself to France and died there, though the nation in honour of whose artistic freedom he had written *Salomé* in French proved less friendly than he had hoped.

Arnold with his praise of the French spirit, and Swinburne with his French poems and enthusiasms, had set recent examples. Morris, particularly for her Gothic architecture, and Rossetti, if only for the poems of Villon, were also lovers of France. Ruth Z. Temple has examined the process of introducing French ideas into England in *The Critic's Alchemy* (1953), and has shown that it is not only the writers of the nineties who derived clearly from French models. James K. Robinson also suggests a longer tradition when he writes in *PMLA* in 1953 of an early period of aestheticism in England, with

> its ambiguous beginnings in Morris and Swinburne, its dependence on the theory of Gautier, the practice of Banville and those early French poets whom he popularised – Ronsard, Marot, Charles d'Orléans and, especially, Villon; its definite beginnings with critics like Besant and Saintsbury, translators like Rossetti, Payne and Lang; to its flowering in a Parnassian cult of fixed French forms, headed by Austin Dobson, and a vogue of Villon translation, climaxing in the work of Payne. This phase of aestheticism, extending from the late sixties to the early eighties, was preoccupied with expression as the chief justification of a work of art. It led naturally to the more extreme aestheticism of the nineties, which not merely

emphasised form but also scouted any work which did not exist for
that work's sake only.   (p. 733)

These English Parnassians, Payne, Dobson, Gosse, Stevenson, and
especially Lang, created a background of interest in French poetry and
poetic theory both by imitation and enthusiastic reporting. George
Moore added his reports of artistic developments in France, a task
taken over to a large extent by Arthur Symons, whose ideas were significantly altered by his visits to Paris. John Gray carried the nineties love
of translation so far that his book of poems *Silverpoints* is almost
swamped by them. The most blatant example of pro-French feeling was
shown by Richard Gallienne, who introduced a fashionable 'Le' into his
name, as if to continue the rôle of parody of current trends which he
acted out in his verse and dress. Max Nordau thought that the aristocra-
tic additions which the writers Barbey d'Aurevilly and Villiers de l'Isle
Adam made to their names were the sign of a degenerate mind.

It was also the habit to call new movements by French names. When
Arthur Mackmurdo's famous chair had inaugurated a new style in pure
and applied art, the Italians would call it *Stile Liberty* to indicate its
English origin, but the English called it *Art Nouveau*. The name in
various countries demonstrates the Janus-like movement's ability to be
seen as simultaneously Decadence and Renaissance; the Viennese called
it *Sezessionstil*, the Germans *Jugendstil*, in Catalan it was *Modernista*,
in Paris the 'Modern Style'. Though the French might derive from
England in the matter of design, the English looked to France in art and
literature. *Vers libre*, which Arthur Symons talks of in his article on
'The Decadent Movement in Literature' in 1893 (27 years before the first
instance recorded by the *OED*, though perhaps not himself the first to
use it), had been developed in France as a natural extension of breaking
rigid forms and, although there had been much metrical experimenta-
tion in England – Symons was thinking primarily of Henley's – it was
the French term which caught the spirit of the period.

Decadence, then, though pruned to an English shape and grafted on
to English stock, has roots in France, and the extent of the French
background can be seen very fully dealt with in Alfred Edward Carter's
book on *The Idea of Decadence in French Literature 1830–1900*
(Toronto, 1958). I do not propose to go over that well-covered ground,
but to follow the history of the word in French and then to follow it in
English, suggesting during the latter what links there are between the
two.

As I said in the last chapter, Decadence was nothing new in the nineteenth century, and the patterns of decline and fall of ancient
civilizations – usually Rome, although Egypt and other civilizations
were available – were at the base of much criticism. Rémy de

Gourmont, the leading Symbolist critic, summarized the view of the late nineteenth century:

> A great many commonplaces have an historic origin. One day two ideas became united under the influence of events, and this union proved more or less lasting. Having seen with its own eyes the death-struggle of Byzantium, Europe coupled these two ideas, Byzantium-Decadence, which became a commonplace. . . . From Byzantium, this association of ideas was extended to the whole Roman Empire, which is now, for sage and respectable historians, nothing but a series of decadences. . . . This commonplace, of Christian origin, has been popularized, in modern times, as everyone knows, by Montesquieu and Gibbon.
>
> (*Decadence and other Essays*, trans. W.A. Bradley, 1922, pp. 8–9)

There was a widespread interest in a general cultural, social, political decadence, but I wish to narrow down the field to literary Decadence and to begin in the 1830s.

It was then that critics of the new Romantic literature attacked it in the name of Classicism, and writers began to view Decadent civilizations not with alarm but with envy; so that Koenraad Swart can see this as a new departure:

> Their unconventional and partly perverse mentality, repudiating traditional morality, rejecting all social restraints, defying society, and taking a morbid delight in corruption, obviously constituted a radical reversal of almost all earlier attitudes towards historical decline. It was this consciously adopted ideology of Satanism, individualism, and estheticism that formed the most important legacy of French Romanticism to the so-called Decadent movement in literature at the end of the nineteenth century. (p. 77)

Eighteen thirty-four will stand as the turning point. It was in that year that Désiré Nisard published his *Etudes de moeurs et de critique sur les poëtes latins de la décadence*. Once a Romanticist himself, Nisard obviously feared the revolutionary and individualistic tendencies of Romanticism (the first edition of 1834 follows the revolution of 1830 and the second edition of 1849 follows the revolution of 1848), and his study of the age of Lucan led him to a comparison with contemporary poets. He admitted that there were differences: the present age had for example more new subjects for poetry:

> Le malaise de la société, le manque de discipline religieuse, la maladie du doute, les ardeurs politiques, une immense liberté de désirer, d'ambitionner, de sentir, d'envier, et presque nulle proportion entre ce qu'on peut et ce qu'on veut; un raffinement d'intelligence qui

augmente les besions; le mal des meilleurs choses, de la liberté, de l'égalité, de la paix, biens humains, donc biens imparfaits; tous les divers aspects de notre société ont donné matière à d'ingénieuses et poétiques analyses des souffrances des âmes.

(2nd edn II, pp. 310–11)

And whereas Rome's Decadence had been an illness cured by the barbarians, that of France had been cured by herself, because of which this true contemporary of Macaulay thought that 'Nous valons, grâce à eux, mieux que nos pères' (p. 315). Nisard was delighted that France had gained strength from what enervates nations, youth from what kills them, and, like all critics who attempt to combine optimism with Decadence, he found that for the France of his day 'la loi des décadences des empires a eu tort pour la première fois' (p. 315). This happiness was, however, only in the political sphere, for he saw that there had indeed been a literary Decadence. His lists of similarities between the Romans and his contemporaries almost set the pattern for later definitions of Decadent literature: a love of erudition and of description which, especially in combination, suggest an insignificance of subject, and 'dans ces descriptions, même intempérance de détails, même recherche des nuances, même esprit de mots, mêmes subtilités, mêmes exagérations, et parmi les exagérations même préférence pour le laid' (p. 316). Further,

Ici et là, à chaque instant, des mots vagues et généraux, que les lois du mètre déterminent, et non le besoin de la pensée.

Ici et là, de laborieux efforts de style pour dissimuler des idées très-communes; et à côté, des negligences choquantes; nul souci de la propriété des mots, avec la prétention de n'employer que le mot propre.

Des deux parts, même abondance d'images; même profusion de métaphores boiteuses; même monotonie; même abus des synonymes, et surtout même manière d'aiguiser le trait, de le réserver pour la fin, de le préparer à l'avance, en y sacrifiant tout ce qui précède.   (p. 317)

Nisard was worried by Hugo's breaking of classical rules to express new ideas, disturbing the alexandrine and enlarging the vocabulary, and he criticized the individualism and lack of popular base of the poetry of his day. When Pater had restated the imprisonment of the individual in his own isolation, this might seem to be the only proper way open to poetry. But it is not the Romantics of Nisard's day that are of interest here so much as the fact that he had provided the specific connection between Decadent Romans and modern poetry, which was turned into praise rather than blame by Gautier and Baudelaire.

It was in 1834 that Gautier published *Mademoiselle de Maupin*, with the Chevalier d'Albert looking to ancient Rome for relief, but what was implicit or partially explicit in Gautier's early work is most clearly stated in that crucial definition of the Decadent style – his 'Notice' to Baudelaire's *Les fleurs du mal* in 1868 (I use the translation from Max Nordau's *Degeneration*):

> The style of decadence . . . is nothing else than art arrived at that extreme point of maturity produced by those old civilizations which are growing old with their oblique suns – a style that is ingenious, complicated, learned, full of shades of meaning and research, always pushing further the limits of language, borrowing from all the technical vocabularies, taking colours from all palettes, notes from all keyboards, forcing itself to express in thought that which is most ineffable, and in form the vaguest and most fleeting contours; listening, that it may translate them, to the subtle confidences of the neuropath, to the avowals of ageing and depraved passion, and to the singular hallucinations of the fixed idea verging on madness. This style of decadence is the last effort of the Word (*Verbe*), called upon to express everything, and pushed to the utmost extremity. We may remind ourselves, in connection with it, of the language of the later Roman Empire, already mottled with the greenness of decomposition, and, as it were, gamy (*faisandée*), and of the complicated refinements of the Byzantine school, the last form of Greek art fallen into deliquescence. Such is the inevitable and fatal idiom of peoples and civilizations where factitious life has replaced the natural life, and developed in man unknown wants. Besides, it is no easy matter, this style despised of pedants, for it expresses new ideas with new forms and words that have not yet been heard. In opposition to the classic style, it admits of shading, and these shadows teem and swarm with the larvae of superstitions, the haggard phantoms of insomnia, nocturnal terrors, remorse which starts and turns back at the slightest noise, monstrous dreams stayed only by impotence, obscure phantasies at which the day-light would stand amazed, and all that the soul conceals of the dark, the unformed, and the vaguely horrible, in its deepest and furthest recesses.   (p. 229)

This concentration on the style of Decadence runs through many of the accounts of it, but the suggestions of corruption and madness in the subject matter are clear enough too. It is not the love of corruption for itself which lies behind this, however, but a desire to use to the full the tremendous powers of the mature language in describing new and hitherto uncharted areas of experience, claiming as its study everything that is part of life, including those new horrors that come with civilization and its movement away from nature into artifice. Baudelaire (again the translation from Nordau's book makes a suggestive connection) agreed with Gautier:

> Does it not seem to the reader, as it does to me, that the language of the later Latin decadence – the departing sigh of a robust person already transformed and prepared for the spiritual life – is singularly appropriate to express passion as it has been understood and felt by the modern poetic world? Mysticism is the opposite pole of that magnet in which Catullus and his followers, brutal and purely epidermic poets, have only recognized the pole of sensuality. In this marvellous language, solecism and barbarism appear to me to convey the forced negligences of a passion which forgets itself and mocks at rules. Words, received in a new acceptation, display the charming awkwardness of the Northern barbarian kneeling before the Roman beauty. Even a play on words, when it enters into these pedantic stammerings, does it not display the wild and bizarre grace of infancy?.   (p. 300)

Whatever Max Nordau says in *Degeneration* about the 'shifting nebulous ideas, its fleeting formless shadowy thought', we have here a fairly clear picture of what the literature of Decadent Rome stood for: an increasing subtlety of language covering a widening range of subject, and a suggestion of the tendency towards the 'spiritual life'. These features are clear in the chief parents of a movement called 'Decadence' and became even clearer in the writings of a group of young poets who, following in the footsteps of the two masters, began in the eighties to call themselves '*les Décadents*'. They aspired to the virtues they claimed to see in late Latin work and used the term as a flag of defiance while the critics used it as a sign of scorn. Wallace Fowlie, in a useful note on Decadence as it was in France, included in his study of *Mallarmé* (1953), describes how in 1886

> the typical *décadent* came to designate the seeker of rare sensation, a combination of dandy and roué, a cultivated dilettante. The stronger word of *maudit* ('accurst') joined with it, when in 1883 *Lutèce* published Verlaine's three studies on Corbière, Rimbaud and Mallarmé. Far from making apology for the *décadent* or the *maudit*, Verlaine aggressively praises the type who, exemplified in the three poets he chose, opposes the civilization in which he lives and is repulsed by his society.   (p. 255)

The work of Verlaine himself, that of Gautier and Baudelaire, the Goncourts and Mallarmé, along with that of the Latin Decadence, received a considerable amount of attention when in 1884 a book was published that put before the French public the most complete picture of the Decadent that they had seen, Joris-Karl Huysmans' *A Rebours*. The hero of the novel, des Esseintes, is held up as the typical Decadent, so it is worth looking in some detail at this character who is often misrepresented by the casual comments of many critics. First, he is a character in fiction, not a historical figure. Second, and most important in looking at his character, one must recognize that the book is not only the Bible of Decadence, but also one of its severest criticisms, a recognition from the first of its necessary failure. All the attempts that des Esseintes makes to escape from the world into artifice fail, since he lacks the leaven of a worldly appetite, just as his tortoise is unable to live under the beautiful but fatal artifice of its decorated shell, and the real flowers that look artificial die in his rooms. Whatever else may be said of des Esseintes, his renunciation of the world is a failure. He must, as his doctor says, choose between death and leading a normal life, enjoying the same pleasures as other people. When artificiality is taken to its logical conclusions, it becomes an impossibility for man, who must then choose death or submission to nature, the former with that touch of heroism that Yeats saw in his friends of the tragic generation. In *A Rebours* there is no middle way, no compromise; the Decadent is grotesque, a caricature from the start.

Not only the man who tries to escape from the natural world is criticized, however, for the society he escapes from is shown as corrupt. All that des Esseintes does is done not from corrupt motives, but from principles which society would have said were the best – honesty, love of intelligence, love of art; the perversity lies in neglecting society's other values and in particular neglecting the materialism which marks this hypocritical society. Des Esseintes dreams of contemporary society, where the

> jovial bourgeois lorded it over the country, putting his trust in the power of his money and the contagiousness of his stupidity. The result of his rise to power had been the suppression of all intelligence, the negation of all honesty, the destruction of all art; in fact, artists and writers in their degradation had fallen on their knees and were covering with ardent kisses the stinking feet of the high-placed jobbers and low-bred satraps on whose charity they depended for a living.   (trans. Robert Baldick, 1959, p. 218)

There is nothing left for des Esseintes but to say 'crumble then, society! perish, old world!' although he awakens to the fact that he must 'rejoin the base and servile riff-raff of the age!' Having seen nothing worthy in society, des Esseintes had turned to art, a gesture which society finds above all insulting, but the book ends with the triumph of nature over artifice, as he looks at his fate in returning to society. It is a gesture more noble than Rastignac's challenge to society at the end of *Le Père Goriot* though it stems from the same hatred; Rastignac joins battle with the world; for des Esseintes the fight is over and only a desire for consoling faith is left:

> 'In two days' time I shall be in Paris,' he told himself. 'Well, it is all over now. Like a tide-race, the waves of human mediocrity are rising to the heavens and will engulf this refuge, for I am opening the flood-gates myself, against my will. Ah! but my courage fails me, and my heart is sick within me! – Lord, take pity on the Christian who doubts, on the unbeliever who would fain believe, on the galley-slave of life who puts out to sea alone, in the night, beneath a firma-ment no longer lit by the consoling beacon-fires of the ancient hope!'
>
> (pp. 219–20)

Unable to escape through artifice, the Decadent finds himself escaping the hateful world through a faith itself grasped at only with doubt and effort. The nobility lies in the stoicism with which he bears the inevitable.

Not everything that the hero of this novel says and does is to be taken as the ideal, any more than in *Gulliver's Travels* (another voyage out of society to test its values) we believe Gulliver, for, although Huysmans sees the vices of contemporary society and shows them up through des Esseintes, the hero is no ideal either, the ideal lying in some balance of the two. We must be aware of the hero as *persona*, for the book is not a manual of conduct, but a picture of the Decadent Dilemma. This would seem to me to be too obvious to stress were it not for the views of Robert Baldick, Huysmans' translator, that 'Des Esseintes is basically a self-portrait' (p. 11), or Nordau's view that he is 'the ideal man of decadent-ism' (p. 309), or the general assumption that the book is a picture of the complete Decadent whom Huysmans wished to make himself and whose characteristics he wished to praise. 'As for Zola,' says Baldick, 'he brushed aside Huysmans' well-meant but dishonest hints that the whole thing was just a literary leg-pull' (p. 10). Huysmans is by no means dishonest, for self-mockery is an essential part of the picture. One incident should suffice to illustrate that the author's attitude is far from self-portraiture, that frequently-quoted example of Decadence when des Esseintes is fed by enemas. As Nordau points out, this is 'diametrically opposed to nature', but nobody can think that this is Huysmans advocating this method of nourishment! It was not done from choice, but from necessity brought about by des Esseintes' abuse of his stomach – again the failure to follow his theories because of his fundamental humanity. The paragraph in which he discovers this method as the ultimate in unnaturalness is carefully placed by the author as the views of the character alone:

The operation was successfully carried out, and Des Esseintes could not help secretly congratulating himself on this experience which was, so to speak, the crowning achievement of the life he had planned for himself; his taste for the artificial had now, without even the slightest effort on his part, attained its supreme fulfilment. No one, he thought, would ever go any further; taking nourishment in this way was undoubtedly the ultimate deviation from the norm.

'How delightful it would be,' he said to himself, 'to go on with this simple diet after getting well again. What a saving of time, what a radical deliverance from the repugnance meat inspires in people without any appetite. What an absolute release from the boredom that invariably results from the necessarily limited choice of dishes! What a vigorous protest against the vile sin of a gluttony! And last but not least, what a slap in the face for old Mother Nature, whose monotonous demands would be permanently silenced!'

And talking to himself under his breath, he went on: 'It would be easy enough to get up an appetite by swallowing a strong aperient. Then, when you felt you might reasonably say: 'Isn't it time for dinner? – I'm as hungry as a hunter,' all you'd have to do to lay the table would be to deposit the noble instrument on the cloth. And before you had time to say grace you'd have finished the meal – without any of the vulgar, bothersome business of eating'.

(pp. 208–9)

If the reader could still be in any doubt that Huysmans means des Esseintes to be laughed at here for his preposterous ideas, Huysmans makes it obvious that he intends the ridiculous. Seeing an enema of a different colour, des Esseintes finds that the doctor has changed the prescription and sets himself the task of composing novel recipes, with a meatless dish for Fridays. How can anyone believe that Huysmans is seriously advocating this as a way of life? When he is well again, des Esseintes goes back to ordinary food, never able to flee society and its ways completely.

His escape is always fraught with these difficulties, and his existence founded upon paradox. Although he escapes into artifice, he continually uses artifice to remind himself of the world. His cabin, with its double window which he could fill with tinted water to simulate different seasons and weathers, was an aid to substitute sensations:

He could then imagine himself between-decks in a brig, and gazed inquisitively at some ingenious mechanical fishes driven by clockwork, which moved backwards and forwards behind the port-hole window and got entangled in artificial seaweed. At other times, while he was inhaling the smell of tar which had been introduced into the room before he entered it, he would examine a series of colour-

> prints on the walls, such as you see in packet-boat offices and Lloyd's agencies, representing steamers bound for Valparaiso and the River Plate, alongside framed notices giving the itineraries of the Royal Mail Steam Packet Line and the Lopez and Valéry Companies, as well as the freight charges and ports of call of the transatlantic mail-boats.   (p. 34)

Yeats later finds himself in this position when he wishes to assume the shape of the golden bird 'out of nature', and both 'Sailing to Byzantium' and 'Byzantium' itself begin in the natural, pass to the artificial, which in turn refers to the natural, not a surprising link when we remember that Yeats's golden bird is after all related to those artificial animals inhabiting the artificial forest of Ludwig II of Bavaria, one of the models for des Esseintes.

The criticism of both contemporary society and of the artificial life which cannot exist separately is effected by exaggerating the division between them in the reactions of a figure who represents one aspect, and his characteristics are writ large enough to summarize briefly. The last degenerate representative of a noble family, des Esseintes has exhausted conventional pleasures, those sins that society more readily forgives, and has fitted out a house, near enough to Paris for the city to lose the temptation of inaccessibility, in which to live apart and indulge his taste for artificiality. His theory of literature is such that his library consists largely of two groups of writers, Decadents ancient and modern. The ancients were late Latin authors who (did he base his chapter on Nisard's book or merely on one like it?) described in a newly-freed language all the detail of everyday life without giving any idea of the author and without comment:

> One section of the bookshelves lining the walls of Des Esseintes' blue and orange study was filled with nothing but Latin works – works which minds drilled into conformity by repetitious university lectures lump together under the generic name of 'the Decadence'.
> The truth was that the Latin language, as it was written during the period which the academics still persist in calling the Golden Age, held scarcely any attraction for him. That restricted idiom with its limited stock of almost invariable constructions; without suppleness of syntax, without colour, without even light and shade. . . . Des Esseintes only began to take an interest in the Latin language when he came to Lucan, in whose hands it took on new breadth, and became brighter and more expressive. The fine craftsmanship of Lucan's enamelled and jewelled verse won his admiration.   (pp. 40, 42)

Among writers in the ornate style he loves are Petronius and Apuleius, so full of his admired intricacy:

This African author gave him enormous pleasure. The Latin language reached the top of the tide in his *Metamorphoses*, sweeping along in a dense flood fed by tributary waters from every province, and combining them all in a bizarre, exotic, almost incredible torrent of words; new mannerisms and new details of Latin society found expression in neologisms called into being to meet conversational requirements in an obscure of Roman Africa.   (p. 44)

Echoes from this chapter sound throughout the Decadence both in France and England.

The modern group of writers in des Esseintes' library is of contemporary or near-contemporary French authors, Baudelaire, Barbey d'Aurevilly, Flaubert, Edmond de Goncourt, Zola, Verlaine, Corbière, Mallarmé, Villiers de l'Isle Adam, and Gautier, all of whom possessed something of the style he saw in his Decadent Romans.

Des Esseintes' pastimes are artificial or centred on art: the contemplation of pictures, especially those with mystic overtones, such as his Moreaus, his Odilon Redon, his El Greco and the fantastic engravings of Jan Luyken; his mouth-organ, a collection of drinks with which he plays a symphony of taste; and his playing with scents and scented harmonies which finally make him fall sick across his window sill. Even his trip to London is completed mentally in a Paris bar. His every action is governed by a desire to be artificial in as much as possible in order to give more 'slaps in the face to old Mother Nature.' It is she who wins in the end, since one by one the delights he finds go jaded as he loses his relationship with the outside world.

That later Decadent writers were to see the element of criticism in the book is obvious from Arthur Symons's suggestion in *Studies in Prose and Verse* (1904) that Huysmans showed

the sterilising influence of a narrow and selfish conception of art, as he represented a particular paradise of art for art's sake turning inevitably into its corresponding hell. Des Esseintes is the symbol of all those who have tried to shut themselves in from the natural world, upon an artificial beauty which has no root there. Worshipping colour, sound, perfume, for their own sakes, and not for their ministrations of a more divine beauty, he stupefies himself on the threshold of ecstasy.   (p. 289)

Symons rejects the 'haschish dream' of that sort of experience, as he claims Huysmans did, for one which gives suggestions of something not visible in the world. This is another form of Symons's claim that Symbolism grew out of Decadence, and that Decadence was 'half a mock-interlude' taking place while Symbolism was growing ready – not a wild suggestion when the central figure of Decadence is a

1. Burne-Jones's self-mocking series of sketches about the impossibility of the artist's finally joining the world of art (1883). *Reproduced by kind permission of the Trustees of the British Museum.*

parody. This self-mocking note of Decadence, conscious of its love 'begotten by Despair / Upon Impossibility', is a fundamental characteristic, uniting aspects of Lionel Johnson, Max Beerbohm, and Aubrey Beardsley, not to mention *Punch* and Adoré Floupette.

This last figure received some official recognition in an article written, not long after the rise to notice of *les Décadents*, for the second supplement of the *Larousse* dictionary and encyclopaedia (1887–90). Scornful of many of the theories of its members, the *Larousse* writer described the origins of the *Décadents*, who had received, he said, little public notice in journals and reviews until 1886, although they had spent 10 years trying to find themselves an audience either at the *Chat Noir* or in their magazines, *Le Décadent* (begun in April 1886 and changed by its editor Anatole Baju to *Le décadisme* in 1888) and later the *Scapin*. Like all new schools they were struggling against indifference, and at the time were gaining their first notoriety. Their declared purpose was to prepare 'les éléments foetusiens de la grande littérature nationale du XIXe siècle', and according to *Larousse* the principal writers among them were Stéphane Mallarmé, Adoré Floupette, René Ghil, Noël Loumo, Anatole Baju, Laforgue, Teneo, and Jean Moréas. It is in key with the satirical tone of the essay that Adoré Floupette figures on the list, since he is a fiction and his book is a witty satire on a movement which demands the satirist whether from within or without. The full title of the book is *Les déliquescences. Poèmes décadents d'Adoré Floupette avec sa vie par Marius Tapora*, and the authors, Henri Beauclair and Gabriel Vicaire, captured the mood by claiming as publisher Lion Vanné (instead of the Léon Vanier who published Verlaine's *Sagesse* and *Jadis et Naguère*) and as the place of publication Byzantium.

The *Larousse* article divides Decadence into two categories, much as Lionel Johnson and Arthur Symons were to do, but its tone is mocking:

> symbolisme et quintessence résument, en effet, assez bien la théorie de cette littérature 'décadente', surtout si par 'quintessence' on entende la recherche des mots étranges, totalement inusités, et par 'symbolisme' l'art de donner à deviner au lecteur les plus obscures énigmes.

The sources that are quoted refer to style, and repeat the by now familiar description of the difficulty of a Decadent style: from Sutter Laumann: 'Les DECADENTS préconisent l'emploi de mots rares, précieux, qu'on va extraire à grand'peine dans les vocabulaires'; and from Anatole France. 'Il reste des DECADENTS attardés qui s'obstinent à peindre avec des mots.' The writer saw clearly enough to which authorities the Decadents turned for example but, unaware of Nisard's criticisms of some of these very authors as Decadent, deplored the use to which the authorities were put. Hugo's style, for example, had included some incomprehensibility of detail, Lamartine's a fluidity and imprecision of contour; but this did not excuse a new school for being more incomprehensible and more imprecise in outlining thought. The search for the rare word was sanctioned by Gautier, but extreme followers had persuaded themselves that Gautier never troubled to have his words also make sense. Even Baudelaire is acceptable, but his theories must not be exaggerated until they are made false. In place of an awareness of the links between the Decadents and Gautier and Baudelaire, the article quotes from a piece by Vir in the *Scapin*, which gives another view of the origin of the Decadents:

> Le grand siècle se contenta, par la voix de Racine, de Corneille et de Molière, de l'expression bien mise des nobles sentiments. Le romantisme ne fut qu'un torrent tumultueux, avec des essais d'aigle et des clameurs guerrières dans l'orage. Puis vint le Parnasse, qui peut-être créa vraiment notre poésie, en cherchant à en faire un parfait thème musical. Mais quelques parnassiens schismatiques (les décadents) voulurent terminer l'oeuvre en la réduisant à une musique évocatrice, fantôme d'un monde mi-réel et mi-céleste, suggestive d'étranges rêves, guitare sonnant au lointain des forêts bleues. Aux sonorités des mots on a ajouté leurs couleurs et leurs odeurs spéciales.

The *Larousse* critic is no exception in finding the systematic synaesthesia of these Decadent writers too much to take, and he objects to the obscurity of language and meaning, quoting from poems including Mallarmé's 'L'après-midi d'un faune'. He concludes that the Decadents confuse the strange and bizarre with the original and that 'les décadents sont des excentriques: ils s'échappent par la tangente.' This view of a contemporary French academic is not entirely unjustified of the extremes of the movement, and it is well to remember Arthur Symons's suspicion of extremes and his ultimate rejection of Decadence.

There is some accuracy in the view that Decadence was an offshoot of Parnassianism. However inaccurately (all great writers make groupings inaccurate), Mallarmé and Verlaine had been numbered among the Parnassians and had published in Parnassian papers, and Verlaine could loosely be called the leader of the new school. Both men published poems which seem almost programmatic in their insistence on Decadent themes. Mallarmé, who was for des Esseintes the most Decadent of contemporary writers, luxuriates in Decadence in his 'Plainte d'automne':

> Depuis que Maria m'a quitté pour aller dans une autre étoile – laquelle, Orion, Altaïr, et toi, verte Vénus? – j'ai toujours chéri la solitude. Que de longues journées j'ai passées seul avec mon chat. Par *seul*, j'entends sans un être matériel et mon chat est un compagon mystique, un esprit. Je puis donc dire que j'ai passé de longues journées seul avec mon chat et, seul, avec un des derniers auteurs de la décadence latine; car depuis que la blanche créature n'est plus, étrangement et singulièrement j'ai aimé tout ce qui se résumait en ce mot: chute. Ainsi, dans l'année, ma saison favorite, ce sont les derniers jours alanguis de l'été, qui précèdent immédiatement l'automne et, dans la journée, l'heure où je me promène est quand de soleil se repose avant de s'évanouir, avec des

rayons de cuivre jaune sur les murs gris et de cuivre rouge sur les carreaux. De même la littérature à laquelle mon esprit demande une volupté sera la poésie agonisante des derniers moments de Rome, tant, cependant, qu'elle ne respire aucunement l'approche rajeunissante es Barbares et ne bégaie point le latin enfantin des premières proses chrétiennes.

Je lisais donc un de ces chers poèmes (dont les plaques de fard ont plus de charme sur moi que l'incarnat de la jeunesse) et plongeais une main dans la fourrure du pur animal, quand un orgue de Barbarie chanta languissament et mélancoliquement sous ma fenêtre.

(Stéphane Mallarmé, *Oeuvres complètes*, ed. Henri Mondor and G. Jean-Aubry, Paris, 1945, p. 270)

Verlaine rehearses similar themes in his sonnet 'Langueur', which appeared in *Le Chat Noir* of 26 May 1883:

> Je suis l'Empire à la fin de la décadence,
> Qui regarde passer les grands Barbares blancs
> En composant des acrostiches indolents
> D'un style d'or où la langueur du soleil danse.
>
> L'âme seulette a mal au coeur d'un ennui dense.
> Là-bas on dit qu'il est de longs combats sanglants.
> O n'y pouvoir, étant si faible aux voeux si lents,
> O n'y vouloir fleurir un peu cette existence!
>
> O n'y vouloir, ô n'y pouvoir mourir un peu!
> Ah! tout est bu! Bathylle, as-tu fini de rire?
> Ah! tout est bu, tout est mangé! Plus rien à dire!
>
> Seul, un poème un peu niais qu'on jette au feu,
> Seul, un esclave un peu coureur qui vous néglige,
> Seul, un ennemi d'on ne sait quoi qui vous afflige!

(Paul Verlaine, *Oeuvres complètes*, ed. Jacques Borel, Paris, 1959)

The editor of Verlaine's complete works, Jacques Borel, points out the parody element of this central Decadent text: this poem

apparaît bientôt comme l'art poétique du Décadisme. Jeu, sans doute, et presque satire: la place du poème dans le cycle parodique de *Jadis et Naguère* n'est pas fortuite. Pourtant, en 1886–1888, Verlaine fait figure de chef d'école. Il feint d'y mal croire. Il ne s'en montre pas moins attentif au mouvement, collabore assidûment au *Décadent* d'Anatole Baju (1886–1888), inaugure ses 'mercredis'. Il se sait à l'origine d'une tentative poétique qui, se détournant à sa suite du Naturalisme et du Parnasse, s'oriente vers l'intime et le secret de l'être, rejette la description pour la suggestion, isole les objets du monde dans la buée de la rêverie, les dépouille de leur valeur de signes, ne tend plus à exprimer des choses que la sensation ou l'impression que le poète en reçoit.

L'admiration des 'Décadents' pour Verlaine ne va pas cependant sans malentendu ni sans confusion. Au contenu intellectuel du Décadisme, le poète reste résolument étranger. C'est dans le domaine des techniques que s'exerce surtout l'influence verlainienne.

(I, pp. 417–18)

Slight differences, as we shall see, from English interpretations of Decadence, but the importance of Verlaine's technique, especially for a poet like Dowson, is unquestionable, and John Gray placed the third line of *'Langueur'* at the beginning of *Silverpoints*. Verlaine was no dogmatic leader, and only belonged to a movement when it suited him to do so. Ghil and Moréas in 1886, Stuart Merrill, Vielé-Griffin and Henri de Régnier in 1887 left him to follow Mallarmé, and to form up under the banner of Symbolism.

It was not long after the publication of *A Rebours* that Symbolism began to shoulder out Decadence as the acceptable term for the modern French writer. In 1885 Paul Bourde made an attack on Moréas who, in his reply in *Le XIXe siècle* of 11 August 1885, suggested the use of the word 'symbolist' to describe what had hitherto been called a 'decadent'. Wallace Fowlie, in his book on *Mallarmé*, adds that 'by this time the general public were confusing 'decadents' and 'symbolists', despite the efforts of those who still called themselves 'decadents'. It was the term Symbolist that prevailed in the end, so that Remy de Gourmont could look back from 1898 and say that

> For ten years, and up to a few weeks ago, artists and writers who refused to rifle the masters were branded decadents and symbolists. This last insult prevailed in the end, being verbally more obscure and consequently easier to handle; it contains, moreover, precisely the same abhorrent notion of non-imitation.

(*Decadence and Other Essays*, trans. W.A. Bradley, 1922, pp. 147–8)

Remy de Gourmont's ideas are in some ways similar to those of Paul Bourget, but he has his own idea of the history of Decadence, and criticizes the inaccuracy of the term:

> Abruptly, about 1885, the idea of decadence entered French literature. After serving to glorify or to ridicule a whole group of poets, it had perched, as it were, upon a single head. Stéphane Mallarmé was the prince of this ironical, almost injurious realm, as it would have been, had the word itself been rightly understood and employed. But, by an eccentricity which is a Latin trait, the academic world, in keeping with its normal but unwholesome

horror when confronted with new tendencies, called thus the fever
for originality which tormented a generation.   (p. 139)

Just as the history of Rome, he argues, has given the example of a
political Decadence, the literature of Decadent Rome has furnished the
example of literary Decadence, as if the two things were connected by
something other than coincidence, an illusion that Montesquieu relied
upon. In de Gourmont's view, the contrary case would seem to be more
accurate: 'It would, perhaps, be nearer the truth to say that political
decadence is the condition most favourable for intellectual flowering'
(p, 142), an idea also held by Henry James. However vague the idea of
political Decadence might be, de Gourmont finds it plain in comparison
to the idea of literary Decadence. For him, as for Yeats or Christopher
Brennan, literary Decadence can only be the absence of a great poet,
when mediocre and imitative talents thrive, so that 'in the last analysis,
the idea of decadence is identical with the idea of imitation' (p. 145), but
in the case of Mallarmé and the group who may be said to follow him
'the idea of decadence has been assimilated to its exact opposite – the
idea of innovation.'

De Gourmont's view is that the critics who have used the term are
ignorant of its meaning, merely using it because they were looking for
an explanation of the movement when *A Rebours* was published, but he
himself is unaware of any earlier history of the term and so starts his
story a little late:

> A parallel imposed itself inexorably between the new poets and the
> obscure versifiers of the Roman decadence praised by des Esseintes.
> The movement was unanimous, and the very ones thus decried
> accepted this opprobrious epithet as a distinction. Once the principle
> was admitted, there was no lack of comparisons. Since no one – not
> even des Esseintes himself, perhaps – had read the depreciated
> poets, it was no trick at all for any critic to compare Sidonius
> Apollinaris, of whom we knew nothing, with Stéphane Mallarmé,
> whom he did not understand. Neither Sidonius Apollinaris nor
> Mallarmé is a decadent, since both possess, in different degrees, their
> own originality; but for that very reason the word was justly applied
> to the poet of *L'Après-midi d'un faune,* for it signified obscurely, in
> the minds of the very persons who employed it, something little
> known, rare, precious, unexpected, new.   (p. 150)

Even when the principle of comparison is admitted, it is worth noting
that de Gourmont was writing at a time when there was a growing
regard for late Latin poets, who were beginning to seem not worse but
merely different from earlier poets. But it the end, he rejected the term,
as so many others did:

It may well be that a poetry full of doubts, of shifting shades, and of ambiguous perfumes, can alone please us henceforward; and, if the word decadence really summed up all these autumnal, twilight charms, we might welcome it, even making it one of the keys of the viol; but it is dead; the master is dead, the penultimate is dead.

(p. 155)

Despite this rejection, the word has a fairly static meaning in French, since it refers to a group of self-styled *décadents*. A.E. Carter's book presents a number of assumptions common to writers from Gautier to the early Gide, which give the movement some coherence, and it would be worth ending this chapter with some account of Carter's argument.

Central to that argument is Carter's view of Decadence as primitivism *à rebours*. He is undoubtedly right in arguing that Decadence is self-consciously artificial, and that from this artificiality stem its main characteristics. Rousseau's arguments could lead to this conclusion; the over-civilization of man producing a decline from the ideal state at the same time as a further alienation from nature and natural things; because of this a Decadent society would be at the peak of artificiality. Carter sees Decadence as a reaction from Rousseau's ideas, first seen in de Sade, and that the first step in Decadent thinking is a rejection of nature, seeing her as the enemy of man, and the pursuit of the abnormal as 'proof of man's superiority to natural law' (p. 5).

Carter traces the history of Decadence through Gautier and Baudelaire, remarking that the 'fusion of the artificial and the modern which is one of the identifying marks of decadence united two fundamentally opposed ideas: a hatred of modern civilization and a love of the refinements modern civilization made possible', a contradiction never solved by Decadent sensibility, so that the movement 'suffered throughout its lifetime from a sort of literary schizophrenia' (p. 6). He sees in Gautier's 'Notice' to *Les Fleurs du mal* the essence of Decadence:

'La déprivation, c'est-à-dire l'écart du type normal, est impossible à la bête, fatalement conduite par l'instinct immuable. C'est par la même raison que les poètes inspirés, n'ayant pas la conscience et la direction de leur oeuvre, lui [i.e. à Baudelaire] causaient une sorte d'aversion, et qu'il voulait introduire l'art et le travail même dans l'originalité.' This passage is the nerve-centre of decadence – as the nineteenth century understood the term. It sums up everything that had been said previously, and contains whatever was said later. The conclusions to which it leads are obvious: Baudelaire liked depravity, which is an essential part of decadence, a last refinement of artificiality, since it is anti-natural. If Gautier was not writing with the Marquis de Sade in mind, at least his thought is the same. That taste for sexual perversions, so characteristic of decadent literature, receives theoretic justification in the 'Notice'. Even painstaking craftsmanship becomes a variety of perversion. To complete the picture, he notes that the setting of Baudelaire's verse is the degenerate capital.   (pp. 14–15)

Artificiality, modernity, and Decadence are seen as associated throughout Decadent literature, and a rough idea of the general conclusions of the book can be conveyed in a selection of its key sentences: the 'calculated, intellectual side of the cult of artificiality is an essential part of decadent sensibility' (p. 12); 'Decadent sensibility developes from the theory that civilization is artificial and corrupt' (p. 26); 'The cult of artificiality begins in the perversion of the Romantic legend, and decadent sensibility is the perversion of a Romantic type' (p. 27); 'the true decadent . . . is neurotic' (p. 28); 'Linked to this sadism is a craving for the *impossible* which Gautier was the first to define as a distinguishing mark of decadent sensibility' (p. 38); 'characteristically decadent themes such as sterility, ennui, artificiality, depraved exoticism' (p. 122); 'the decadent style, with the possible exception of Huysmans' work, produced nothing of value: at best it is amusing, at worst unreadable' (p. 143); 'the excessive, bookish culture of the decadence, its morbid introspection, its perverse attitudinizing, its sterility, neurosis, and its studied boredom' (p. 122); 'the word "decadence" as it is used in the foregoing pages has a special meaning, implying not merely deterioration, but deterioration which is somehow both corrupt and alluring' (p. 144). The book concludes with a reiteration of the original idea that the Decadent is the exact opposite of the Noble Savage.

Of course there are many minor writers and much minor detail in Carter's account, but the major landmarks remain the same, though I have introduced the founding figure of Nisard; Baudelaire is the decisive writer, crystallizing Gautier's earlier views by declaring in response to Pontmartin's attack on Poe that 'if Poe was decadent he was quite legitimately so' (p. 145). It is this acceptance of the term by writers that marks the crucial step.

The term developed in relation to the writers in France in the nineteenth century. It was brought into common use about the middle of that century. defined influentially by Huysmans in 1884, and rejected in favour of Symbolism by the end of the century. Its most popular period in France was in the 1880s, and it is late in this period that the term crossed the Channel to England.

3 Decadence as a Critical Term in England

The history of Decadence in England has many points in common with the story in France, but there are significant differences, caused not only by the expected confusions about what exactly Decadence was, but also and perhaps more by the lack of any coherent group of writers who accepted the name and fought for it. The climate of censorship was also different and more severe than in France, so that there are not the extremes of French Decadence. In England it was a term flourished, used, abused, worried over and, with Wilde's conviction, hastily abandoned. But for five or six years it kept certain writers in the public eye and certain literary and theoretical problems under consideration.

The earliest definition of the term is in Du Cange's *Glossarium ad Scriptores Mediae et Infimae Latinitatis* (1678), which defines the word as decline, quoting a passage from the *Chronicon Beccense* where the word refers quite neutrally to the tumbledown state of mills and farms. The term is itself late Latin, a derivative from *cadere*. It is first found in English in the sixteenth century, recorded in *The Complaynt of Scotland* (1549, chapter 7), where 'My triumphant stait is succumbit in decadens.' The stress here is on the second syllable, perhaps under the influence of the associated word decay, and this pronunciation remained until well into the 1890s when *Punch* published a poem with the lines

> 'Good boys and girls' we've all become, and modern
>   men and maidens see
> The world with such prosaic eyes, Romance is
>   in decadency.

(13 May 1893, p. 219)

In the final lines of Dowson's 'Transition' the word probably has this stressing still:

> Short summer-time and then, my heart's desire,
>   The winter and the darkness: one by one
> The roses fall, the pale roses expire
>   Beneath the slow decadence of the sun.

The *OED* of 1897 comments that the pronunciation with the stress on the first syllable – the natural stress in English – is 'now considered more scholarly.' This change of pronunciation indicates a growing familiarity with the term, or perhaps even further imitation of the French example. 'Decidence' – the more correctly derived term – is known in English from an early date (1646 in Sir Thomas Browne's *Pseudodoxia Epidemica* III, ix, p. 127) but never found the popular favour of the other word.

Since there are several adequate synonyms of 'decay', the impetus which gave rise to the word's popularity in the late nineteenth century obviously came from some special application, and perhaps was the result of foreign influence; though its immediate currency again suggests that the phenomenon it describes was well-known before the word was found to name it. Just as (so H.A. Skinner tells us in *The Origin of Medical Terms*, 2nd edn, Baltimore, 1961) 'degeneration' was unknown 'as a specific medical term before 1860' but soon found a place in medical language, so the word 'Decadence' was present in the language, but its use infrequent until the middle years of the nineteenth century. It was not used to describe a literary phenomenon, however, but rather as a convenient term for the historian, a term to use specifically of a declining civilization; But even then it was regarded with some suspicion. In 1871 J.B. Mayor in the *Journal of Philology* (pp. 347–8) wrote of the word with rather unscholarly warmth that 'I am afraid it is no longer possible to extinguish this barbarous Gallicism which has been accepted now by so many of our best writers.' He argues that the word 'obtrudes itself into ground already occupied by 'decay', 'decline' and other words', and that the main reason for the word becoming generally known and used is its appearance in the title of Montesquieu's book. He does add that ' "decadence" seems to have made little way in England until the last quarter of a century, when, possibly owing to the influence of Comte, it came into fashion, apparently to *denote* decline, and *connote* a scientific and enlightened view of that decline on the part of the user.' How far things were to change from that 'scientific and enlightened view'! The *OED* of 1897 tends to agree with Mayor, defining the meaning as 'applied to a particular period of decline in art, literature, etc. e.g. the Silver Age of Latin Literature (chiefly a French use).' It quotes from Stubbs's *Constitutional History of England* the comment that 'the men of the decadence, not less than the men of the renaissance, were giants of learning', as if to make clear that a decadent culture does not necessarily accompany a decadent empire, a point which Désiré Nisard and Remy de Gourmont were both careful to make.

The term, although accepted even by the 'best writers' of the mid century, would perhaps not have had the popularity it did had it not been for Walter Pater. He used the term and was interested in many associated ideas, and he was the one man who claimed the respect of the new generation of the nineties as a whole. In 1873 he wrote of the poems of du Bellay that the Renaissance was 'thus putting forth in France an aftermath, a wonderful later growth, the products of which have to the full that subtle and delicate sweetness which belongs to a fine and comely decadence, just as its earliest phases have the freshness which belongs to periods of growth in art.' Again, when writing of 'Mr Gosse's Poems' in the *Guardian* in 1890:

> for a writer of his peculiar philosophic tenets, at all events, the world itself, in truth, must seem irretrievably old or even decadent. Old, decadent, indeed, it would seem with Mr. Gosse to be also returning to the thoughts, the fears, the consolations, of its youth in Greece, in Italy. (*Essays from the Guardian*, 1901, p. 115)

More significant than these comments, Pater praises the late Roman age in his seminal book *Marius the Epicurean* (1885), the golden book of many writers for some time. Here his carefully cadenced and delicately phrased sentences inevitably associate the ideas of style and decadence. And Pater not only translates from the highly ornate Latin of Apuleius the story of Cupid and Psyche (also translated by another stylist, Robert Bridges, in 1885), but also has some comments to make on Apuleius's book that are remarkably similar to those of Huysmans I have quoted earlier. Having described the delicately formed and perfumed exterior of Flavian's copy of the book, Pater says that

> the inside was something not less dainty and fine, full of the archaisms and curious felicities in which that generation delighted, quaint terms and images picked fresh from the early dramatists, the lifelike phrases of some lost poet preserved by an old grammarian, racy morsels of the vernacular and studied prettinesses: – all alike, mere playthings for the genuine power and natural eloquence of the erudite artist, unsuppressed by his erudition, which, however, made some people angry, chiefly less well 'got-up' people, and especially those who were untidy from indolence. . . . And at least his success was unmistakable as to the precise literary effect he had intended, including a certain tincture of 'neology' in expression – *nonnihil interdum elocutione novella parum signatum* – in the language of Cornelius Fronto, the contemporary prince of rhetoricians. What words he had found for conveying, with a single touch, the sense of textures, colours, incident! 'Like jewellers' work! Like a myrrhine vase!' – admirers said of his writing.
> (*Marius the Epicurean*, 1885, chap. V)

It is worth digressing from a strict chronology at this point to put directly against this passage and that of Huysmans already referred to, another passage describing a book, this one from Wilde's *The Picture of Dorian Gray*. Wilde, as he admitted at his trial, was referring to *A Rebours* (see *The Trials of Oscar Wilde*, ed. H. Montgomery Hyde, 1948, p. 130), but the general pattern and the literary references are markedly similar:

> It was a novel without a plot, and with only one character, being, indeed, simply a psychological study of a certain young Parisian, who spent his life trying to realise in the nineteenth century all the passions and modes of thought that belonged to every century except his own, and to sum up, as it were, in himself the various moods through which the world-spirit had ever passed, loving for their mere artificiality those renunciations that men have unwisely called virtue, as much as those natural rebellions that wise men still call sin. The style in which it was written was that curious jewelled style, vivid and obscure at one, full of argot and of archaisms, of technical expressions and of elaborate paraphrases, that character-ises the work of some of the finest artists of the French school of *Symbolistes*. There were in it metaphors as monstrous as orchids, and a subtle in colour. The life of the senses was described in the terms of mystical philosophy. One hardly knew at times whether one was reading the spiritual ecstasies of some mediaeval saint or the morbid confessions of a modern sinner. It was a poisonous book. The heavy odour of incense seemed to cling about its pages and to trouble the brain. The mere cadence of the sentences, the subtle monotony of their music, so full as it was of complex refrains and movements elaborately repeated, produced in the mind of the lad, as he passed from chapter to chapter, a form of reverie, a malady of dreaming, that made him unconscious of the falling day and creep-ing shadows.
>
> (*The Complete Works of Oscar Wilde*, 1966, p. 101)

Even Wilde did not accept the book, as many seem to suppose, whole-heartedly, for Dorian Gray says of it, 'I didn't say I liked it, Harry. I said it fascinated me. There is a great difference.'

And to compound the story of art feeding upon itself, Beerbohm's definition of Decadent qualities in his 'A Letter to the Editor' of the second *Yellow Book* depends on Wilde:

> There are signs that our English literature has reached that point, when, like the literatures of all the nations that have been, it must fall at length into the hands of the decadents. The qualities that I tried in my essay to travesty – paradox and marivaudage, lassitude, a love of horror and all unusual things, a love of argot and archaism and

the mysteries of style – are not all these displayed, some by one, some by another of les jeunes écrivains? Who knows but that Artifice is in truth at our gates and that soon she may pass through our streets? Already the windows of Grub Street are crowded with watchful, evil faces.

There is indeed an increasing self-consciousness, and an interest in artificiality and the creations of man, that would lead to the literariness of Lionel Johnson, the poems on paintings, the increasing concentration on form as subject, and the criticism of the *Yellow Book* within its own pages.

It was before the publication of Wilde's book that a newer interpretation of the word 'decadence' was brought into English, perhaps its earliest appearance being in an essay by Havelock Ellis in the *Pioneer* for October 1889. Swinburne and other Francophiles would have been familiar with the beliefs and names of French groups, but I know of no reference to Decadence in Swinburne. For his generation as a whole, reference to German writers, to Heine and Goethe, is far more common than mention of French authors, Gautier or Baudelaire. In October of 1889 Ellis wrote 'A Note on Paul Bourget'; Bourget (whom I have placed here rather than in the survey of French Decadence in order to make the link with Ellis) was the author of two books on contemporary writers, *Essais de Psychologie Contemporaine* (1881) and *Nouveaux Essais de Psychologie Contemporaine* (1885), which have a scientific approach which would attract Ellis. In them he studies authors who particularly embody various aspects of modern writing, Baudelaire, Leconte de Lisle, Tourgéniev, Amiel, Renan, Flaubert, Taine, Stendhal, Dumas fils, Edmund and Jules de Goncourt. He comes to the melancholy conclusion that all their work is profoundly pessimistic, a later expression of *le mal du siècle* (just as Symons was to see things as the results of the *maladie fin de siècle*), a result of tiredness with life and an attitude that all effort is vain. In the essay on Baudelaire, Bourget discusses the *Théorie de la Décadence*, and this section forms the point of departure for Ellis's comments. Bourget had stated that: 'Par le mot de décadence, on désigne volontiers l'état d'une société qui produit un trop petit nombre d'individus propres aux trauvaux de la vie commune' (*Essais de Psychologie Contemporaine*, Paris, 1920, I, p. 19). Ellis translates the whole passage when he writes of decadence:

> Bourget uses this word as it is generally used (but, as Gautier pointed out, rather unfortunately) to express the literary methods of a society which has reached its limits of expansion and maturity – 'the state of society,' in his own words, 'which produces too large a number of individuals who are unsuited to the labours of common life. A society should be like an organism. Like an organism, in fact,

it may be resolved into a federation of smaller organisms, which may themselves be resolved into a federation of cells. The individual is the social cell. In order that the organism should perform its functions with energy it is necessary that the organisms composing it should perform their functions with energy, but with a subordinated energy, and in order that these lesser organisms should themselves perform their functions with energy, it is necessary that the cells comprising them should perform their functions with energy, but with a subordinated energy. If the energy of the cells becomes independent, the lesser organisms will likewise cease to subordinate their energy to the total energy and the anarchy which is established constitutes the *decadence* of the whole. The social organism does not escape this law and enters into decadence as soon as the individual life becomes exaggerated beneath the influence of acquired well-being, and of heredity. A similar law governs the development and decadence of that other organism which we call language. A style of decadence is one in which the unity of the book is decomposed to give place to the independence of the page, in which the page is decomposed to give place to the independence of the phrase, and the phrase to give place to the independence of the word'.

(*Views and Reviews. First Series*, 1932, pp. 51–2)

The italicizing of the word, and Ellis's whole tone of explaining some concept new to the language, gives some basis for the suggestion that this may indeed be the first time the word is used with this application in English. Summing up Bourget's ideas, Ellis emphasizes style rather than subject, and includes some more names in the heterogeneous collection of writers who at one time or another fall into that category:

A decadent style, in short, is an anarchistic style in which everything is sacrificed to the development of the individual parts. Apuleius, Petronius, St Augustine, Tertullian, are examples of this *decadence* in ancient literature; Gautier and Baudelaire in French literature; Poe and especially Whitman (in so far as he can be said to have a style) in America; in English literature Sir Thomas Browne is probably the most conspicuous instance; later De Quincey, and, in part of their work, Coleridge and Rossetti.   (*Views and Reviews*, pp. 52–3)

Like Pater and like his friend Arthur Symons, Ellis insists on the style of Decadence rather than its content, but he does note the difficulty of the word when he notes that 'the style of decadence sometimes tends to represent what Baudelaire calls "la phosphorescence de la pourriture" ' (p. 53).

Ellis, like most of the men who were to write on the topic, was familiar with France; not so Lionel Johnson, whose knowledge of

France was largely academic, but who in April 1891 wrote an article for volume VI of the *Century Guild Hobby Horse*, 'A Note upon the Practice and Theory of Verse at the Present Time Obtaining in France', an article subtly illuminated by the appearance opposite its final page of Dowson's 'Cynara' (the same volume had as its frontispiece a reproduction of G.F. Watts's painting 'A Roman Lady in the Decadence of the Empire'). Johnson first identifies in France a 'spirit of excellent curiosity' (Arnold's term soon to be used by Symons) and, having spoken of older French schools, goes on to write of the new, again with the manner of explaining new ideas and relying heavily on French sources:

> But we have now to say the few words, possible to an English writer, upon the last, the newest, of the French schools: and it cannot be without great caution, great deference, great submission, that I must speak. So sincerely do I feel this; so well do I recognize the difficulty of criticism and the peril of wrong judgment, incident to writers upon a foreign literature: that I will stand aside, and let a more competent writer define the schools, to which belong, not, it may be thought, too happily, the names of *décadence* or of *symbolisme*. Here is a concise view of them, by M. Antoni Lange:
>
> 'Manque d'Idées et de Formes neuves dans la littérature contemporaine: même chose en peinture et musique avant le Plein-air et le Wagnérisme. Un désir littéraire nouveau parmi l'Europe: la France, avec ses 'Décadents' qu'elle insulte, ouvre la voie.
>
> 'Histoire: chute du Romantisme, Parnassiens, le Naturalisme, Le Naturalisme a les *tabulae praesentiae et absentiae* – métier et préparation, – et non *comparationis* que possède le Symbolisme, qui est philosophique.
>
> 'Baudelaire, Verlaine, Mallarmé.
>
> 'Paul Verlaine et son école: Jean Moréas, Jules Laforgue, Gustave Kahn, etc. Cette école n'est pas sortie du Romantisme et le continue.
>
> 'L'école Symboliste et instrumentiste: école de Stéphane Mallarmé, dont René Ghil, Stuart Merrill, Henri de Régnier, Francis Vielé-Griffin, Emile Verhaeren, Georges Khnopff, c'est l'École Nouvelle.
>
> 'Forme et matière: symbole et musique.
>
> 'Matière, La poétique nouvelle: le TRAITÉ DU VERBE. Le tout de la théorie symboliste est dans ces mots de Mallarmé: ". . . [sic] brut et immédiat ici, là essentiel . . ." [sic] La Poésie est un Symbole.
>
> 'Le point philosophique de l'École: évolution, perfectionnement de l'humanité, Dieu et religion rationels, vénération de la Raison, le sentiment dans l'intellect, oubli du Moi, universalisme des Symbolistes.
>
> 'Forme. Forme stricte, Enrichissement de la langue. Musique de la

langue Française, son histoire: Hugo, Gautier, Banville, Sully-Prudhomme, Baudelaire, Verlaine, Mallarmé.

'Audition colorée. Une langue unissant les formes poétiques, éloquente, plastique, pictorale et musicale: l'INSTRUMENTATION PARLÉE de René Ghil.

'Conclusion: C'est là l'École nouvelle: "elle est en sa période d'orage et de guerre. Elle deviendra une source d'universalisme actif et créateur pour le siècle qui vient, car il y a en elle les rayons de la Vérité." '

Now that is a most remarkable statement: we are here presented with a theory and a practice of poetry, involving, it would seem, Wagner's music, and Bacon's induction, and a host of scientific or philosophical things. It must either be very absurd: or very serious. I speak for myself: having read, pondered, and discussed, many volumes of this poetry, I do not find it absurd: on the contrary, I am somewhat disposed, to think it a little too serious. But that is a fault, venial indeed, in this hasty and impatient age.

In English, *décadence* and the literature thereof, mean this: the period, at which passion, or romance, or tragedy, or sorrow, or any other form of activity or of emotion, must be refined upon, and curiously considered, for literary treatment: an age of afterthought, of reflection. Hence come one great virtue, and one great vice: the virtue of much and careful meditation upon life, its emotions and its incidents: the vice of over subtilty and of affectation, when thought thinks upon itself, and when emotions become entangled with the consciousness of them.

In English, *symbolisme*, and its literature, mean this: a recognition, in things, of a double existence: their existence in nature, and their existence in mind. The *sun sets*: what is the impression of that upon your mind, as you say the words? Clearly, that is the 'true truth' of the thing; its real and eternal significance: not the mere natural fact, but the thing, as it is in thought. So, literature is the evocation of truth from the passing show of things: a view, curiously like many philosophical views, from the days of Heraclitus to the days of Kant.

Now, in either of these schools, poetry becomes a matter of infinite pains, and of singular attention; to catch the precise aspect of a thing, as you see or feel it; to express, not the obvious and barren fact, but the inner and fruitful force of it; this is far from easy, far from trivial.   (pp. 63–5)

This is a fascinating article, written at a time when Johnson was looked up to as the theoretician of a group of young poets and one of their most able critics. From a purely verbal point of view, it is noticeable that he uses the French forms of Decadence and Symbolism, though one should not make too much of that since Johnson is rather a conservative writer. From the point of view of content, one must note the clarity of his definitions, his stress on the 'deliberate *science*' of the French poets, and his insistence on the need for technique. The magazine may well have had a small circulation, but it would have reached most of those writers who would be significant in the nineties.

About the same time as this article was published, another contributor to the *Century Guild Hobby Horse* showed the horror with which some Victorians looked at Decadence. In 'Michael Field's' diary for 1891, the fervent comment on the evening of Census Sunday, 5 April, was 'For oneself the prayer From decadence, Good lord deliver us!' It is probable then that the term was becoming popular a little before Johnson's article.

The conjunction of English and French traditions can be seen in Johnson's final paragraph, which may derive from his reading in French, but could equally well derive from Pater, who had written in the Preface to the *Renaissance* that

> To define beauty, not in the most abstract, but in the most concrete terms possible, to find, not a universal formula for it, but the formula which expresses most adequately this or that special manifestation of it, is the aim of the true student of aesthetics.
>
> 'To see the object as in itself it really is,' has been justly said to be the aim of all true criticism whatever; and in aesthetic criticism the first step towards seeing one's object as it really is, is to know one's own impression as it really is, to discriminate it, to realise it distinctly.   (pp. vii–viii)

It is not far from here to Symons's description of Decadence, nor is it far from here to Eliot's 'objective correlative' which he defines in the penultimate paragraph of his 1919 essay on *Hamlet* as a 'set of objects, a situation, a chain of events which shall be the formula of that *particular* emotion.'

The two or three years after 1891 saw an explosion in the popularity of the word itself, though the ideas described as Decadent look familiar. Bourget had said the Decadents were pessimistic; *Punch* depicted 'Post Prandial Pessimists':

> Scene – *The Smoking-room at the Decadents.*
> *First Decadent (M.A. Oxon).* 'After all, Smythe, what would life be without coffee?'
> *Second Decadent (M.A. Camb.)* 'True, Jeohnes, true! And yet, after all, what is life *with* coffee?   (15 October 1892)

Obviously Decadence comes with an education, but by December of

1892 it is just part of the battle of the sexes in 'Snubbing a Decadent':

He.   'A – don't you find existence an awful bore?'

She.   'A – well, *some* people's existence – most decidedly!'

Punch in fact drew a great deal of copy from Decadent poets in these years, among which Owen Seaman's satires, later published as *The Battle of the Bays* (1894), must stand high. The highest concentration of references to Decadence was in 1894. On 7 July 'Our Decadents' in the person of Flipbutt, a famous young art-critic, mistook a child's drawing for an impressionist work. On 14 July 'Our Female Decadents' preferred to sit out dances with an energetic but clumsy dancer. In the same issue, a playlet called 'Select Passages from a Coming Poet' contained pieces called 'Disenchantment' and 'Abasement'. It is not difficult to see the poetry being satirized here:

> My love has sickled into Loath,
>   And foul seems all that fair I fancied –
> The lily's sheen a leprous growth,
>   The very buttercups are rancid

or in 'Abasement':

> With matted head a-dabble in the dust,
> And eyes tear-sealèd in a saline crust,
> I lie all loathly in my rags and rust –
> Yet learn that strange delight may lurk in self-disgust.

To this last a character remarks, 'I rather like that – it's so very decadent!' On 27 October 'Our Decadents' (obviously a popular series) stand rather aesthetically saying:

Algy. 'What's the matter, Archie? You're not looking well!'

Archie. '*You* wouldn't look well, if you'd been suffering from insomnia every afternoon for a week!'

And the Christmas number rounded off the year with its 'Britannia à la Beardsley (*By our 'Yellow' Decadent*)'.

　　While *Punch* was making fun, the discussion about Decadence went on. Richard Le Gallienne expanded the discussion of the subject in the *Century Guild Hobby Horse* in 1892. Indeed, in 1892 and 1893 he was often occupied with the topic. In letters to the pages of the *Daily Chronicle*, he (among nearly 2,000 correspondents) discussed Christianity and Decadence, and from these letters came his *Religion of a Literary Man* (1893) in which there is a violent attack on '*décadent*' art. Le Gallienne keeps the French word, as he had done in the poem 'The Décadent to his Soul', which he published in his *English Poems* (1892), obviously in an attempt to keep the blight away from English poetry. The introductory poem 'To the Reader' complains that

> Art was a palace once, things great and fair,
> And strong and holy, found a temple there:
> Now 'tis a lazar-house of leprous men.

'The Décadent to his Soul' makes a more specific attack. At one time the *Décadent* had thought that

> The body were enough,
> The body gives me all.

But seeing the attractive soul, he smiled evilly and

> dreamed of a new sin:
> An incest 'twixt the body and the soul.

So the *Décadent*

> used his soul
> As bitters to the over dulcet sins,
> As olives to the fatness of the feast –
> She made those dear heart-rending ecstasies
> Of minor chords amid the Phrygian lutes,
> She sauced his sins with splendid memories,
> Starry regrets and infinite hopes and fears;
> His holy youth and his first love
> Made pearly background to strange-coloured vice.

The accuracy of Le Gallienne's analysis is obvious if one puts this poem against Dowson's work, especially 'Cynara' which Le Gallienne knew. He quite rightly points to the tension between ideal and real, but sees it as perverse rather than tragic:

> Sin is no sin when virtue is forgot.
> It is so good in sin to keep in sight
> The white hills whence we fell, to measure by –
> To say I was so high, so white, so pure,
> And am so low, so blood-stained and so base;
> I revel here amid the sweet sweeet mire
> And yonder are the hills of morning flowers:
> So high, so low; so lost and with me yet;
> To stretch the octave 'twixt the dream and deed,
> Ah, that's the thrill!

Finally, Le Gallienne wishes to keep the soul and body separate, weeping for both because

> The man was once an apple-cheek dear lad,

The soul was once an angel up in heaven.

O let the body be a healthy beast,
And keep the soul a singing soaring bird;
But lure thou not the soul from out the sky
To pipe unto the body in the sty.

Le Gallienne does not write a good poem, but it is perceptive of important features of Decadent writing, in particular the Decadent paradox.

Unfortunately he does not notice the paradox in his own book, between his stolidly English attitude in poems like the two I have mentioned and the Decadent view in 'Beauty Accurst'. E.K. Chambers brought this out among other points in a review of Le Gallienne's book for the *Academy*, which places Decadence effectively:

The title of Mr Le Gallienne's book is designed, one gathers, to be a protest against certain latter-day tendencies in literature; and the protest is amplified in an address 'To the Reader', and in a very striking, clever poem called 'The Décadent to his Soul'. Mr Le Gallienne wishes us clearly to understand that he is on the side of the angels, and that he is not tarred with the brush of Verlaine, that his inspiration is manly and normal, not abnormal and morbid. . . . But whom is Mr Le Gallienne attacking? Is the note of decadence so strong in our younger poets, in those in whose hands the future of our poetry rests? If Mr Le Gallienne will look for a moment beyond the borders of the Rhymers' Club, he will surely see that it is not. Mr Robert Bridges, Mr William Watson, Mr Alfred Austin, Mrs Woods – they are sane and healthy and 'English' enough; they have not made Cayenne pepper of their souls. And what has Mr Le Gallienne to say for 'Beauty Accurst' – la très belle *Beauté maudite*? Then again, the antithesis of 'English' and 'Décadent' is not a true one.

(*Academy*, 19 November 1892, p. 451)

Le Gallienne rather weakly replied to this review, claiming he had in mind 'the tendency of modern English letters' rather than the 'work of any particular poet, the influences in the air, mainly critical as yet, which will inevitably, one may fear, affect the youngest generation of poets' (p. 485).

Certainly he was frequently concerned with those influences in his criticism, attempting in a variety of reviews to define Decadence to his own liking. His usual argument was that Decadence failed to 'see life steadily and see it whole', though his poem had complained of remembering virtue in the midst of sin. In his 'Considerations suggested by Mr. Churton Collins' "Illustrations of Tennyson" ' in the *Century Guild Hobby Horse* (vol. VII, 1892), Le Gallienne took up the argument from

Lionel Johnson earlier in the same magazine, and tried to think out the question of literary Decadence.

> But what is decadence in literature? It seems largely to be confused with a decadence in the style of literature, which is not quite the same thing. Even that decadence is continually misunderstood – euphuism and quite proper organic refinements of style being continually confused with each other. Mr. Collins, and many others, continually assume that the mere exercise of conscious art in literature, the care of the unique word, the use of various literary means to literary ends, as alliteration and onomatopoeia, constitute decadence. To say this is to be forced to the absurd conclusion that the nearer an instrument approaches perfection, the more it becomes adapted to the uses for which it is designed, the less its value. The only decadence in style are euphuism and its antithesis, slang. . . .
>
> But decadence in literature is more than a question of style, nor is it, as some suppose, a question of theme. It is in the character of the treatment that we must seek it. In all great vital literature, the theme, great or small, is always considered in all its relations near and far and above all in relation to the sum total of things, to the infinite, as we phrase it; in decadent literature the relations, the due proportions, are ignored. One might say that decadence consists in the euphuistic expression of isolated observations. Thus disease, which is a favourite theme of *décadents*, does not in itself make for decadence: it is only when, as often, it is studied apart from its relations to health, to the great vital centre of things, that it does so. Any point of view, seriously taken, which ignores the complete view, approaches decadence.
>
> To notice only the picturesque effect of a beggar's rags, like Gautier; the colour-scheme of a tipster's nose, like Mr. Huysmans; to consider one's mother merely prismatically, like Mr. Whistler – these are examples of the decadent attitude.
>
> At the bottom, decadence is merely limited thinking, often insane thinking.   (pp. 80–1)

It may be the result of answering Lionel Johnson's attitude that this article is French orientated, but the same attack on French models is implicit in Le Gallienne's *The Religion of a Literary Man* (1893), especially since *décadence* is still set apart by its accent and italics as an unwanted import from France.

Speaking of the religious senses, he says that

> The Sense of Beauty, however, is not necessarily a religious sense – save in so far as it gives birth to the sense of wonder, of love, of gratitude. Curiously enough, in our own day, among what we call

décadent artists, we find its influence not, as one would have expected, as a spiritualising, but as a materialising, an actually degrading, influence. Even when, as I make bold to say of its worst forms, *décadent* art is not merely the expression of moral mental and spiritual disease, lusts that dare no other operation finding vent in pictorial and literary symbolism, even when it retains a certain innocence and health, it does its best to limit its appeal to what we call the sensual faculties. It merely addresses the sensual eye and ear the more obviously, and endeavours desperately to limit beauty to form and colour, scornfully ignoring the higher sensibilities of heart and spirit. (p. 89)

It is an accurate enough description of certain theories of art then current to say that they are concerned with the sensual faculties. The 'Conclusion' to the *Renaissance*, about which Le Gallienne is so enthusiastic elsewhere, states that life itself is only realized through these faculties, and implies that symbols would be useless if there were no means of apprehending them. On the question of the morality of art, Le Gallienne is a little confused, wishing for the moral and yet understanding the need for the art of his day to be free from the restraint of conventional morals.

Not, of course, that I mean for a moment that art must be definitely moral or didactic. It has nothing to do with morals – only, so so to say, with spirituals. Many people seem to confuse the moral and the spiritual. As a matter of fact the spiritual must often of necessity be the immoral. A man's subject may be as so-called 'immoral' as he pleases so that he is able to treat it spiritually, or shall we say symbolically, in its relation to the whole of life. (p. 92)

He continues to argue that artists may claim to be dealing only with form and colour, but they cannot hope to paint a person without implying more than form and colour, as in the case of Whistler's portrait of his mother, because 'In the empire of life, art is but a province, and, like the artist, is subject to greater laws than its own' (p. 93).

The arguments may be a little lacking in sharpness, but Le Gallienne had a good nose for a popular subject, and this was a popular book, running to over 5,000 copies. His main claim is something of a reiteration of his *Hobby Horse* article about the lack of proportion:

This *décadence* is simply the result of that modern disregard of proportion of which I shall have to speak again. It would almost seem that the relative spirit has carried us so far that we have come to deny not only ultimates, but relations also. *Décadence* is founded on a natural impossibility to start with. It attempts the delineation of certain things and aspects *in vacuo*, isolated from all their relations to other things and their dependence on the great laws of life. Its position is as absurd as that of an artist who should say: I will paint this figure in but two dimensions, and will give it no length; or one who would say: I will paint this summer landscape, but omit all reference to sunlight. So hardly less vainly does the *décadent* attempt to ignore certain conditions of his theme, which, actually, it is impossible to ignore.   (pp. 90–1)

And so we are treated to Baudelaire's prismatic hues of corruption once again. Le Gallienne fails to notice that the impossibility of the task is recognized by Decadent writers and is itself a cause of much of the parody and the anguish in Decadent writing.

Because of Le Gallienne's popularity, let me reproduce two further sections from his book which are not so commonly reprinted as his other versions of Decadence. First, he acknowledges that his book will be rejected by

> the typical literary man of the period, who sips his absinthe (with a charmingly boyish sense of sin), and reads Huysmans. To discuss such antiquated matters as God, Love, and Duty, when one might be wrangling over Degas, or grappling with a sonnet by Mallarmé!
>
>   (pp. 9–10)

Obviously the Decadent again, who is further analysed in a section called 'The Dream of the Décadent':

> But in other guises, that dog-fighter is still with us. His latest evangel has been that of the demi-monde and the music-hall. Soon, he has prophesied, 'domesticity' with all its irksome restraints, shall be no more. Repent, for a Walpurgis night is at hand when men and women shall once more run on all fours as dogs, and revel in the offal of the streets. O happy era of liberty, when the talon is free of the sheath for ever, and lust may run without his muzzle; when every one may be as indecent as his heart wishes, and he who loves the gutter may lie therein without reproach; when no man takes off the hat to a woman or a church, but all may wear it jauntily on one side, through the length and breadth of the land, may smoke and drink unmoved before the sacred passion-play of life, and expectorate with a fine carelessness, none daring to make them afraid! Such is the dream of the poor little sensual 'dog-fighter' of our days. Instead of dogs he sells us beastly and silly novels, poetry he dare not expose for sale at Farringdon market, and pathetic 'advanced' science which runs thus: 'It is a sad mission to cut through and destroy with the scissors of analysis the delicate and iridescent veils with which our proud mediocrity clothes itself. Very terrible is the religion of truth. The physiologist is not afraid to reduce love to a play of stamens and

pistils, and thought to a molecular movement. Even genius, the one human power before which we may bow the knee without shame, has been classed by not a few alienists as on the confines of criminality, one of the tetralogic forms of the human mind, a variety of insanity.' But shall we despair of man's soul because, forsooth! a Lombroso cannot find it, or of love because Paul Verlaine is a satyr, of religion and law because a mad poet fires his little pistol at Westminster. I think not. What are all these men but dirty children building their mud-pies, and soon oblivion, like an indignant mother, shall send them all to bed.

The spring of a new era is in the air – an era of faith. That prophesied Walpurgis night is already behind us; and except in the imagination of a handful of ill-conditioned writers, artists, and 'thinkers', who have written and painted and 'thought' for each other, it never had even any potential existence.   (pp. 103–5)

The passage is interesting for its detail, and for placing Le Gallienne against both Verlaine and Lombroso – where would he stand when he read Nordau's Lombroso-inspired attacks on Verlaine?

Le Gallienne is himself trapped in the Decadent dilemma, writing on obviously Decadent themes in his 'Beauty Accurst' and 'A Ballad of London', while longing for religious acceptability and expressing his faith in a separate book on religion and Literature. How appropriate then for him to review John Gray, a poet who expressed the opposing sides of his character in his *Silverpoints* and his *Spiritual Poems* (1896). Reviewing the former when it came out in 1893, Le Gallienne found it not Decadent, a curious conclusion when one considers that it is often regarded as the epitome of Decadent book-production, that it imitates and translates from Decadent poets like Baudelaire and Verlaine, and even uses the line from the Decadent poem 'Langueur' to set the tone. Le Gallienne reiterates his earlier ideas about proportion, and gives a detailed picture of what he associates with Decadence:

Mr Gray's poems are not so decadent as he would have us suppose. They are luxurious to the last degree, they are subtly cadenced as the song the sirens sang, they will dwell over-unctuously on many forbidden themes – 'many whisper things I dare not tell' – they are each separately dedicated to every more or less decadent poet of Mr Gray's acquaintance, and their *format*; an adaptation of the Aldine italic books, is of a far-wrought deliciousness.

But in spite of his neo-Catholicism and his hot-house erotics, Mr Gray cannot accomplish that gloating abstraction from the larger life of humanity which marks the decadent.

(*Retrospective Reviews*, 1896, I, pp. 230–1)

And having quoted a stanza ending 'What bonny hair our child will have!' he concludes 'Is this not absurdly domestic in a decadent? Really Mr Gray must check these natural impulses.' The luxuriousness of the poem, the perhaps literally deathly pallor of the lady, seem to have escaped him. The lady is another of those attractive and impossible women – 'Bud and fruit are always ripe' as Gray has it (p. xviii) – of the Decadent ideal.

Le Gallienne follows the general pattern of writers who were both involved in the controversy of the 1890s and wrote of it later, in that he is less willing in 1926 to have the writers of the period gathered under the flag of Decadence. In his *The Romantic '90s* (1926) he says that

> *The Yellow Book* has become the symbol of the period, and the two or three writers and artists to whom the word 'decadence' may perhaps be applied have been taken as characteristic of a time which was far from being all 'yellow', or 'naughty', or 'decadent'.   (p. 122)

In the end, all that he sees the group of writers most closely associated with Decadence to have in common is a publisher, John Lane. Vincent O'Sullivan, who published books in the nineties with the imprint of Leonard Smithers and designs by Beardsley, shares this rejection of the label in his *Opinions*, blaming it all on Arthur Symons who, he says, 'though he was perhaps the only decadent in London . . . has managed to pass into history as the leader of a definite movement called Decadent' (pp. 198–9).

Symons is unquestionably the central Decadent writer. Intimate with Havelock Ellis, whose early essay on Bourget may have introduced the topic to this country, Symons went to Paris in 1889 and 1890 and consolidated his ideas about contemporary French schools of literature. Ellis, with whom he went, was finding out what was going on in medical and anthropological quarters, while Symons was getting first-hand information on trends in art and literature, but they must have shared each other's interests (there is an intriguing possibility of close links between medical and scientific discoveries and the vocabulary of Decadence). During their stay, they met many of the leaders of the Decadent movement, and others associated with it, Verlaine, Mallarmé, Rodin and Odilon Redon, and Huysmans, to whom they were introduced by Remy de Gourmont.

It was thus with first-hand knowledge of the facts and with Havelock Ellis's comments on Bourget's interpretation of Decadence that Symons began to use the term, but he is by no means whole-heartedly in support of either '*Décadents*' or '*Symbolistes*' in these early days, as one can see from his review of Verlaine's *Bonheur*:

He has done what Goncourt has done in his prose: he has

contributed to the destruction of a classical language, which, within its narrow limits, had its own perfection. But how great a gain there has been, along with this inevitable loss! In the hands of the noisy little school of *Décadents*, the brain-sick little school of *Symbolistes*, both claiming Verlaine as a master, these innovations have of course been carried to the furthest limits of caricature.

(*Academy*, 18 April 1891, p. 362)

Edmund Gosse defends this position of Symons's in the *Academy* for 7 January 1893, saying that 'if the school has had a single friend in England, it has been Mr. Arthur Symons, one of the most brilliant of the younger poets; and even he has been interested, I think, more in M. Verlaine than in the Symbolists and Décadents proper' (p. 5). But in 1893 Symons seems more disposed to accept the title of Decadent, although he still makes reservations about the extremes, in his article on 'The Decadent Movement in Literature', in *Harper's New Monthly Magazine* (LXXXVII, November 1893).

This article, more than any other, whether by Le Gallienne, Johnson or Ellis, has had the most far-reaching effect on subsequent accounts and criticisms of the Decadent movement in England. For the first time the movement was not merely described, but vigorously defended and praised, and the movement was seen as a European rather than a merely French phenomenon. Walter Pater was linked with the school and, in more detail, W.E. Henley was praised for doing in English the things that the French Decadents had done. Again the controversialist of the nineties developed into a less partial observer in the twentieth century, for when the essay was reprinted in *Dramatis Personae* (1925), all matter describing the Decadence in England is ommitted. Perhaps after the response to the Wilde trial, Henley could hardly be said to deserve the name of Decadent.

I make no apology for quoting at length from this central statement of Decadent ideas. It is the most extended, authoritative and influential statement and, more important, it dates from the central years of the movement. Symons explains his terms in the opening paragraphs:

The latest movement in European literature has been called by many names, none of them quite exact or comprehensive – Decadence, Symbolism, Impressionism, for instance. It is easy to dispute over words, and we shall find that Verlaine objects to being called a Decadent, Maeterlinck to being called a Symbolist, Huysmans to being called an Impressionist. These terms, as it happens, have been adopted as the badge of little separate cliques, noisy, brainsick young people who haunt the brasseries of the Boulevard Saint-Michel, and exhaust their ingenuities in theorizing over the works they cannot write. But, taken frankly as epithets which express their own meaning, both Impressionism and Symbolism convey some notion of that new kind of literature which is more broadly characterized by the word Decadence.   (p. 858)

The last sentence is a little unhelpful, but, probably deriving his ideas about classical Decadences as much from Lionel Johnson as from his own reading in those Decadent authors, Symons does give some particular qualities that help to define Decadence:

> The most representative literature of the day – the writing which appeals to, which has done so much to form, the younger generation – is certainly not classic, nor has it any relation with that old antithesis of the Classic, the Romantic. After a fashion it is no doubt a decadence: it has all the qualities that mark the end of great periods, the qualities that we find in the Greek, the Latin, decadence: an intense self-consciousness, a restless curiosity in research, an over-subtilizing refinement upon refinement, a spiritual and moral perversity. If what we call the classic is indeed the supreme art – those qualities of perfect simplicity, perfect sanity, perfect proportion, the supreme qualities – then this representative literature of to-day, interesting, beautiful, novel as it is, is really a new and beautiful and interesting disease.   (pp. 858–9)

For Symons at this time, Decadence is both a style and an attitude towards content, both characterized by their newness, their lack of relation to what has gone before, although he does pick up and express forcibly that idea which had been present in Baudelaire which associates corruption both of language and subject with Decadence: 'Healthy we cannot call it, and healthy it does not wish to be considered.' Diseased or not, Symons defends Decadent art against the classic, since it depicts what it must, life as it is around it:

> For its very disease of form, this literature is certainly typical of a civilization grown over-luxurious, over-inquiring, too languid for the relief of action, too uncertain for any emphasis in opinion or in conduct. It reflects all the moods, all the manners, of a sophisticated society; its very artificiality is a way of being true to nature: simplicity, sanity, proportion – the classic qualities – how much do we possess them in our life, our surroundings, that we should look to find them in our literature – so evidently the literature of a decadence?   (p. 859)

He takes the word Decadence as 'most precisely expressing the general sense of the newest movement in literature' and defines its qualities as novelty, artificiality, self-consciousness, over-subtlety, complexity and a spiritual and moral perversity.

Decadence he divides into the two branches of Symbolism and Impressionism, both of which seek *la vérité vraie*, Impressionism by representing things as they appear to the senses, and Symbolism by penetrating the surface to reach the inner meaning of things. In order to keep pace with these searching theories, which demand an endeavour after the perfect expression and a rejection of the ready-made in both language and form, a new style had to be developed.

> In France, where this movement began and has mainly flourished, it is Goncourt who was the first to invent a style in prose really new, impressionistic, a style which was itself amost sensation. It is Verlaine who has invented such another new style in verse. (p. 859)

And it is this development of style that forms the argument of the subsequent pages on the Goncourts and Verlaine.

> What the Goncourts have done is to specialize vision, so to speak, and to subtilize language to the point of rendering every detail in just the form and colour of the actual impression. (p. 860)

Verlaine in verse has done the same, defining the ideal of poetic art in his 'Art Poétique' where he cried for 'rien que la Nuance.' While Verlaine has managed to 'fix the last fine shade', Mallarmé has become the theoretician. In his paragraphs on Mallarmé's language, Symons makes the familiar comparison with Latin Decadence:

> Mallarmé's contortion of the French language, so far as mere style is concerned, is curiously similar to the kind of depravation which was undergone by the Latin language in its decadence. It is, indeed, in part a reversion to Latin phraseology, to the Latin construction, and it has made, of the clear and flowing French language, something irregular, unquiet, expressive, with sudden surprising felicities, with nervous starts and lapses, with new capacities for the exact noting of sensation. Alike to the ordinary and to the scholarly reader, it is painful, intolerable; a jargon, a massacre. (p. 862)

Mallarmé's Decadence is seen almost purely as style and form, his experiments with rhythm leading naturally to the 'freak or the discovery of "le vers libre" ' (p. 863), though mere technical virtuosity is still not what makes a poet.

Symons's account of the Decadent movement as he prints it in *Dramatis Personae* ends with some comments on Maeterlinck, Villiers de l'Isle Adam and Huysmans:

> Joris Karl Huysmans demands a prominent place in any record of the Decadent movement. His work, like that of the Goncourts, is largely determined by the *maladie fin de siècle* – the diseased nerves

that, in his case, have given a curious personal quality of pessimism
to his outlook on the world, his view of life.   (p. 865)

Symons sees des Esseintes as the typical Decadent, 'the effeminate,
over-civilized, deliberately abnormal creature who is the last product
of our society: partly the father, partly the offspring, of the perverse art
that he adores' (p. 866). Self-born like Jay Gatsby, or connected with
art as father or son, man becomes gathered into the artifice of eternity.
A Rebours is for Symons not merely an expression of Huysmans but an
expression of an epoch, which a 'style which carries the modern experiments upon language to their furthest development' (p. 866).

> Barbaric in its profusion, violent in its emphasis, wearying in its
> splendour, it is – especially in regard to things seen – extraordi-
> narily expressive, with all the shades of a painter's palette.
> Elaborately and deliberately perverse, it is in its very perversity that
> Huysman's work – so fascinating, so repellent, so instinctively
> artifical – comes to represent, as the work of no other writer can be
> said to do, the main tendencies, the chief results, of the Decadent
> movement in literature.   (p. 866)

So he sums up Decadence and so he later leaves it. But at the time
when he had been its chief voice in England he had continued the article
with an examination of the Decadent movement as it was seen outside
France and more particularly in England. The list of European writers
goes to Holland for the Sensitivists, such as Couperus in *Ecstasy*, to
Italy for Luigi Capuana, and for Gabriele d'Annunzio in 'that marvel-
lous, malarious *Piacere*', to Spain for Senora Pardo-Bazan, to Norway
for Ibsen, with the Impressionism of *Hedda Gabler* and the Symbolism
of *The Master Builder*. As for the English Decadents

> The prose of Mr. Walter Pater, the verse of Mr. W.E. Henley – to
> take two prominent examples – are attempts to do with the English
> language something of what Goncourt and Verlaine have done with
> the French.   (p. 866)

Pater and Henley are certainly not the two writers a modern critic
would choose to call Decadent, but are here given the name for their
style:

> And *Marius the Epicurean*, in its study of 'sensations and ideas' (the
> conjunction was Goncourt's before it was Mr. Pater's), and the
> *Imaginary Portraits*, in their evocations of the Middle Ages, the age
> of Watteau – have they not that morbid subtlety of analysis, that
> morbid curiosity of form, that we have found in the works of French
> Decadents?   (p. 867)

Henley's poetry is a fulfilment of Verlaine's demand for 'sincerity and the impression of the moment followed to the letter', and Symons adds that 'the poetry of Impressionism can go no further, in one direction, than that series of rhymes and rhythms named *In Hospital*' (p. 867). Symons's odd choice of Henley, ruling out deliberate attempts to involve him with a group which he would dislike, is explained by the summary, curiously predictive of Eliot's critical ideas of impersonality:

> He has written verse that is exquisitely frivolous, daintily capricious, wayward and fugitive as the winged remembrance of some momentary delight. And, in certain fragments, he has come nearer than any other English singer to what I have called the achievement of Verlaine and the ideal of the Decadence: to be a disembodied voice, and yet the voice of a human soul. (p. 867)

The rejection of the later section of the essay is related to Symons's rejection of the term altogether in favour of Symbolism. In the last *Savoy* in December 1896, Smithers announced Symons's book to be called *The Decadent Movement in Literature*, listing its chapters as Introduction, Paul Verlaine, the Goncourts, J.K. Huysmans, Villiers de l'Isle Adam, Maurice Maeterlinck, Conclusion. His later book, whose title is changed only in one word, *The Symbolist Movement in Literature*, contains essays on Verlaine, Mallarmé, Maeterlinck, Villiers, and Huysmans, in fact all those whom he had previously termed Decadent, with the exception of Goncourt (whom he added in 1919, though one must not make too much of post 1908 alterations).

In 1899 in *The Symbolist Movement in Literature*, he repudiates the term Decadent, and explains away the whole movement as merely preparing the way for something more important:

> Meanwhile, something which is vaguely called Decadence had come into being. That name, rarely used with any precise meaning, was usually either hurled as a reproach or hurled back as a defiance. It pleased some young men in various countries to call themselves Decadents, with all the thrill of unsatisfied virtue masquerading as uncomprehended vice. As a matter of fact, the term is in its place only when applied to style; to that ingenious deformation of the language, in Mallarmé, for instance, which can be compared with what we are accustomed to call the Greek and Latin of the Decadence. No doubt perversity of form and perversity of matter are often found together, and, among the lesser men especially, experiment was carried far, not only in the direction of style. But a movement which in this sense might be called Decadent could but have been a straying aside from the main road of literature. Nothing, not even conventional virtue, is so provincial as conventional vice; and

the desire to 'bewilder the middle-classes' is itself middle-class. The interlude, half a mock-interlude, of Decadence, diverted the attention of the critics while something more serious was in preparation. That something more serious has crystallised, for the time, under the form of Symbolism, in which art returns to the one pathway, leading through beautiful things to the eternal beauty.   (pp. 6–7)

This is the language of Yeats in the Preface to *Poems* (1895). Decadence is almost a scapegoat, but the dismissal highlights the rapid rise and fall of the popularity of Decadence even with its central figure.

Not that the word dropped out of use. Symons had disclaimed its application to matters other than style, but it had occurred with other applications in his own writing. In an essay 'On English and French Fiction' reprinted in *Dramatis Personae* (1925), he speaks of the 'subtle decadence of *Dorian Gray*' (p. 81) while concentrating on the subject of the book. In the essay 'Confessions and Comments' he writes of the novels of George Moore that they are 'entertaining, realistic, and decadent; and certainly founded on modern French fiction' (p. 132). Nine pages later he writes of 'that perverse, decadent, delicately depraved study of the stages in the education of the young Parisian girl, *Chérie*' (p. 141). The subject matter is of some relevance when he takes Sir Richard Burton as his subject:

> Certainly Burton leaves out nothing of the nakedness that startles one in the verse of Catullus: a nakedness that is as honest as daylight and as shameless as night. When the text is obscene his translation retains its obscenity; which, on the whole, is rare: for the genius of Catullus is elemental, primitive, nervous, passionate, decadent in the modern sense and in the modern sense perverse.   (p. 247)

The self-consciousness, a characteristic of Decadent literature, marks this criticism and its use of the term. Even in 1897 Symons had realized that Decadence had ceased to express the main trend in literature, significantly in an essay on W.E. Henley called 'Modernity in Verse' (reprinted in *Studies in Two Literatures*, 1924). For Symons, modernity had taken the place of Decadence as the quality of Henley's work, and the essay amounts to a retraction of his earlier position in the *Harper's* article. From a position where he tentatively accepted Decadence as a description of content and style, Symons retreated to using the term only of style, and then abandoned it as a temporary phase, only half serious.

Max Beerbohm was never wholly serious, but does confirm the bias towards style and the debt to Pater in his essay 'Be it Cosiness' in *The Pageant* in 1896:

> Not that even in those more decadent days of my childhood did I

admire the man [Pater] as a stylist. Even then I was angry that he should treat English as a dead language, bored by that sedulous ritual where-with he laid out every sentence as in a shroud – hanging, like a widower, long over its marmoreal beauty or ever he could lay it at length in his book, its sepulchre.   (p. 230)

Beerbohm's self-conscious style is both criticism and parody at once. In the first *Yellow Book*, in April 1894, Beerbohm had connected Decadence and artifice, in particular the artifice of make-up, while making that uncomfortable comparison between the end of the Victorian era and the decline of Rome:

For behold! The Victorian era comes to its end and the day of *sancta simplicitas* is quite ended. The old signs are here and the portents to warn the seer of life that we are ripe for a new era of artifice. Are not men rattling the dice-box and ladies dipping their fingers in the rougepot? At Rome, in the keenest time of her *degringolade*, when there was gambling even in the holy temples, great ladies (does not Lucian tell us?) did not scruple to squander all they had upon unguents from Arabia.   (pp. 65–6)

This essay, 'a bomb thrown by a cowardly decadent' in the eyes of its critics and in Max's eyes a flippant burlesque, is almost the swan-song of the movement. Telescoping his view of history, Max viewed 1880 and his youth as the distant past and, while Beardsley was yet working, said farewell to the 'Beardsley period'. And the *Yellow Book*, commonly held to be the epitome of the Decadence, changed drastically after volume IV.

Before that volume, the *Yellow Book* had focussed the discussion of Decadent literature for supporter and critic alike. *Punch* recognized this immediately and published frequent parody. On 2 February 1895 Beardsley's illustrations and Beerbohm's essay '1880' in the fourth *Yellow Book* were the main targets of a passage supposedly 'From the Queer and Yellow Book':

1894
(*By Max Mereboom.*)

'Linger longer, LUCY,
    Linger longer, LOO.
How I'd like to linger longer,
    Linger longer, LOO!' – *Old Ballad.*

I suppose there is no one that has not wished, from Time to Time, that someone else had lived in another Age than his own. I myself have often felt that it would have been nice to live in 1894; to have seen the '*Living Pictures*' at the old *Empire*, to have strained my Eyes for a glimpse of *Mrs. Patrick Campbell*, broken my Cane applauding *May Yohé*, and listened to the *Blue Hungarians* while dining, on a Sunday, at that quaint old Tavern *the Savoy*. At that time the Beauties from New York had not quite lost their Vogue. CHRISTOPHER COLUMBUS, who discovered the United States, left it to the Prince of WALES to invent their inhabitants: personally, I am more implected with their Botany; and am, indeed, at this moment, engaged in a study of the Trees in America. Much of this remote Period must remain mobled in the Mists of Antiquity, but we know that about then flourished the Sect that was to win for itself the Title of the '*Decadents*'. What exactly this Title signified I suppose no two entomologists will agree. But we may learn from the Caricatures of the day what the *Decadents* were in outward semblance; from the Lampoons what was their mode of life. Nightly they gathered at any of the Theatres where the plays of Mr. WILDE were being given. Nightly, the stalls were fulfilled by Row upon Row of neatly-curled Fringes surmounting Button-holes of monstrous size. The contrasts in the social Condition of the time fascinate me. I used to know a boy whose mother was actually present at the 'first night' of *Charley's Aunt*, and became enamoured of *Mr. Penley*. By such links is one Age joined to another!

I should like to have been at a Private View of the '*New English Art Club*'. There was *Crotchet*, the young Author of the *Mauve Camellia*; there were *Walter Sickert*, the veteran R.A.; *George Moore*, the romanticist; *Charles Hawtrey*, the tragedian, and many another good fellow. The period of 1894 must have been delicious.

Perhaps in my Study I have fallen so deeply beneath the Spell of the Age, that I have tended to underrate its unimportance. I fancy it was a Sketch of a Lady with a Mask on, playing the piano in a Cornfield, in a low dress, with two lighted Candles, and signed '*Aubrey Weirdsley*', that first impelled me to research.

But to give an accurate account of the Period would need a far less brilliant Pen than mine; and I look to JEROME K. JEROME And to Mr. CLEMENT SCOTT.   (p. 58)

As this parody, which so often depends on mere quotation, suggests, the idea of the Decadent derives as much from caricature as fact.

It is not accident, however, that links the *Yellow Book* with Decadence. In the first place it had a sensational impact, inspiring a sense of horror difficult to recapture. 'Michael Field' recorded that the book was

full of cleverness such as one expects to find in those who dwell below light and hope and love and aspiration. The best one can say of any tale or of any illustration is that it is clever – the worst one can say is that it is damnable.   (BM Add. MS 46782, f. 70)

The tone may be a little exaggerated, but those two ladies did consider
themselves part of the literary world of the day, knew a number of
writers, and even submitted a poem to the *Yellow Book* whose return
they hastily requested when they saw the book itself. Their feelings
were of course supported by those who demanded the dismissal of
Beardsley after the Wilde scandal, and the tone of the *Yellow Book* after
volume IV shows that the publisher and editor knew that this was a
daring and Decadent periodical. The same thing is indicated by Lane's
taking over the publishing of the *Yellow Book* alone after the second
volume; Mathews had always been the more reticent of the two.

There was a balance of less shocking material in the first *Yellow
Book*, which was obviously put in to lessen the impact, among which
material Arthur Waugh's 'Reticence in Literature' is important. Waugh
dates the 'present tendency to literary frankness' (p. 213) from the early
work of Swinburne, and argues that his work has lasted because of its
music and in spite of its content, an argument common among Victorian editors; like R.H. Stoddart who admits in his *Selections from the
Poetical Works of A.C. Swinburne* (New York, 1884) that the poems
'could not have come from a healthy mind: they are morbid, feverous,
diseased, – sick unto death with the awful sickness of the soul' (p. xvi)
but adds that 'He is a wonderful musician, if nothing else' (p. xvii).
Waugh repeats the common comparison with Rome, but adds a new
idea in a comparison with Restoration drama, suggesting perhaps the
way in which the term Decadence would come to be used by later critics
of earlier seventeenth-century drama to describe the disintegration of
line and the increasing brutality and corruption of subject:

> But the new movement did not stop there. If, in the poet we have
> been discussing, we have found the voice among us that corresponds
> to the decadent voices of the failing Roman Republic, there has
> reached us from France another utterance, which I should be inclined
> to liken to the outspoken brutality of Restoration drama.   (p. 216)

Waugh's complaints stem like Le Gallienne's from his view of this
literature's lack of proportion, but Waugh does manage to include in his
criticisms the apparently opposed groups of effeminate writers and the
activists:

> The two developments of realism of which we have been speaking
> seem to me to typify the two excesses into which frankness is inclined
> to fall; on the one hand, the excess prompted by effeminacy – that is
> to say, by the want of restraint which starts from enervated sen-
> sation; and, on the other, the excess which results from a certain
> brutal virility, which proceeds from coarse familiarity with indul-

gence. The one whispers, the other shouts; the one is the language of
the courtesan, the other of the bargee. What we miss in both alike is
that true frankness which springs from the artistic and moral
temperament; the episodes are no part of a whole in unity with itself.

(p. 217)

Waugh refuses to mention names, either of writers or of movements,
and so one must deduce to whom is referring, but it seems likely that the
Decadent is his target when he says that

the latest development of literary frankness is, I think, the most
insidious and fraught with the greatest danger to art. A new school
has arisen which combines the characteristics of effeminacy and
brutality. In its effeminate aspect it plays with the subtler emotions
of sensual pleasure, on its brutal side it has developed into that class
of fiction which for want of a better word I must call chirurgical. In
poetry it deals with very much the same passions as those which we
have traced in the verse to which allusion has been made above; but,
instead of leaving these refinements of lust to the haunts to which
they are fitted, it has introduced them into the domestic chamber,
and permeated marriage with the ardours of promiscuous
intercourse. (pp. 217–18)

Waugh's conclusion is, of course, that reticence is necessary to great
art.

Hubert Crackanthorpe, whose story followed the article by Waugh
in volume I, and who was a champion of freedom of speech and subject,
wrote a reply with the same title 'Reticence in Literature' for volume II.
His first defence, based on the division between real and ideal, suggests
that there has been a variation between two religions, the worship of
beauty called idealism, and the worship of truth called realism. 'The
pendulum of production is continually swinging, from degenerate
idealism to degenerate realism, from effete vapidity to slavish sordidity'
(p. 260). Nor can either extreme be separated from some alloy of the
other, and it is the individual rather than the theory which is important,
for 'Realism, as a creed, is as ridiculous as any other literary creed'
(p. 261). And, although there is inevitable friction between an
advanced writer and the general public, the age is so hurried that there
has been a swift decline in opposition to the new freedom of subject
matter.

Crackanthorpe, in a manner he may have learned from Beerbohm,
even defends the Philistine critic as a salutary corrective to excess, while
the 'artistic objector to realistic fiction' is the real danger.

Sometimes, to listen to him you would imagine that pessimism and
regular meals were incompatible; that the world is only ameliorated

by those whom it completely satisfies, that good predominates over evil, that the problem of our destiny had been solved long ago. You begin to doubt whether any good thing can come out of this miserable, inadequate age of ours, unless it be a doctored survival of the vocabulary of a past century. The language of the coster and the cadger resound in our midst, and though Velasquez tried to paint like Whistler, Rudyard Kipling cannot write like Pope. And a weird word has been invented to explain the whole business. Decadence, decadence: you are all decadent nowadays. Ibsen, Degas, and the New English Art Club; Zola, Oscar Wilde, and the Second Mrs Tanqueray. Mr Richard Le Gallienne is hoist with his own petard; even the British playwright has not escaped the taint. Ah, what a hideous spectacle. All whirling along towards one common end. And the elegant voice of the artistic objector floating behind: '*Après vous le déluge*'. A wholesale abusing of the tendencies of the age has ever proved, for the superior mind, an inexhaustible source of relief. Few things breed such inward comfort as the contemplation of one's own pessimism – few things produce such discomfort as the remembrance of our neighbour's optimism. (p. 266)

Crackanthorpe does not concentrate on style, maintaining a more Paterian or Zolaesque idea that temperament creates style, for realist and idealist alike. On the other hand, he does not allow that subject matter is of vast importance. As he concludes:

The truth is, and, despite Mr Waugh, we are near recognition of it, that nowadays there is but scanty merit in the mere selection of any particular subject, however ingenious or daring it may appear at first sight; that a man is not an artist, simply because he writes about heredity or the *demi-monde*, that to call a spade a spade requires no extraordinary literary gift, and that the essential is contained in the frank, fearless acceptance by every man of his entire artistic temperament, with its qualities and its flaws. (p. 269)

Yet, for all the protestations, the *Yellow Book* was connected with Decadence, mainly because of the lack of reticence in the subject matter of its drawings, poems and stories.

Only one major statement about Decadence in the nineties remains, that in Max Nordau's *Degeneration*, which came with a timing little short of miraculous, but it is worth mentioning a few comments from other countries before considering Nordau's comprehensive criticism. In Australia, Christopher Brennan, poet and scholar of some repute, came to his own definition of Decadence. In the *Australian Magazine* of 29 April 1899 he wrote of 'The English Decadents':

Decadents, in the primary sense of the word, as I understand it, artists in whose hands a noble tradition becomes enfeebled, shows signs of age and wear, are, in England, Mr William Watson and Mr Stephen Phillips: both classicists.

(Reprinted in *The Prose of Christopher Brennan*, ed. A.R. Chisholm and J.J. Quinn, Sydney, 1962, p. 201)

Watson, with his part in the Beardsley dismissal from the *Yellow Book*, would not have been pleased to find himself a Decadent. Brennan adds in the issue of 6 July that 'The essential of decadent art is that it lacks plan, and that its beauty resides in accidental detail' (p. 211) and that 'The decadent poet, being happy only in details, and neglecting proportion, easily falls into the vices of over-elaboration and preciosity, with obscurity as a result' (p. 216). Brennan obviously kept in touch with the movements sufficiently to agree with Havelock Ellis and Lionel Johnson.

In America too there were signs that Decadence had not gone unnoticed. The Boston *Knight Errant* led the way for a number of American minority periodicals which owe much both in form and idea to the *Century Guild Hobby Horse* and ideas current in England in the late nineteenth century. (See Ian Fletcher's unpublished doctoral dissertation, *Union and Beauty*, Reading, 1965, for detail on this and other periodicals.) One of the two principal figures connected with the *Knight Errant*, Ralph Adams Cram, had privately printed in 1893 a book with the short title *The Decadent* (Cambridge, Mass., 1893) and the long explanatory subtitle *Being the gospel of inaction: wherein are set forth in romance form certain reflections touching the curious characteristics of these ultimate years, and the divers causes thereof*. His hero Aurelian welcomed the inevitable fall of civilization and the book, with its mixture of Huysmans and Wilde, is mainly of interest here for its recording the pervasiveness of Decadent influence.

In the New York *Forum* of 1893 Frederic Harrison published an article on 'Decadence in Modern Art' reprinted in *Realities and Ideals* (1908) and, although he was concerned with graphic art and not literature, his complaints are the ones that are typical of critics using the term. Decadence for him consists in sordid realism and emphasis on technique – 'If *technique* is right, all is right' is his version of the Decadent view – and he condemns the idea behind this that art should represent anything that exists. Like many English moralists who write on Decadence, he claims that the purpose of art is to increase the beauty and happiness of life, which Decadent art fails to do, but he does find some hopeful signs visible, particularly in France. He ends with this fervent attack, rather on the lines of 'Michael Field's' view:

But amongst these new groups, raging to be 'original' both here and in France, there are some to whom beauty – nobleness of aspect or feeling – even decency – are a mockery and an offence; some whose ideal it is to be dull or to be eccentric, or to be brutal. For such there is no hope in this world or the next. (p. 320)

The view and the attitude were to be amplified and given European publicity in Max Nordau's book *Entartung* in 1893.

The English translation, *Degeneration* (1895), and the vigorous attacks and defences that it occasioned, form the centrepiece of the nineties controversy about the subject. Not only does it range over the whole of Europe to glean its examples of Decadent artists, but it also makes use of medical theories in much the same way as some of the French realistic novelists had done. It contained most of the conventional responses to Decadent art, but it provided the moral judgments with a backing of medical and psychological theory that seemed formidable. Critics who were slightly biased against Decadence in art were immediately won over. An extreme view can be seen in the reviewer in the *World*, quoted in advertisements before Nordau's *Conventional Lies of Our Civilization* (1895):

> That the melancholy phenomena exhibited by the 'mystics' and 'symbolists', the 'décadents' and the 'ego-maniacs' of latter-day literature and art have been due to some strange epidemic of mental declension, was evident to most thinking persons before Nordau turned the pitiless searchlight of his analytical genius upon those several orders of art eccentrics.

What is most effective about the book is that almost all except the opinion is accurate; there is no comparable review of Decadent European literature, and certainly not at that early date. But it is not surprising that such a damning view of literature, one that promises that literature's place in society will grow less and less significant, should have found opponents, and not necessarily among the Decadent writers. Bernard Shaw, for example, would not normally be classed as Decadent (although his review first appeared in the American Anarchist paper *Liberty* on 27 July 1895, under the heading 'A Degenerate's View of Nordau'), but his defence, or rather his attack on Nordau's methods and conclusions, is convincing. Yet even his *The Sanity of Art* does not dismiss finally one of Nordau's major themes, that of the insanity of genius.

Symons, as in his essay on de Nerval, would make the equation. Rimbaud had wished for a systematic derangement of all the senses. Macaulay had written in 1825 that 'Perhaps no person can be a poet, or even enjoy poetry, without a certain unsoundness of mind.' And Wilde even tried to make use of it, pleading in a letter to the Home Secretary that sexual misdemeanours are diseases and 'In the works of eminent men of science such as Lombroso and Nordau, to take two instances out of many, this is specially insisted on with reference to the intimate connection between madness and the literary and artistic temperament' (*The Letters of Oscar Wilde*, ed. Rupert Hart-Davis, 1962, p. 402), and Wilde seeks justification from the book that helped in the case against him by pointing out that Nordau had 'devoted an entire chapter to the petitioner as a specially typical example of this fatal law.' Havelock Ellis, in *The New Spirit* (1890), says that 'it may be that what we call "genius" is something abnormal and distorted, like those centres of irritation which result in the pearls we likewise count so precious' (p. 11). It is a commonplace of Romantic theory.

In his Preface for *The Sanity of Art* (1908), Shaw remarked with an ingenuous air that

> neither the pleadings nor the criticisms dispose of the main question as to how far genius is a morbid symptom. I should rather like Dr Nordau to try again; for I do not see how the observant student of genius from the life can deny that the Arts have their criminals and lunatics as well as their sane and honest men.   (p. 11)

The 1895 article in *Liberty* shows Shaw in a more belligerent spirit:

> Is there not something deliciously ironical in the ease with which a splenetic pamphleteer, with nothing to shew for himself except a bookful of blunders tacked on to a mock scientific theory picked up at second hand from a few lunacy doctors with a literary turn, should be able to create a European scandal by declaring that the greatest creative artists of the century are barren and hysterical madmen?

Shaw does nevertheless maintain that genius is as subject to moral laws as anyone else, although he also argues that progress in morals is made by going against the accepted code.

> Every step in morals is made by challenging the validity of the existing conception of perfect propriety of conduct; and when a man does that, he must look out for a very different reception from the painter who has ventured to paint a shadow brilliant lilac, or the composer who ends a symphony with an unresolved discord. Heterodoxy in art is at worst rated as eccentricity or folly: heterodoxy in morals is at once rated as scoundrelism, and, what is worse, propagandist scoundrelism, which must, if successful, undermine society and bring us back to barbarism after a period of decadence like that which brought imperial Rome to its downfall.
>
>   (*The Sanity of Art*, pp. 38–9)

Shaw is clear, witty, and cool, in an argument where these virtues are not too common.

Other replies to *Degeneration*, apart from innumerable responses in the newspapers, were Alfred Egmont Hake's *Regeneration* (1895), and William Hirsch's *Genius and Degeneration* (translated from the German, 1897), the former implying in its name the common co-presence of ends and beginnings, the paradoxical interchangeability of Decadence and newness.

Nordau's book views Decadence as merely a small part of the whole field of ego-mania. Of course in a post-Romantic period Nordau has little difficulty in finding writers who seem interested in themselves. So the Parnassians in France, the Diabolists, Ibsen and Nietzsche are all lumped together with Decadents and Aesthetes as Ego-maniacs. Nordau follows the history of Decadence more accurately than most of his predecessors had, through Baudelaire, Gautier, and Huysmans, and he ridicules quite rightly the supposed parallels with the Roman Decadence. He approves Bourget's interpretation of Decadence, but he includes Bourget among the Decadents because he can admire Baudelaire while realizing that the Decadent is not concerned with social aims. In fact, after a lengthy examination of *A Rebours* Nordau comes to a conclusion not unlike Carter's in *The Idea of Decadence in France* that the Decadent seeks exactly the opposite of what the multitude seeks, he is 'an ordinary man with a *minus* sign' (p. 306). Nordau spends some time on a diatribe against Maurice Barrès and his *culte du moi* before he comes to the English Decadents, whom he equates with the Aesthetes as A.J. Farmer would do in his *Le Mouvement Esthétique et 'Décadent' en Angleterre*. Swinburne would probably have been the starting point in this section but for his 'mysticism' and his place among the PreRaphaelites, and the honour goes to Wilde:

> The ego-mania of decadentism, its love of the artificial, its aversion to nature, and to all forms of activity and movement, its megalomaniacal contempt for men and its exaggeration of the importance of art, have found their English representative among the 'Aesthetes', the chief of whom is Oscar Wilde.   (p. 317)

Wilde's chief offence seems to be his personal eccentricity, particularly his clothing, since his plays and poems 'are feeble imitations of Rossetti and Swinburne, and of dreary inanity. His prose essays, on the contrary, deserve attention, because they exhibit all the features which enable us to recognise in the "Aesthete" the comrade in art of the Decadent' (p. 319). And from these essays Nordau draws up his list of Decadent characteristics in Wilde: the way he despises nature; his ego-mania; his despising popular opinion; his ideal of the inactive life; his admiration for immorality, sin and crime, as in the essay on

Wainwright; his 'slight mysticism in colours'; his central glorification of art; and perhaps most damning from Nordau's point of view, the idea that 'Aesthetics are higher than ethics' (p. 322, quoting from Wilde's *Intentions*).

Nordau shows up the weakness in his earnestness when he writes of Wilde's theories. Wilde seems for once to agree with him on the point that life imitates art, but Nordau staunchly refuses to see the tone of Wilde's assertions and takes him quite literally:

> Wilde does not refer to the fact, long ago established by me, that the reciprocal relation between the work of art and the public consists in this, that the former exercises suggestion and the latter submits to it. What he actually wished to say was that nature – not civilized men – develops itself in the direction of forms given in by the artist.
>
> (p. 321)

And so Nordau takes Wilde's assertion that painters have changed the climate and created London fogs as a statement 'so silly as to require no refutation. It is sufficient to characterize it as artistic mysticism' (p. 322). In general, Nordau's attitude, his insensitivity, his literalness, and his willingness to make any characteristic represent degeneracy without proof that it is a necessary and not accidental characteristic, combine to vitiate his conclusions. He quite rightly notes the anti-natural tendencies of the groups of writers he discusses, but in his insistence on the morality of art he heavily underscores the emphasis placed by its critics on the content of Decadent art. He is not ashamed of mixing art and life himself and insists in his conclusions on the actual degeneracy of these writers:

> Insensible to its tasks and interests, without the capacity to comprehend a serious thought or a fruitful deed, they dream only of the satisfaction of their basest instincts, and are pernicious – through the example they set as drones, as well as through the confusion they cause in minds insufficiently forwarned, by their abuse of the word 'art' to mean demoralization and childishness. Ego-maniacs, Decadents and Aesthetes have completely gathered under their banner this refuse of civilized peoples, and march at its head. (p. 337)

The book's influence can be guaged from its popularity, seven editions in a year, but there was an aptness in its time of publication that may well have boosted its sales, for it came out in the year of Wilde's trials. The attack on Wilde, accusing him of perverting the young and innocent, can scarcely have made his case easier when he was brought to trial in April. The book came out on 22 February, four days after the Marquis of Queensberry had left his libellous card at the Albermarle, and five editions of the book had been printed before the end of the second trial. Nordau's ideas and accusations are heard again, more shrilly, in the *National Observer* of 6 April 1895, in an article possibly written by Charles Whibley, and obviously endorsed by the editor, W.E. Henley. This is before the second trial:

> There is not a man or woman in the English-speaking world possessed of the treasure of a wholesome mind who is not under a deep debt of gratitude to the Marquess of Queensberry for destroying the High Priest of the Decadents. The obscene impostor, whose prominence has been a social outrage ever since he transferred from Trinity Dublin to Oxford his vices, his follies, and his vanities, has been exposed, and that thoroughly at last. There must be another trial at the Old Bailey, or a coroner's inquest – the latter for choice; and the Decadents, of their hideous conceptions of the meaning of Art, and of their worse than Eleusinian mysteries there must be an absolute end.

(Reprinted in H. Montgomery Hyde, *Famous Trials, Seventh Series: Oscar Wilde*, 1962, p. 156)

Decadence was by now more than style; and more than content; it had become life. Montgomery Hyde adds other details which prove that the persecution of Wilde was more than artistic, and more than theoretic:

> Meanwhile messages of congratulation were pouring in on Queensberry. On being informed by one of the Sunday newspapers that a further pile of messages was waiting for him, the delighted Marquess said: 'You know, I have not much to do with distinguished people, but I had a very nice letter from Lord Claud Hamilton, and a kind telegram from Mr Charles Denby, the actor, with "Hearty Congratulations", et cetera. Various clubs have telegraphed also. Here is a message: "Every man in the City is with you. Kill the – !" '

(p. 156)

The weight of feeling against anything associated with the name of Decadence made it impossible for any movement with the name to continue. Symbolism was there to take its place as it had done with no prompting in France; and, although many writers stuck by Wilde both in ideas and deeds, the Decadent movement had received a mortal blow.

The strength of feeling against Wilde can be seen by the comments quoted above, written the day after his first arrest. Before he was committed for trial, *Punch* of 13 April 1895 had printed some verses 'Concerning a Misused Term':

> *viz., 'Art' as recently applied to a certain form of Literature.*
> Is this, then, 'Art' – ineffable conceit,
>   Plus worship of the Sadi-tinted phrase,

Of pseud-Hellenic decadence, effete,
   Unvirile, of debased Petronian ways?

Is *this* your 'Culture', to asphyxiate
   With upas-perfume sons of English race,
With manhood-blighting cant-of-art to prate,
   The jargon of an epicene disgrace?

Shall worse than pornographic stain degrade
   The name of 'Beauty', Heav'n imparted dower?
Are *they* fit devotees, who late displayed
   The symbol of a vitriol-tinted flower?

And shall the sweet and kindly Muse be shamed
   By unsexed 'Poetry' that defiles your page?
Has Art a mission that may not be named,
   With 'scarlet sins' to enervate the age?

All honour to the rare and cleanly prints,
   Which have not filled our homes from day to day
With garbage-epigrams and pois'nous hints
   How aesthete-hierophants fair Art betray!

If such be 'Artists', then may Philistines
   Arise, plan sturdy Britons as of yore,
And sweep them off and purge away the signs
   That England e'er such noxious offspring bore!

Wilde may be said to have been judged before he was tried, but the whole Decadent movement was on trial with him.

The trial and the accompanying adverse publicity for Decadence were devastatingly effective. By 11 May *Punch* could see degeneration as a thing of the past. 'A Philistine Paean' sang of the change of atmosphere:

> At last! I see signs of a turn in the tide,
>   And O, I perceive it with infinite gratitude,
> No more need I go with a crick in my side
>   In attempts to preserve a non-natural attitude.
> *Something* has changed in the season, *somewhere*:
> I'm sure I can feel a cool whiff of fresh air!

After Nordau, the poem discovered that 'Egomania is *not* the last word of latter-day wisdom', and that High Art was maudlin, not decent, mad, unclean, impure. At last the Philistine did not feel obliged to admire the literature of the egomaniac, mystical High Art school, though he did feel a little baffled at the inclusiveness of the condemnation:

I am not *quite* sure that I *quite* understand
How they've suddenly found all our fads are degenerate;
Why MAETERLINCK, IBSEN, VERLAINE, SARAH GRAND,
    TOLSTOI, GRANT ALLEN, ZOLA, are 'lumped' – but, at
    any rate,
I know I'm relieved from one horrible bore,-
I need not admire what I hate any more.

With all this feeling concentrated against the ideas for which Decadence had been held to stand, it is not unnatural that the writers who still subscribed to some of those ideas should seek a new label which would describe their beliefs without the overtones of moral scorn and censure which inevitably attached themselves to Decadence. It is difficult to find after 1895 any example of the term used with the approval it had before, as with Lionel Johnson, or even as an approximate label as Symons had used it.

In the *Savoy*, which inherited from the *Yellow Book* the unfortunately implicated Beardsley, many of the interesting writers, and much of the unsavoury reputation, it was necessary to deny association with Decadence, though Symons staunchly defended its theories elsewhere. Symons's statements in the *Savoy* of November 1895 make the position clear:

> We have no formula and we desire no false unity of form or matter. We have not invented a new point of view. We are not Realists or Romanticists or Decadents. For us, all art is good which is good art.

And even *Punch* seems to have lost interest in the idea of Decadence under the pressure of more important items on the international field.

The rise and fall of the Decadent movement in England was in the main confined to the years from 1889 to 1897; it was certainly over by the end of the century. Some of the chief figures of that movement died with the century, setting a permanent seal on that sense of an ending: Dowson, Wilde, Johnson, Crackanthorpe, Beardsley. Beerbohm retired from the struggle, and even Symons renounced the name. The novelty of Decadence had worn off, and Symbolism took its place.

One can put some order into the subject of Decadence apart from the historical order by seeing the discussion tending towards distinct polarities. First there is the pole of the critic, who equates modern literature with that of Roman Decadence as a way of showing tendencies to be avoided; the attitude is a moral one, and attacks largely on the grounds of subject, though with occasional criticisms of style, especially when the vocabulary in which that style is defended implies decay or disease. Second there is the pole of the writer, who sees a Decadent literature as appropriate to a time of Decadence, but, maintaining the irrelevance of art to morality, concentrates on matters of style and technique. Nordau is the culmination of the first type, though he no longer makes the parallel with Rome, and founds his arguments on Darwinian models and an extension of Lombroso's work. Symons is the epitome of the second type. Unfortunately, the adherents of the movement made their case difficult by using a name which implied a degeneracy which was, without need of proof, an undesirable state; and the case was made worse by the continued hints of immorality or disease in their subjects. The built-in moral overtones of Decadence finally invalidated the term, and the writers moved towards the available and less loaded notion of Symbolism.

The term had never been completely satisfactory, nor had it ever been completely clear. But it had provided a useful focus and has gone on providing a focus ever since. Despite a willingness to acknowledge its inadequacy, critics have found themselves unable to abandon it because it fits something, whether works, writers, attitudes, or merely the need of the time. It will always be an approximation, a label rather than a definition, but to see what features it might describe, I shall look at a number of writers who are grouped beneath its flag.

4 Ernest Dowson

Everyone agrees that Ernest Dowson was central to the Decadence. The compendious *A Literary History of England* concludes a chapter on 'Aestheticism and "Decadence" ' with 'the typical figure of Ernest Dowson', while a detailed review of two editions of Dowson's work said that 'it can be claimed for him, no less than Beardsley or Wilde, that he stood in a symbolic relationship to his age.' Between these extremes of generalization and close particularity, critics share the assumption that Dowson is at the heart of the Decadent movement. And so he is. The Decadent Dilemma runs through his whole work; it shapes his whole life; and curiously it shapes even the way that critics think about him, some creating or embroidering a romantic myth and others attempting to stick firmly to the verifiable facts.

The plain facts of Dowson's life are sufficient to single him out as a rather romantic figure without any help from the myth-makers. Born at Lee in Kent in 1867, he spent an irregular childhood as he followed his consumptive parents to various continental retreats in an effort to find some cure for their illness. His education was equally irregular, though he had a useful introduction to French through living in France and even having to learn some of his other subjects through the medium of French. His father gave him enough of an introduction to Latin to make him able to impress a number of men who knew him, though the tags and Paterian phrases which he uses in his poems indicate a very superficial knowledge in comparison to Lionel Johnson's. The undisciplined but in some subjects well-informed student which this education made him went up to Oxford in 1886 where for five terms he read Classics at Queen's. It is difficult to say why Dowson, who had been academically sound enough to read for an honours degree and who was enjoying a not untypical student life, should suddenly decide in the middle of his Honours Moderations examinations that he would not sit the rest of his papers but would leave the university. It may have been his pessimism and melancholy; it may have been what he used to call his 'ooflessness' since his father's financial affairs were in decline; it may have been his restlessness and a dissatisfaction with university life; or he may simply have felt that he had not done well in his examinations. Whatever the reason, he went down at the end of term in March 1888.

University could not have been completely unattractive. He had studied literature for a time and discussed it with congenial company. He had made permanent friendships there: he met Lionel Johnson, later a fellow member of the Rhymers' Club, and he met Arthur Moore, with whom he was to collaborate on a number of novels. *The Passion of Dr Ludovicus*, which they completed in 1889, was a 'shocker' and it was probably fairly treated in not finding a publisher. *Felix Martyr*, their next book, was probably never completed, and although *A Comedy of Masks* (1893) and *Adrian Rome* (1899) were published, they are prose works with elegant fragments rather than successful novels, since neither writer was very strong on plot. Indeed Dowson's particular genius finds expression much more aptly in the short prose pieces which are well described by the collective title they were given when they were published in 1895, *Dilemmas; Stories and Studies in Sentiment*. Dowson was an enthusiast for dilemmas. It was at Oxford that he began to write seriously and, although he was known and wished to be thought of as a writer of prose, it was appropriately his poem 'Sonnet to a Little Girl' which was his first published work, appearing in *London Society* for November 1886. Arthur Symons wrote in September 1884 of *London Society* that 'the beast of an editor "does not pay for verse!" ', and Dowson never made a great deal out of his poems or his prose. Even from the edition of 600 copies of *Dilemmas*, the contract suggests that he would make a maximum of £15 on the English edition.

When he went down from Oxford, Dowson began gradually to make a name for himself. He became for a time in 1889 the unpaid sub-editor of a failing weekly called *The Critic*, the chief attraction of which post and one he took liberal advantage of, was that it allowed him free seats for the theatre. His stories began to appear in magazines, *The Temple Bar*, *Macmillan's*, and *The Century Guild Hobby Horse*. Finally he moved to magazines at the heart of the Decadence, *The Yellow Book* and *The Savoy*, edited by Arthur Symons and Aubrey Beardsley, key figures in charge of a key publication. Dowson shared the notoriety of these publications, and many of his young contemporaries felt that of their number it was he who would achieve fame as a poet. Yeats, for example, wrote in his *Autobiographies* that he suggested collecting poems for *The Book of the Rhymers' Club* (1892) because he wanted to have printed copies of two of Dowson's poems which up to then he had only known from his reading. The second collection of the Rhymers' Club in 1894 reprinted Dowson's most notorious poem, his *'Non sum qualis eram bonae sub regno Cynarae'*, of which Dowson had written to his friend Sam Smith when it was to appear in the *Century Guild Hobby Horse* for April 1891: 'I have seen the proofs of my 'Cynara' poem for the April Hobby. It looks less indecent in print, but I am still nervous! though I admire Horne's audacity' (*Letters*, p. 190). This audacity of the editor has to be measured against such things as the imprisonment of Vizetelly for publishing a popular translation of Zola, or by W.H. Smith's refusal to sell George Moore's *Esther Waters*, or the same firm's similar shocked response to a Blake design in the *Savoy*. When the *Savoy* ceased publication — partly as a consequence of that closing of outlets — Dowson earned money mainly as a translator, though he still published original works, including *Dilemmas* (1895), *Verses* (1896) and *Decorations* (1899).

His literary activity must be set against a background of family and social complications. His father owned a dry dock in the Limehouse district, though he was not very interested in running it and recognized that the dock was losing business. It had been let to the Dry Dock Corporation of London, but when they went bankrupt in 1888 Dowson's father recovered the dock, and father and son were going to run it (relying substantially on the foreman) until it could be let again. That Dowson was under no illusion as to its condition can be recognized from the picture of Blackpool Dock in Dowson and Moore's *A Comedy of Masks* (1893), which is a scarcely-disguised version of the decadent Bridge Dock:

> . . . as time went on and the age of iron intervened, and the advance on the Clyde and the Tyne had made Thames shipbuilding a thing of the past, Blackpool Dock had ceased to be of commercial importance. No more ships were built there, and fewer ships put in to be overhauled and painted; while even these few were for the most part of a class viewed at Lloyd's with scant favour, which seems, like the yard itself, to have fallen somewhat behind the day.

Dowson's help in the unpoetic job of book-keeping was persistent but did not solve the underlying problem. Whether rumour is right that his father committed suicide because of worry about the dock and his declining health, or whether we believe the death certificate which mentions only natural causes, Dowson's father died in August 1894 and his mother, never very stable, hanged herself six months later. His younger brother left for the United States soon afterwards. Dowson kept on working both at his creative work and his translations. His interest in the dock declined and he left it in 1895, being something of a wanderer ever afterwards. Though the firm was finally wound up in 1902 and Dowson's estate on his death valued at over £1,000, he saw precious little of the money and lived the last years of his life in a scarcely genteel shabbiness. Some of his money was derived from the series of translations for Leonard Smithers, at which he worked regularly and hard. In 1897 Dowson deposited £45 with Smithers to be doled out at no more than £2 a week, while the family money which was his due was tied up in legal delays which cause a sorry burden of poverty spiced with frustrated anticipation of solvency in the later letters. Though Dowson's love of girls is different in some ways from Wilde's view of youth as a virtue (though both owe something to Pater), the two men were friends in France after Wilde's release from gaol, and both were chronically short of money. Dowson was in difficulties when his illness, whose terrible effects he had seen in his parents, made it impossible for him to work. His friend R.H. Sherard found him wandering around in a pitiful condition and took him home to his cottage in Catford, where he and his wife nursed Dowson, with medicines paid for by another friend. Dowson died there six weeks later on 23 February 1900.

This is to leave out of the factual account the most famous part of all, his love for the young girl, Adelaide Foltinowicz, to whom he dedicated *Dilemmas* (1895) and to whom he wrote a dedicatory preface for *Verses* (1896). She was born in 1878, the daughter of a Polish restaurant keeper, and Dowson met her first in 1889. She was not the first of his enthusiasms for girls, though she was the most important. His early sequence of 'Sonnets of a Little Girl' is dated 1885 in his manuscript book of poems, his 'Poésie Schublade', and suggests his early love for this childish ideal:

> a child's tender love.
> Ah do not doubt it – all things die and wane,
> Save this alone; this only lasts above,
> The lingering rule of weariness and pain,
> This love alone is stingless and can calm
> Life's fitful fever with its healing balm.

He had published an essay on 'The Cult of the Child' in *The Critic* in August 1889, and earlier in 1889 he had conducted an 'episode' as he called it with a young waitress. He had tried to keep it platonic, had begun to regard it as an inconvenience, but when it finished in June, he reported to his friend Moore that 'it has quite spoofed me quite'. Even in the letter of 9 November 1889 in which we find Dowson's first mention of 'Missie' as he called her, he is enthusing to Moore about Minnie Terry, a child actress of whom Dowson collected photographs and momentoes. Dowson spent a good deal of time at the Foltinowicz's restaurant just to be near to his Adelaide, growing more and more committed to her until he finally declared himself in 1893, just before her 15th birthday. The time was one of great tension and stress since her father was obviously dying and indeed died within the week, and it is no surprise that Adelaide's mother suggested that things should be left for a year or two. But even then Dowson was not very hopeful, for his letter explaining it to his friend continues: 'For the rest I am not very sanguine; if she liked me less or had not known me so long, I believe, my chance would·be much better.' He was quite right for, although he remained devoted, or perhaps one should use his self-description 'idolatrous', she regarded him merely as a friend. He wrote to Victor Plarr in May 1896, 'Missie writes to me fairly often, *friendly* letters, which give me sleepless nights and cause me to shed morbid and puerile tears. But she is very kind.' In 1897 he even moved into rooms above the restaurant, though by now it must have been obvious that she was not to marry him as he had at one time – perhaps – hoped. She married Augustus Noelte who also lived there and had been a waiter but worked as a tailor at the time of the marriage in September 1897; they had two daughters and she died in December 1903 from septicaemia following an abortion. Dowson last mentions her in a letter of June 1896:

> My Missie is well; they have resumed their restaurant again but are trying to sell it outright. There is nothing in the world which you could do for me, for which I should be more grateful than to go & see them, & write to me of them. I have broken my heart over her, but she remains, none the less, my sole interest in life.

He later sent a present with Moore who attended the wedding, and wherever he travelled he noted the place and the date on the page of *Dilemmas* which bears the dedication 'To Missie (A.F.)'.

The 'Dowson legend' is not satisfied with these facts, however, and weaves around them stories based on hearsay, rumour, or mere invention, stories which still appear as facts in some books on the period. Dowson emerges as a raddled Keats, a pale and tragic figure who almost deliberately failed to outlive the century and the decade to which his work belongs and which it so effectively represents. He is characterized by a languid withdrawal from all effort, while at the same time he is seen as an energetic lecher and a lover of drink and squalor. One finds reports about his taking of drugs, his chronic drinking and his chasing after women all of which seem designed to make him seem a lurid example of a highly-coloured Decadent poet.

At the root of the legend lies the account of Dowson written by Arthur Symons; and substantially nourishing it are the anecdotes in *Autobiographies* by W.B. Yeats, who insisted in his *Memoirs* that he had 'no intimate knowledge of Dowson but through' Symons (p. 93). Neither Symons nor Yeats would claim his account as a bare factual record. 'I have changed nothing to my knowledge; and yet it must be that I have changed many things without my knowledge', wrote Yeats in his Preface to *Reveries over Childhood and Youth*, and the method of depending on memory and remembering only those heightened moments of experience is bound to distort. Nonetheless, their confessedly one-sided picture has often been taken as a true account and a complete character study.

Symons began the mythification in 'A Literary Causerie: on a Book of Verses', which he published in the *Savoy* of August 1896. Writing of him 'with some of that frankness which we reserve usually for the dead', Symons reported that 'his favourite form of intoxication had been haschisch' at Oxford, but that he had given that up for 'readier means of oblivion'. Subsequent writers have often taken Symon's tale of Dowson's drug experiments and elaborated them into an addiction, though Symon's did not know Dowson until three years after he left Oxford. As for drinking, that too has assumed such proportions that Dowson is pictured as a complete dipsomaniac. Symons may well have started this too with his account of Dowson's drinking 'the poisonous liquors of those pot-houses which swarm about the docks.'

Yeats does not conceal the derivation of his accounts from gossip, and we can see a process of elaboration in the transition from Yeats's *Memoirs* to his *Autobiographies*; but he tells the stories since they help to create his picture of Dowson who is, like so many of the biographies of that book, one of Yeats's vicarious potential autobiographies. Acknowledging readily that he derives his information from a 10-year-old tale, Yeats makes an irresistible picture:

> Dowson wrote a protest against some friend's too vivid essay upon the disorder of his life, and explained that in reality he was living a life of industry in a little country village; but before the letter arrived that friend received a wire, 'Arrested, sell watch and send proceeds' – Dowson's watch had been left in London – and then another wire, 'Am free'. Dowson, or so ran the tale as I heard it ten years after, had got drunk and fought the baker, and a deputation of villagers had gone to the magistrate and pointed out that Monsieur Dowson was one of the most illustrious of English poets. 'Quite right to remind me', said the magistrate; 'I will imprison the baker.'

Yeats's idea of the sensual Dowson is supported by another tale, and again it is worth stressing that Yeats is not so much interested in the facts as that the tale – they have that fictional roundness best described by the word 'tale' – was told:

> Then there came a wonderful tale repeated by Dowson himself, whether by word of mouth or by letter I do not remember. Wilde had arrived in Dieppe, and Dowson pressed upon him the necessity of acquiring 'a more wholesome taste'. They emptied their pockets on to the café table, and though there was not much, there was enough if both heaps were put into one. Meanwhile the news had spread, and they set out accompanied by a cheering crowd. Arrived at their

destination, Dowson and the crowd remained outside, and presently Wilde returned. He said in a low voice to Dowson, 'The first these ten years, and it will be the last. It was like cold mutton' – always, as Henley had said, 'a scholar and a gentleman', he now remembered that the Elizabethan dramatists used the words 'cold mutton' – and then aloud so that the crowd might hear him, 'But tell it in England, for it will entirely restore my character'.

These are fine stories and capture a good deal of the spirit of the period whether they are true or not. It is not always possible to find evidence which will sort out the truth from the hearsay, and allowance must also be made for the tendency of writers like Symons and Yeats to describe their subjects at moments of intensity. Nonetheless, most writers tend to follow Symons and Yeats, assume there is no smoke without fire, and give Dowson's character accordingly.

Time and again, friends or admirers of Dowson have risen up and protested against the picture of the degenerate, drunken womanizer. Edgar Jepson began it when he protested in an article called 'The Real Ernest Dowson' in 1907 in the *Academy* against the accusations made by Symons. He claimed that Symons 'had neither the knowledge nor the experience to understand Dowson' and added that Dowson did not love the sordid, nor feel at home in East End pothouses. Symons's lurid account of 'The poisonous liquors of those pot-houses which swarm about the docks' seems to forget that it is natural to have a drink in a pub near to the dock where you happen to work and that the liquor came from the same manufacturers as that drunk by Symons himself at the Crown. Unfortunately Jepson was not completely able to claim that he understood Dowson either. They had quarrelled 10 years earlier over the publication of Dowson's *Verses*. Jepson tried to do Dowson a good turn by getting profitable terms from the publisher without asking Dowson whether he might try. Dowson was so annoyed that he immediately transferred the book to Leonard Smithers to publish and wrote to Moore that he and Jepson were 'on terms of extreme hostility'. Jepson's justification of Dowson apparently went unnoticed since he had to repeat it in his book of 1933, *Memories of a Victorian*, though it still had little effect. Dowson appeared elsewhere as Symons had so temptingly portrayed him. This was all the more surprising since there had appeared in 1914 a book by another friend of Dowson's, a much closer friend, the Librarian of the Royal College of Surgeons, Victor Plarr, a man of simple thoroughness, who spoke from undeniable authority. This book of reminiscences, *Ernest Dowson 1888–1897*, was based on the eight years that he had known Dowson well, during which time he had known him under the influence of drink only once. This is quite likely to be true; one would get drunk with a man like Symons much more readily than with a man like Plarr. But despite his defence, on this and other matters, Plarr did nothing to halt the flow or change the nature of caricatures derived form Symons, and he may well have added fuel to the fire by admitting that he was concealing some information for Dowson's sake.

W.R. Thomas, a friend of Dowson's Oxford days, wrote reminiscences of Dowson in 'Ernest Dowson at Oxford' in *The Nineteenth Century* in April 1928. This account again stressed the attractive qualities of Dowson's personality, and incidentally suggested the duality which everyone saw in Dowson: 'his frail body was almost free from the power of the flesh, though its psychological study interested him.' Thomas was at pains to dispel the picture of Dowson as drunk and haschisch taker, pointing out he was typically undergraduate in his drinking habits and noting that the second experiment with whisky was a failure not to be repeated and the third and last experiment with haschisch sent them rushing to a chemist for an emetic.

The thirties saw two attempts other than Jepson's to clarify the picture. First, a level-headed introduction by Desmond Flower to the *Poetical Works of Ernest Dowson* (1934), the best edition of his poems, recognized some of the injustice in Symon's picture and put it straight on some points. But still, four years later someone again felt compelled to take up cudgels on the side of the undegenerate Dowson. John Gawsworth, in a talk to the Royal Society of Literature, later published as 'The Dowson Legend', defended Dowson from most of the attacks, but attributed to him at least some of the blame because he behaved in such a way as to make the rumours possible.

The war might have distracted attention from this defence, because mistakes were still being made, but there was less excuse after 1943. In that year and in a revised form in 1944 and 1967, Mark Longaker's biography of Dowson appeared. Despite its faults, it is largely accurate and ponderously solid; it again goes through the attacks and defences of his character, and comes out in favour of a rather pleasant individual, certainly not conforming to the pictures of the conventional caricature, nor to the portraits of Symons or Yeats. Even this has not prevented numerous critics from depending for their versions of Dowson on the old distorted pictures. So much so that in 1964 another American, Russell Goldfarb, felt it necessary to reiterate the old complaint that critics misinterpret Dowson by reading the poetry in terms of the life, and are in any case mistaken about the life they are interpreting by. It still goes on. The centenary of Dowson's birth, 1967, saw the publication of a literary history with the mythical picture – 'His febrile, sordid and lonely, pathetic and tragically short life was in strictest harmony with *fin de siècle* aestheticism' – and it also saw the publication of three books which ought to clarify the picture once and for all:

reprints of Desmond Flower's *The Poetical Works of Ernest Dowson* and of Mark Longaker's *Ernest Dowson* and, most important of all, Desmond Flower and Henry Maas's *The Letters of Ernest Dowson*.

What we must do in consequence of the collected *Letters* is shift our ground a bit. Dowson was obviously more warmly loved by his friends and much more hardworking than his detractors had thought; but he was also fundamentally involved in creating the image of himself that the mythologizers have been blamed for. He is the true Decadent in making for himself a biography to fit his view of art, and in helping to foster the notion of the artist with the Decadent Dilemma.

Yeats's stories, so wonderful as to seem like fiction, have a solid basis in truth. The editors of *The Letters of Ernest Dowson* have located and published the *Procès verbal* which demonstrates that at least the basis of one story is true; Dowson had indeed 'got drunk and fought the baker'. And Arthur Symons, as we knew, checked with Dowson before publishing his article about the poet, but exactly what the checking was had not been clear. Symons's article seems to me to stand up well against the critics of it and I shall quote a substantial piece:

A book of delicate, mournful, almost colourless, but very fragrant verses was lately published by a young poet whom I have the privilege to know somewhat intimately. Whether a book so essentially poetic, and at the same time so fragile in its hold on outward things, is likely to appeal very much to the general public, for which verse is still supposed to be written, it scarcely interests me to conjecture. It is a matter of more legitimate speculation, what sort of person would be called up before the mind's eye of any casual reader, as the author of love-poetry so reverent and so disembodied. A very ghostly lover, I suppose, wandering in a land of perpetual twilight, holding a whispered 'colloque sentimental' with the ghost of an old love:

> 'Dans le vieux parc solitaire et glacé
> Deux spectres ont évoqué le passé.'

That is not how I have seen my friend, for the most part; and the contrast between the man as I have seen him and the writer of verses as I read them, is to me the most attractive interest of a book which I find singularly attractive. He will not mind, I know, if I speak of him with some of that frankness which we reserve usually for the dead, or with which we sometimes honour our enemies; for he is of a complete indifference to these things, as I shall assure myself over again before these lines are printed.

I do not remember the occasion of our first meeting, but I remember seeing him casually, at railway stations, in a semi-literary tavern which once had a fantastic kind of existence, and sometimes, at night, in various parts of the Temple, before I was more than slightly his acquaintance. I was struck then by a look and manner of pathetic charm, a sort of Keats-like face, the face of a demoralized Keats, and by something curious in the contrast of a manner exquisitely refined, with an appearance generally somewhat dilapidated. That impression was only accentuated, later on, when I came to know him, and the manner of his life, much more intimately. I think I may date my first real impression of what one calls 'the real man' – as if it were more real than the poet of the disembodied verses! – from an evening in which he first introduced me to those charming supper-houses, open all night through, the cabmen's shelters. There were four of us, two in evening dress, and we were welcomed, cordially and without comment, at a little place near the Langham; and, I recollect very hospitably entertained. He was known there, and I used to think he was always at his best in a cabmen's shelter. Without a certain sordidness in his surroundings, he was never quite comfortable, never quite himself; and at those places you are obliged to drink nothing stronger than coffee or tea. I liked to see him occasionally, for a change, drinking nothing stronger than coffee or tea. At Oxford, I believe, his favorite form of intoxication had been haschisch; afterwards he gave up this somewhat elaborate experiment in visionary sensations for readier means of oblivion; but he returned to it, I remember, for at least one afternoon, in a company of which I had been the gatherer, and of which I was the host. The experience was not a very successful one; it ended in what should have been its first symptom, immoderate laughter. It was disappointing, and my charming, expectant friends, disappointed.

Always, perhaps a little consciously, but; at least always sincerely, in search of new sensations, my friend found what was for him the supreme sensation in a very passionate and tender adoration of the most escaping of all ideals, the ideal of youth. Cherished, as I imagine, first only in the abstract, this search after the immature, the ripening graces which time can but spoil in the ripening, found itself at the journey's end, as some of his friends thought, a little prematurely. I was never of their opinion. I only saw twice, and for a few moments only, the young girl to whom most of his verses were to be written, and whose presence in his life may be held to account for much of that astonishing contrast between the broad outlines of his life and work. The situation seemed to me of the most exquisite and appropriate impossibility. She had the gift of evoking, and, in its way, of retaining, all that was most delicate, sensitive, shy, typically poetic, in a nature which I can only compare to a weedy garden, its grass trodden down by many feet, but with one small, carefully-tended flower-bed, luminous with lilies. I used to think, sometimes, of Verlaine and his 'girl wife', the one really profound passion, certainly, of that passionate career; the charming, child-like creature, to whom he looked back, at the end of his life, with an unchanged tenderness and disappointment: 'Vous n'avez rien compris à ma simplicité', as he lamented. In the case of my friend there was, however, a sort of virginal devotion, as to a Madonna; and I think had things gone happily, to a conventionally happy ending, he would have felt (dare I say?) that his ideal had been spoilt.

But, for the good fortune of poets, things never do go happily with them, or to conventionally happy endings. So the wilder wanderings began, and a gradual slipping into deeper and steadier waters of oblivion. That curious love of the sordid, so common an affectation of the modern decadent, and with him so expressively genuine, grew upon him, and dragged him into yet more sorry corners of a life which was never exactly 'gay' to him. And now, indifferent to most things, in the shipwrecked quietude of a sort of self-exile, he is living, I believe, somewhere on a remote foreign sea-coast. People will complain, probably, in his verses, of what will seem to them the factitious melancholy, the factitious idealism, and (peeping through at a few rare moments) the factitious suggestions of riot. They will see only a literary affectation where in truth there is as poignant a note of personal sincerity as in the more explicit and arranged confessions of less admirable poets. Yes, in these few, evasive, immaterial snatches of song, I find, implied for the most part, hidden away like a secret, all the fever and turmoil and the unattained dreams of a life which has itself had much of the swift, disastrous, and suicidal energy of genius.

For Mark Longaker this is obviously a cruel blow to Dowson and a travesty of his life:

> Suffering, and detached as he was from his friends, Dowson was by no means indifferent to Symons' statements concerning his personal affairs and the oblivion which would soon overtake him. He was too ill and dispirited at the time to strike back, and furthermore there was little of the polemic in his nature when it came to such deeply affecting matters; but Yeats and others have reported that he wrote a letter of protest in which he stated that his life was not devoid of industry. A letter has turned up, probably the one mentioned by Yeats, in which Dowson writing directly to Symons who had evidently sent him the proofs of the 'Causerie' asked him to tone down some of the detail. Among other things, Dowson objected to Symons's describing his appearance as dilapidated.

But that will not do. Again Yeats in a verifiable case was right for the most part, and the letter, which is dated 'le 5 Juliet', was written only five days before Dowson and a drunken friend went and burst in on the baker. Perhaps there was indeed a telegram arriving before the letter, 'Arrested, sell watch and send proceeds', as Yeats reports (Dowson certainly redeemed a pawn some months later). Although the baker was not imprisoned, he withdrew the charges. But more significant than this insight into Yeats's method and memory is the insight which is provided by Dowson's response to Symons's article:

My dear Symons,
  My thanks for your charming letter & the article, à propos of myself & my work. You are right in assuming my complete indifference as to what things may be said of me over yonder, & I am content to be found of sufficient interest personally, to be the subject of your chronique. Would you, however, mind, toning down certain ~~sentences~~ phrases on the 3rd page of your proof which I return forthwith to you – sentences which would – if the veil of your article ~~is~~ were penetrated – give an erroneous & too lurid account of me: for ~~am~~ have I not been peacefully rusticating these five months en pleine campagne? The sentence 'Abroad in the *shadier* quarters of foreign cities etc down to 'Gay' to him' is the one which I have in my mind & suggests the too hopelessly disreputable. *Could you, without spoiling your article*, change that sentence into an expression of the fact that my wanderings in foreign cities are a result of my chronic restlessness – for indeed I have long since outgrown mine old 'curious love of the sordid', & am grown the most pastoral of men? I should be grateful if you would do this, not so much for my own feeling, as for the benefit of sundry of my friends, who might otherwise be needlessly pained (as for instance Image, who heard exaggerated rumours of my life in Paris & was at the pains to write a most kind grieved and paternal letter.).
  If at the same time you would suppress a too alcoholic reference to the cabman's shelter – (for the 'refused admittance was to outsiders generally & not personal) substitute 'readier means of oblivion' or some such phrase for 'oblivion of alcohole', & if you *could* possibly find a less ignoble word than 'very dilapidated', there is nothing in your article which I have any objection to your publishing.
  It is always of curious interest to get any genuine idea of the manner in which others see you, & I am fortunate in my chronicler. I am especially charmed with the sympathy & tact with which you touch on what you rightly call my 'supreme sensation'. And for your conclusion ~~the~~ I take off my hat to the compliment – the 'genius' is perhaps too partial & beaucoup trop flatteur, but, as no one is better

aware than myself, I have alas! always had, alas! too much of that 'swift, disastrous & suicidal energy' which destroyed our dear & incomparable Verlaine. (*Letters*, pp. 371–2)

There is no desire to 'strike back' here, but a willing acquiescence in Symons's portrayal, and a thankfulness at finding an understanding appreciation of him when he foresees, as he tells Symons in the same letter, that 'I am to dispute the honour with you of being the most abused versifier in England'.

Dowson, then, is not as well served by his defenders as they might have thought. Gawsworth was perhaps nearest when he said that

Having examined a considerable amount of evidence, and considered its fluctuations and metamorphoses, in search for the truth, I am now prepared to side with Plarr and Mr. Jepson in their reasonable good opinion; with this reservation, however, that Dowson's careless mode of living and indifference to the expectations of society laid him open, perhaps to a tithe of the criticism and reproach that he has received.

But one must go further and see Dowson as striving for a mythical status which Symons captures. He must have seen Symons's essay as accurately identifying the central element of his work, the split between the real and the ideal and the lament at the consciousness of it. That lament is morality bemoaning the irrelevance of art; it is the response of the conscience to art for art's sake.

Symons notes the depth of the split between the life of the man and the poet one imagines behind the verses, as if to illustrate Yeats's 'The Choice':

The intellect of man is forced to choose
Perfection of the life, or of the work,
And if it take the second must refuse
A heavenly mansion, raging in the dark.

When all that story's finished, what's the news?
In luck or out the toil has left its mark:
That old perplexity an empty purse,
Or the day's vanity, the night's remorse.

Equally he stresses the separation of the 'poetic' book from the 'outward things' on which it has such a tenuous hold, which reflect the 'exquisitely refined' manner contrasted with the 'dilapidated' appearance (obviously it was because he needed this contrast that he could not accede to Dowson's request to find another word for 'dilapidated'). And Symons's treatment of Dowson's 'supreme sensation' which Dowson found so tactfully done, notes its growth from an abstract ideal and the division between that ideal and the real. It is much less tactful in the Memoir to Symons's edition of *The Poems of Ernest Dowson* (1905):

> Sober, he was the most gentle, in manner the most gentlemanly of men; unselfish to a fault, to the extent of weakness; a delightful companion, charm itself. Under the influence of drink, he became almost literally insane, certainly quite irresponsible. He fell into furious and unreasoning passions; a vocabulary unknown to him at other times sprang up like a whirlwind; he seemed always about to commit some act of absurd violence. Along with that forgetfulness came other memories. As long as he was conscious of himself, there was but one woman in the world, and for her he had an infinite tenderness and an infinite respect. When that face faded from him, he saw all the other faces, and he saw no more difference than between sheep and sheep.

Dowson was certainly not unacquainted with prostitutes ('*Vraiment*, it is only the third occasion since I returned to this sad country that I have dealt with a whore', he wrote to Conal O'Riordan in April 1897) but he does not emerge as a devoted womanizer from his letters, not one who by policy 'found harlots cheaper than hotels' as Pound would have it. The picture is important to his place as a Decadent poet, however, and Yeats, in using the same material, makes Dowson's an image of his own behaviour, something to place alongside his own barren passion:

> My devotion might as well have been offered to an image in a milliner's window, or to a statue in a museum, but romantic doctrine had reached its extreme development. Dowson was in love with a girl in an Italian restaurant, courted her for two years; at first she was too young, then he too disreputable; she married the waiter and Dowson's life went to wreck. Sober he looked on no woman; drunk he picked the cheapest whore. 'He did not even want them clean', said a friend. 'I have been faithful to thee, Cynara, in my fashion'
> *(Autobiographies* p. 399)

The importance of all this is to emphasize that for Dowson the artificial is the approach to the ideal and that he almost did wish for an ideal to worship as un-real as an image in a milliner's window, or a statue in a museum. His source of inspiration was as often art as life and from art came the pattern for his life, his love and his poetry.

Those who complain of reading the poems in terms of the life seem to forget that the life is Dowson's creation too. In an outburst in a letter to Arthur Moore the day before Christmas 1889 he bemoaned the general depression of the season and suggested:

Shall we write a novel – the study of a man *two-sided,* i.e. by temperament etc, humanus, pleasure loving, keenly sensible to artistic impressions, & to the outward & visible beauty of life – & at the same time morbidly conscious of the inherent grossness & futility of it all – & so trace the struggle between his sensibility & his fanaticism – until the latter has spoilt the whole of art & nine tenths of life for him, & made him either a suicide, a madman, or simply a will-less, disgustful, drunken debauchee. I don't see any other possible dénouement for our novel.   (*Letters,* p. 122)

And in March of the same year he had asked Moore for the source of a quotation, which he obviously felt was accurate for him since he gave it to Edgar Jepson some years later to put by his name: 'The small things of life are odious to me & the habit of them enslaves me: the great things of life are eternally attractive to me & indolence & fear puts them by' (*Letters,* pp. 51–2). He even suggested that the dog in Aesop's fable which tried to grasp the shadow, preferred it wisely (*Letters,* p. 45).

Similarly Dowson seems to have designed his love in the abstract and Symons saw, and I think rightly suggests that Dowson also saw, the impossibility of his love. Dowson wrote more than once of the 'factitious' nature of modern love, and wished his love to be more literary: 'I am quite content to let the affair develop itself in the way – I prefer – on paper', he wrote of the episode with the barmaid, whom he insisted on calling Lena rather than her real name. And his love of children is paradoxically a love for the artificial, as one can see in his essay on 'The Cult of the Child' which he wrote just before he met Adelaide:

. . . there is no greater fallacy than the assumption . . . that a child's acting is necessarily inartistic. In our opinion it is generally the reverse. At the risk of appearing paradoxical, we must even assert that there is every reason why a child's acting should be artistic – more artistic even than that of most 'grown ups'. The men and women who are naturally actors and actresses are, as we know by painful experience, in the exception. But in childhood we are all spontaneously dramatic. Without effort children take up poses the most delightfully naive in the world. Tragedy, comedy, romantic drama, they play it all by turns. A child who is a real child and not a precocious little prig, a child who has entered into its inheritance, lives all its real life in the kingdom of pretence. It is only when we have turned our first decade that we begin to grow out of the 'passion for making believe'. Anyone who has been a sympathetic observer of a little girl with her doll must admit the truth of this. What dramas! what romances! what a wealth of histrionic power is lavished on the wooden puppet! . . .

As Montaigne says, 'the play of children is not performed in play, but to be judged as their most serious action.' . . .

Indeed, it is not suprising that an age which is, after all, chiefly pessimist, an age which is so deeply disillusioned, should turn with an immense delight to the constant charm of childhood. Sentimental unrealities *à la* Buchanan no longer appeal to us; our realism has made us difficult, and, profoundly disgusted with the result of our scepticism, we naturally hail the more eagerly the one unimpeachable consolation which our scepticism cannot touch. And not less in the drama than in the rest of art the cult of the child should have a place, so that just as we seek relief from the sombre and relentless psychology of M. Paul Bourget in the realism of the nursery, the charming pages of Mrs. Ewing, we may find it now and again across the footlights, and acknowledge, as we must all have done a year ago, when we applauded the exertions of the charming little player who performed the *title-rôle* in Mrs. Winter's play of *Bootle's Baby*, that art can still offer us the counterfeit presentment of one exquisite relation.   (*Letters* pp. 433–5)

Minnie, the star of *Bootle's Baby*, gave way to Missie. What Symons found in his music-halls and Yeats in his masks, Dowson found in his little girls, a place where life became art and thus the more life; and although Dowson never joined Symons in a liking for the ballet, they shared a love of the stage's artifice. Perhaps even the change from girlhood to womanhood was seen by Dowson as a change from the world of artifice to the real world. The whole complexity of the relationship of art to life, ideal to reality, is summed up in the opening words of his preface to *Verses*: 'To you, who are my verses'.

Certainly the inspiration of the poems is a mixture of ideal and literary precedent. Not since Gray has a poet made such a success of putting a succession of echoes to a mournful tune; and the extent of his borrowings can be seen by some simple if perhaps lengthy comparisons, which show not only how extensively he borrowed but also how distinct is his own creation. We know from W.R. Thomas (in his 'Ernest Dowson at Oxford') that Swinburne, Poe and Baudelaire were the poets in whom Dowson was most interested in his university days. Indeed one could construct an interesting poem:

> There comes an end to summer,
>   To spring showers and hoar rime;
> His mumming to each mummer
>   Has somewhere end in time,
> And since life ends and laughter,
>   And leaves fall and tears dry,

Who shall call love immortal,
　　When all that is must die?

We are not sure of sorrow,
　　And joy was never sure;
To-day will die to-morrow;
　　Time stoops to no man's lure;
And love, grown faint and fretful,
With lips but half regretful
Sighs, and with eyes forgetful
　　Weeps that no loves endure.

And all my days are trances
　　And all my nightly dreams
Are where thy grey eye glances
　　And where thy footstep gleams –
In what ethereal dances,
　　By what eternal streams.

The first stanza is from Dowson's 'To His Mistress', the second from
Swinburne's 'The Garden of Proserpine', and the third from Poe's
Dowsonesquely-titled 'To One in Paradise'. Not much separates the
Dowson and the Swinburne in the balancing of line with line, pairing of
alliterative groups, the strong syntactical break in the middle, the alter-
nating masculine and feminine rhymes, even the ideas. Swinburne's
stanza does have that triple rhyme in its second half which adds a lift
before the dying fall, a stanza form which Dowson uses in 'Praeterita',
but the similarities are more remarkable than the differences. Dowson
always sounds more distinctly Swinburnian in this stanza, where the
lines are too short, urgent and regular for his usual hesitant appeal. It is
in this stanza too that Dowson sounds most like Poe. Although Symons
reported that Dowson said to him that his ideal of a line of verse was
Poe's 'The viol, the violet, and the vine' and had a theory 'that the letter
"v" was the most beautiful of the letters, and could never be brought
into verse too often', neither the poet nor the theory seems to have had
more than a passing influence, perhaps only in 'A Coronal' with its
opening antithesis of innocence and indulgence in 'Violets and leaves of
vine' or in the only mention of Poe in Dowson's letters: 'I have been
lolling over Poe's "Valueless Verse" this afternoon.' Or were the 'leaves
of vine' from *Hedda Gabler* which so impressed Dowson in 1891 and
from which he uses the 'vine leaves in your hair' allusion twice in letters
to Moore? (*Letters*, pp. 202 and 204.)
　The strongest influence is undoubtedly Swinburne. 'A Ballad of
Burdens' for example provided material for more than one of Dowson's
poems. It is a virtuoso piece with nine stanzas and an envoi ending with
the same line, but it can be adequately tasted in its first stanza:

> The burden of fair women. Vain delight,
>   And love self-slain in some sweet shameful way,
> And sorrowful old age that comes by night
>   As a thief comes that has no heart by day,
>   And change that finds fair cheeks and leaves them grey,
> And weariness that keeps awake for hire,
>   And grief that says what pleasure used to say;
> This is the end of every man's desire.

Vanity of desire and ambition, futility and the inevitability of age are themes dear to Dowson and he clearly remembers them in 'Dregs':

> The fire is out, and spent the warmth thereof,
> (This is the end of every song man sings!)
> The golden wine is drunk, the dregs remain,
> Bitter as wormwood and as salt as pain;
> And health and hope have gone the way of love
> Into the drear oblivion of lost things.
> Ghosts go along with us until the end;
> This was a mistress, this, perhaps, a friend.
> With pale, indifferent eyes, we sit and wait
> For the dropt curtain and the closing gate:
> This is the end of all the songs man sings.

In place of Swinburne's formulaic and parallel abstracts and his generalizing tendency, Dowson concentrates on images, responding perhaps to Pater's assertion that 'the first condition of the poetic way of seeing and presenting things is particularisation.' But Dowson's eye is just as firmly on literary as on non-literary experience. He seems to remember not only Swinburne but also Robert Bridges, whose 'Elegy on a Lady, whom Grief for the death of her Betrothed Killed' says that 'on the banks of the forgetful streams, / The pale indifferent ghosts wander, and snatch / The sweeter moments of their broken dreams.' Swinburne's eighth stanza called forth many echoes:

> The burden of dead faces. Out of sight
>   And out of love, beyond the reach of hands,
> Changed in the changing of the dark and light,
>   They walk and weep about the barren lands
>   Where no seed is, nor any garner stands.

In Dowson's 'Vanitas' the echo is particularly strong:

> Beyond the need of weeping,
>   Beyond the reach of hands,
> May she be quietly sleeping,

> In what dim nebulous lands?
> Ah, she who understands!

And other of Dowson's poems, with their barren or hollow lands, their contrasts of seedtime and harvest, show this barren land to have been a particularly fertile source.

Swinburne's 'Forsaken Garden' depicts a still land:

> Not a breath there shall sweeten the seasons hereafter
>   Of the flowers or the lovers that laugh now or weep,
> When as they that are free now of weeping and laughter
>   We shall sleep.

Dowson slows this anapaestic surge, whose enthusiasm always threatens to compromise its desire for rest, and in a measured stanza preserves some of the images and marries them with the theme and atmosphere of Horace's ode (*Odes* I, iv) from which he took his title:

> *Vitae summa brevis spem nos vetat incohare longam*
>
> They are not long, the weeping and the laughter,
>   Love and desire and hate:
> I think they have no portion in us after
>   We pass the gate.
>
> They are not long, the days of wine and roses:
>   Out of a misty dream
> Our path emerges for a while, then closes
>   Within a dream.

Swinburne's 'The Oblation' again has a play with word and rhythm which contradicts the statement:

> Ask nothing more of me, sweet;
>   All I can give you I give,
>   Heart of my heart, were it more,
> More would be laid at your feet:
>   Love that should help you to live,
>   Song that should spur you to soar.
>
> All things were nothing to give
>   Once to have sense of you more,
>   Touch you and taste of you sweet,
> Think you and breathe you and live,
>   Swept of you wings as they soar,
>   Trodden by chance at your feet.
>
> I that have love and no more
>   Give you but love of you, sweet:
>   He that hath more, let him give;

> He that hath wings, let him soar;
>   Mine is the heart at your feet
>   Here, that must love you to live.

In 'Amor Umbratilis' Dowson seems to derive his oblation from Swinburne (to whom he made a reference in his notebook copy of the poem), but his stanza is completely different, with its long third line carrying in each stanza the gesture towards the loved one which falls into silence and frustration in the last line. Dowson also protests far less, gently moving to his wistful paradox without appearing to make it a brazen stance:

> A gift of Silence, sweet!
>   Who may not even hear:
> To lay down at your unobservant feet,
>   Is all the gift I bear.
>
> I have no songs to sing,
>   That you should heed or know:
> I have no lilies, in full hands, to fling
>   Across the path you go.
>
> I cast my flowers away,
>   Blossoms unmeet for you!
> The garland I have gathered in my day:
>   My rosemary and rue.
>
> I watch you pass and pass,
>   Serene and cold: I lay
> My lips upon your trodden, daisied grass,
>   And turn my life away.
>
> Yea, for I cast you, sweet!
>   This one gift, you shall take:
> Like ointment, on your unobservant feet,
>   My silence, for your sake.

If it derives from Swinburne, the passion is cooled, slowed down, made unassertive; it is a masochism of self-denial, not self-laceration.

One could go on at much greater length on the subject of Dowson's obvious debt to Swinburne, particularly to the first series of *Poems and Ballads*. One could compare Swinburne's 'Before Parting' and Dowson's 'Nuns of the Perpetual Adoration' which both see the bitter and the sweet of the world and talk of the world's lack of care in treading on flowers; one could compare 'Félise' with Dowson's 'Villanelle of Marguerites' since both turn on fortune-telling from flowers using a translation of the French words for the counting off of the petals, 'Un peu, passionément, pas du tout'; one could point to Swinburne's 'A

Leave-Taking' and Dowson's 'A Last Word' with their repetitions of 'Let us go hence'; or one could note the Swinburnian 'Libera Me', which nods even more vigorously towards its source under its manuscript title 'Hymn to Aphrodite'. There are in fact so many similarities of line or phrase that it is more important to stress the fundamental shift which allows Dowson to retain a distinct voice. Desmond Flower maintained that 'Swinburne's legacy to Dowson was one of tone rather than metre', but in modifying and removing the stress and *élan* of Swinburne's rhythms Dowson simultaneously modifies the tone, and emphasizes the note of withdrawal while retaining a series of phrases and images which help to keep reality at a distance.

Dowson's intimate knowledge of French and his love of prose may well have affected his modifications of Swinburne, and there are suggestions that both his language and his idealism owed much to Pater and to that 'Golden Book' of the period, Pater's *Marius the Epicurean*. Certainly Yeats, in a passage in which Dowson figures strongly, wonders whether that book 'or the attitude of mind of which it was the noblest expression, had not caused the disaster of my friends. It taught us to walk upon a rope tightly stretched through serene air, and we were left to keep our feet upon a swaying rope in a storm' (*Autobiographies*, pp. 302–3). There is in the *Letters* ample evidence of respect for the man Dowson regarded as 'the finest artist now with us', but two titles of Dowson's poems indicate something of the particular elements that caught Dowson's eye. 'Ad Domnulam Suam' and 'Amor Umbratilis' both derive from Pater's book. 'Domnulam', which Mark Longaker was 'unable to find elsewhere in Latin love poetry', comes from a letter of Marcus Aurelius which Pater quotes when describing Aurelius's care for his children:

> Yet when his children fall sick or die, this pretence breaks down, and he is broken-hearted: and one of the charms of his letters still extant, is his references to those childish sicknesses, – 'On my return to Lorium,' he writes, 'I found my little lady – *domnulam meam* – in a fever.'

Dowson's earlier version indeed used the more personal 'ad domnulam meam' but one can observe Dowson's intermingling of literature and life as he sees his own 'little lady' in Paterian terms in writing to Arthur Moore:

> I dine almost invariably in Poland now. The atmosphere of the place has the most cheering effect on me. The dear child becomes daily more kind & gracious. The other day she came & sat by me & conversed with great affability all the time I was there. She is really the most quaint & engaging little lady – & she can play the fiddle

very prettily. Do you remember, par exemple, Pater's note in 'Marius' – to the effect that when one's pain in life seems just a stupid, brutal outrage on us & one can seek refuge from it, at best, only in a mere 'general sense of goodwill, somewhere, perhaps' – sometimes the discovery of that goodwill if it is only 'in a not unfriendly animal may seem to have explained & actually justified the existence of our pain at all'. That is really almost true. Certainly the mere friendliness of a child has some such effect on me – seems to me at times to be not merely a set-off against one's innumerable unliquidated claims against life but a quite final satisfaction of them – an absolute end in itself – Corollorary [sic] (& my apology for dilating to you so much on quite trivial incidents) – that there is really after all nothing so important as that one should be constantly trying to multiply these moments & to make them last.

(*Letters*, p. 137–8)

It was the purpose of art, Pater had said, to make these moments last, but was the source of the moments always life? How much did Dowson, and how much did Symons in his picture of Dowson, derive from passages in Pater like this one which gave Dowson his word for 'Amor Umbratilis'?

Thus the boyhood of Marius passed; on the whole, more given to contemplation than to action. Less prosperous in fortune than at an earlier day there had been reason to expect, and animating his solitude, as he read eagerly and intelligently, with the traditions of the past, already he lived much in the realm of the imagination, and became betimes, as he was to continue all through life, something of an idealist, constructing the world for himself in great measure from within, by the exercise of meditative power. A vein of subjective philosophy, with the individual for its standard of all things, there would be always in his intellectual scheme of the world and of conduct, with a certain incapacity wholly to accept other men's valuations. And the generation of this particular element in his temper he could trace up to the days when his life had been so like the reading of a romance to him. Had the Romans a word for *unworldly*? The beautiful word *umbratilis* perhaps comes nearest to it; and, with that precise sense, might describe the spirit in which he prepared himself for the sacerdotal function hereditary in his family – the sort of mystic enjoyment he had in the abstinence, the strenuous self-control and *ascêsis*, which such preparation involved.

Surely Dowson's idealism, his sense of dedication among the distractions of the world, his longing for the image of Cynara, have that Decadent consciousness of their literary sources.

The fundamental division of his whole existence and his yearning idealism are characteristic of all of Dowson's work, whatever its sources, and this is true of his most famous poem '*Non sum qualis eram bonae sub regno Cynarae*', where most clearly one can see Symons's division between the real and the 'supreme sensation', between the one woman and the cheapest whore:

> Last night, ah, yesternight, betwixt her lips and mine
> There fell thy shadow, Cynara! thy breath was shed
> Upon my soul between the kisses and the wine;
> And I was desolate and sick of an old passion,
>   Yea, I was desolate and bowed my head:
> I have been faithful to thee, Cynara! in my fashion.
>
> All night upon mine heart I felt her warm heart beat,
> Night-long within mine arms in love and sleep she lay;
> Surely the kisses of her bought red mouth were sweet;
> But I was desolate and sick of an old passion,
>   When I awoke and found the dawn was gray:
> I have been faithful to thee, Cynara! in my fashion.
>
> I have forgot much, Cynara! gone with the wind,
> Flung roses, roses, riotously with the throng,
> Dancing, to put thy pale, lost lilies out of mind;
> But I was desolate and sick of an old passion,
>   Yea, all the time, because the dance was long:
> I have been faithful to thee, Cynara! in my fashion.
>
> I cried for madder music and for stronger wine,
> But when the feast is finished and the lamps expire,
> Then falls thy shadow, Cynara! the night is thine;
> And I am desolate and sick of an old passion,
>   Yea hungry for the lips of my desire:
> I have been faithful to thee, Cynara! in my fashion.

This strikingly original and individual poem is in a sense still resounding with echoes: echoes of Swinburne's lines, perhaps, from the second stanza of 'A Ballad of Burdens' where the 'burden of bought kisses' is counted

> Between the nightfall and the dawn threescore,
>   Threescore between the dawn and evening;

more certainly echoes of Baudelaire, whose poem XXXII from *Les Fleurs du Mal* was also the source of Arthur Symons's 'To One in Alienation':

Une nuit que j'étais près d'une affreuse Juive,
Comme au long d'un cadavre un cadavre étendu,
Je me pris à songer près de ce corps vendu
A la triste beauté dont mon désir se prive.

Je me représentai sa majesté native,
Son regard de vigueur et de grâces armé,
Ses cheveux qui lui font un casque parfumé,
Et dont le souvenir pour l'amour me ravive.

Car j'eusse avec ferveur baisé ton noble corps,
Et depuis tes pieds frais jusqu'à tes noires tresses
Déroulé le trésor des profondes caresses,

Si, quelque soir, d'un pleur obtenu sans effort
Tu pouvais seulement, ô reine des cruelles!
Obscurcir la splendeur de tes froides prunelles.

Dowson's is more immediate than Baudelaire's, not 'une nuit' but 'yesternight', and is more conscious of some affection in its 'warm heart' as she lay 'night-long within mine arms in love and sleep' as opposed to Baudelaire's grotesque 'au long d'un cadavre un cadavre étendu' and impersonal 'ce corps vendu'. But if the indebtedness is not absolute it is unquestionable. Also possible is a recollection from Gautier, the 'Maître et ami' to whom *Les Fleurs du Mal* is dedicated, whose 'A une robe rose' describes how

ces plis roses sont les lèvres
De mes désirs inapaisés.

And we ought to note Victor Plarr's view in his *Ernest Dowson* that 'Horace suggested, but Propertius inspired' (p. 57, n. 1).

However, the poem is central to the nineties not simply because it collects fashionable predecessors, or has a new music, a shift in rhythm, a technical excellence, but because it voices the dilemma which was the great subject of the period.

T.S. Eliot admitted a debt to 'Cynara'. Geoffrey Tillotson had suggested that Eliot's phrase 'Falls the shadow' in 'The Hollow Men' recalled Dowson. Eliot thought primarily of technique in the response he made in the *TLS*: 'The derivation had not occurred to my mind, but I believe it to be correct, because the lines . . . have always run in my head, and because I regard Dowson as a poet whose technical innovations have been underestimated' (10 January 1935).

Eliot may have made broader associations. His poem, with its literally Decadent theme of 'This is the way the world ends', is concerned as Dowson's is with the inability to unite the two elements, the ideal and the real, concerned that is with a dissociated sensibility. Eliot had found a way of putting things together in the Symbolist image, or the 'observation' as he might have named it; and he had ways of making it impersonal.

> Between the idea
> And the reality
> Between the motion
> And the act
> Falls the Shadow
>   *For Thine is the Kingdom*
>
> Between the conception
> And the creation
> Between the emotion
> And the response
> Falls the Shadow
>   *Life is very long*
>
> Between the desire
> And the spasm
> Between the potency
> And the existence
> Between the essence
> And the descent
> Falls the Shadow
>   *For Thine is the Kingdom*
>
> For Thine is
> life is
> For Thine is the
>
> *This is the way the world ends*
> *This is the way the world ends*
> *This is the way the world ends*
> *Not with a bang but a whimper.*

Is this not a comment on the poets of the nineties, wistfully regretting their inability to achieve their object, finding 'death's twilight kingdom/ The hope only/ Of empty men'? Dowson might almost himself be a Hollow Man, saying in 'A Last Word':

>   vain things alone
> Have driven our perverse and aimless band.
> Let us go hence, somewhither strange and cold
> To Hollow Lands where just men and unjust
> Find end of labour, where's rest for the old,
> Freedom to all from love and fear and lust.

Eliot even manages to capture in his snatches of religion and the life-weary 'Life is very long' the late-nineteenth-century mixture of hope and disillusion, that sense that, as for des Esseintes, satisfaction lies only in the prospect of death or the Church, there being no reconciliation of the artificial ideal and the sensual ordinary world.

This idealism among distractions of the world is the central axis around which Dowson's poetry revolves. It is obvious in his 'Nuns of the Perpetual Adoration':

> Calm, sad, secure; behind high convent walls,
> These watch the sacred lamp, these watch and pray:
> And it is one with them when evenings falls,
> And one with them the cold return of day.
>
> . . .
>
> Outside, the world is wild and passionate;
> Man's weary laughter and his sick despair
> Intreat at their impenetrable gate:
> They heed no voices in their dream of prayer.

In this poem we have the development to include specifically religious contrast with the world, and we also have the image of the rose of the world set against the star of the heavens, a change in symbol but no change in significance from those opposites of 'Cynara'.

> They saw the glory of the world displayed;
> They saw the bitter of it, and the sweet;
> They knew the roses of the world should fade,
> And be trod under by the hurrying feet.
>
> Therefore they rather put away desire,
> And crossed their hands and came to sanctuary;
> And veiled their heads and put on coarse attire;
> Because their comeliness was vanity.
>
> And there they rest; they have serene insight
> Of the illuminating dawn to be:
> Mary's sweet Star dispels for them the night,
> The proper darkness of humanity.

'Benedictio Domini' rehearses the same theme: and in the same rhyme and metre:

> Without, the sullen noises of the street!
> The voice of London, inarticulate,
> Hoarse and blaspheming, surges in to meet
> The silent blessing of the Immaculate.
>
> . . .

> Strange silence here: without, the sounding street
>   Heralds the world's swift passage to the fire:
> O Benediction, perfect and complete!
>   When shall men cease to suffer and desire?

And 'Carthusians' does substantially the same, though lengthening the line to the Alexandrine, which Dowson managed to use without it falling into the usual pitfalls that led Pope to liken it to a wounded snake:

> We fling up flowers and laugh, we laugh across the wine;
>   With wine we dull our souls and careful strains of art;
> Our cups are polished skulls round which the roses twine:
>   None dares to look at Death who leers and lurks apart.
> Move on, white company, whom that has not sufficed!
>   Our viols cease, our wine is death, our roses fail:
> Pray for our heedlessness, O dwellers with the Christ!
>   Though the world fall apart, surely ye shall prevail.

One even feels that there are poems which are paired to balance the two opposing types of love. 'Amor Umbratilis' celebrates the Cynara side, ideal, desired, and cold:

> I watch you pass and pass,
>   Serene and cold: I lay
> My lips upon your trodden, daisied grass,
>   And turn my life away.

'Amor Profanus' is not quite the 'bought red mouth', but is fully within the *carpe diem* tradition, even if there is a spectral attractiveness about the threatened alternatives:

> Ah, Lalage! while life is ours,
> Hoard not thy beauty rose and white,
> But pluck the pretty, fleeting flowers
> That deck our little path of light:
> For all too soon we twain shall tread
> The bitter pastures of the dead:
> Estranged, sad spectres of the night.

Desmond Flower refers the reader to Horace's *Odes*, I,22, but there is something more to the name than that. We do have the passion, but there is the possibility that Dowson was thinking more of the Lalage of *Odes*, II,5. Here we have the much more Dowsonesque figure:

> Nodum subacta ferre iugum valet
> cervice, nondum munia comparis
>   auquare nec tauri ruentis
>   in venerem tolerare pondus.

The poem is more ironic than would at first appear, just as in 'Cynara' itself the apparent contrast of sinful and pure love is undercut by the 'hungry for the lips of my desire', which sounds like Shakespeare's Troilus as he awaits Cressida. Despite the qualifications, however, 'Amor Umbratilis' and 'Amor Profanus' form the two sides that occurred together in other poems.

Even the poems that are superficially different from Dowson's usual mode are clearer when seen as aspects of Dowson's central theme. 'To One in Bedlam' is not just a poem in a slightly different style, which is rather more detached than is usual in Dowson – he is as a rule much more closely involved in the situation – it is another exploration of the contrast he perceives elsewhere. Here he sees the madman rather than the priest as the one possessed of a higher knowledge than ordinary man. But the images are the same; again the stars are there as the ideal ('There are "stars" in poem after poem of certain writers of the 'nineties as though to symbolise an aspiration towards what is inviolate and fixed', wrote Yeats), again the roses, but not this time the 'roses of the World' but 'moon-kissed roses', again the wine but now 'enchaunted wine' rather than the wine with which in 'Carthusians' 'we dull our souls'.

> With delicate, mad hands, behind his sordid bars,
> Surely he hath his posies, which they tear and twine;
> Those scentless wisps of straw, that miserably line
> His strait, caged universe, whereat the dull world stares,
>
> Pedant and pitiful. O, how his rapt gaze wars
> With their stupidity! Know they what dreams divine
> Lift his long, laughing reveries like enchaunted wine,
> And make his melancholy germane to the stars!?
>
> O lamentable brother! if those pity thee,
> Am I not fain of all thy lone eyes promise me;
> Half a fool's kingdom, far from men who sow and reap,
> All their days, vanity? Better than mortal flowers,
> Thy moon-kissed roses seem: better than love or sleep,
> The star-crowned solitude of thine oblivious hours!

The contrasts of 'vanity' and mortality, of the 'dull world' and his 'star-crowned solitude' restate the other poems' subject, substituting madness for love or sleep as the route of escape. Coleridge and Yeats had seen the poet as madman but Dowson adds the imprisonment, the 'strait, caged universe' out of which he is 'rapt' by the non-wordly, the 'divine' and the 'enchaunted'. Again in this poem a seemingly straightforward antithesis is undercut, since what is promised is 'half a fool's kingdom', not quite the ideal one might ask for, the fool's paradise, not necessarily the heaven of desire.

Dowson's longest verse piece. 'The Pierrot of the Minute', dragged from him in three weeks in 1892, revolves around the same theme, and epitomizes it in the figure of Pierrot. In an essay on Beardsley which Yeats called a masterpiece, Symons describes how 'Pierrot is one of the types of our century, of the moment in which we live.' He describes Pierrot as

> passionate; but he does not believe in great passions. He feels himself to be sickening with a fever, or else perilously convalescent; for love is a disease, which he is too weak to resist or endure. He has worn his heart on his sleeve so long, that it has hardened in the cold air. He knows that his face is powdered, and if he sobs it is without tears; and it is hard to distinguish, under the chalk, if the grimace which twists his mouth awry is more laughter or mockery. He knows that he is condemned to be always in public, that emotion would be supremely out of keeping with his costume, that he must remember to be fantastic if he would not be merely ridiculous. And so he becomes exquisitely false, dreading above all things that 'one touch of nature' which would ruffle his disguise, and leave him defenceless. Simplicity, in him, being the most laughable thing in the world, he becomes learned, perverse, intellectualising his pleasure, brutalising his intellect; his mournful contemplation of things becoming a kind of grotesque joy, which he expresses in the only symbols at his command, tracing his Giotto's O with the elegance of his pirouette.
>
> (*Studies in Seven Arts*, 1924, pp. 96–7)

Dowson again expresses the typical. He concentrates in this poem more on the aspirations than upon the trials of this world. One only finds the worldly gaiety in such lines as those of Pierrot before he sleeps to be wakened by Love:

> Tired am I, tired, and far from this lone glade
> Seems mine old joy in rout and masquerade.
> Sleep cometh over me, now I will prove
> By Cupid's grace, what is this thing called love.

But the striving for immortality, the impossible union, is there:

> *The Lady.*   Who is this mortal
>   Who ventures to-night
>   To woo an immortal,
>   Cold, cold the moon's light.

And Pierrot recognizes clearly and is clearly warned what he is risking.

'Unveil thyself', he tells the veiled lady, although 'thy beauty be/Too luminous for my mortality'. She warns:

> Mortal, beware the kisses of the moon!
> Whoso seeks her she gathers like a flower –
> He gives a life, and only gains an hour.   ·

The hour is rather frittered away, she telling him that he will never find his heart again nor find love 'In some earthly Pierette', and he teaching her of the ways of scandal at court, before the time runs out and he begins to sleep as the lady sings over him the sentence on such as he:

> Dream thou hast dreamt all this, when thou awake,
> Yet still be sorrowful for a dream's sake.
> . . .
> I come no more, thou shalt not see my face
> When I am gone to mine exalted place:
> Yet all thy days are mine, dreamer of dreams,
> All silvered over with the moon's pale beams:
> Go forth and seek in each fair face in vain,
> To find the image of thy love again.
> All maids are kind to thee, yet never one
> Shall hold thy truant heart till day be done.
> Whom once the moon has kissed, loves long and late,
> Yet never finds the maid to be his mate.
> Farewell, dear sleeper, follow out thy fate.

The playlet uses images very much akin to those of 'To One in Bedlam': line 151 asks for 'white music' to 'stir his tired veins like magic wine' which, even rhythmically, is similar to the poem's 'Lift his long, laughing reveries like enchaunted wine'; the poem's 'moon-kissed roses' relate to the playlet's line 139, 'Mortal, beware the kisses of the moon', to the lines at the end of the play quoted above ('Whom once the moon has kissed . . .'), and to lines 293–4, 'Moon-kissed mortals seek in vain/ To possess their hearts again!'

In general the play is slight, though it works pleasantly with suitable music, for which of course it provides ample room. The rewards of the hour are, like the rewards of Faustus in Marlowe's play, impossible to represent, since they are an insight into eternity. The Lady may ask her maidens to

> work such havoc on this mortal's brain
> That for a moment he may touch and know
> Immortal things, and be full Pierrot.

But the things which Pierrot wishes for seem very mundane or unconvincing, and the style full of reminiscences. It perhaps does not deserve

Beardsley's description of it as 'that foolish book', but it is lacking in that rhythmical subtlety which is generally so satisfying in Dowson's poems. Beardsley's illustrations to the play, none of them featuring the lady, represent a rather baffled Pierrot in a luxurious garden, a somewhat rakish figure holding an hourglass, a very furtive and a very self-involved Pierrot. The cul-de-lampe, in Beardsley's *Rape of the Lock* style expresses effectively something of the sense of expulsion from the garden of Dowson's play with Pierrot's expression of mixed wonder and regret, while the cover design of a Pierrot crowned with what we presume are moon-kissed roses suggestively depicts him flying upward in a transport while the hourglass in his hand measures the fleeting hour. The 'rapt gaze' of the drawing probably renders the experience more successfully than the play.

Many writers and critics have noted Dowson's achievement. Pound was much impressed by Dowson, whom he thought a 'very fine craftsman', praise indeed from '*il miglior fabbro*'. T.S. Eliot, as I have said, thought Dowson's technical innovations underestimated and considered '*Non sum qualis eram*' as 'the one poem in which, by a slight shift of rhythm, Ernest Dowson freed himself' from the poetic diction of English verse of his time, just as Yeats said of his own 'Innisfree' that it was 'my first lyric with anything in its rhythm of my own music. I had begun to loosen rhythm as an escape from rhetoric and from that emotion of the crowd that rhetoric brings.' And Yeats himself described Dowson's poems as 'not speech but perfect song, though song for the speaking voice' (*Autobiographies*, p. 301). Geoffrey Tillotson, having noted that Dowson's most important contributions to 'the way poetry has developed since, are Dowson's experiments and achievements in rhythm', adds that his loosening of rhythm 'was mainly carried out in the Alexandrine'. Presumably he too is thinking primarily of 'Cynara' and the handful of other poems in this metre.

Certainly Dowson was interested in the music of his poems; he reported on 20 March 1891 to Arthur Moore that he had been 'writing verses, in the manner of the French 'symbolists': verses making for mere sound, & music, with just a suggestion of sense, or hardly that; a vague Verlainesque emotion.' The comment recalls Symons's view of Verlaine in *The Symbolist Movement in Literature*: words, writes Symons,

> transform themselves for him into music, colour, and shadow; a disembodied music, diaphanous colours, luminous shadow. They serve him with so absolute a self-negation that he can write *romances sans paroles*, songs almost without words, in which scarcely a sense of the interference of human speech remains. The ideal of lyric poetry, certainly, is to be this passive, flawless medium for the deeper consciousness of things, the mysterious voice of that mystery

which lies about us, out of which we have come, and into which we shall return.

Dowson was enough of a lover of Pater to wish to follow his belief that 'all art constantly aspires towards the condition of music', but it may be that he was somewhat superficial in his understanding, not penetrating to the significance of the unification of the manner and the matter which Symons and Yeats reached in the dancer image. 'It was at the time when one or two of us sincerely worshipped the ballet; Dowson, alas! never', wrote Symons in the Memoir of Dowson. With his prose also, Dowson was enough of a disciple of Flaubert to write to Horne that he could adopt some suggested alterations but that 'some I should wish to on their intrinsic merits, but fear, that in doing so, I should undeniably destroy the rhythm' (*Letters*, p. 256). Imitating Poe in 'Violets and leaves of vine', Dowson includes symbols of frail, retiring innocence and drink, the two opposing forces again, but in his 'Villanelle of the Poet's Road' he adds to them the bridging element of music or poetry:

> Unto us they belong,
>   Us the bitter and gay,
> Wine and woman and song.

Something musical is going on in the poems, but exactly how it is achieved is a complex matter, and perhaps eventually impossible to define. There is of course a complex alliterative and repetitive pattern, as anyone can see by looking at 'To One in Bedlam'. This is nothing like Swinburne's jangling juxtapositions of similar sound that jump to their positions like a well-drilled band; it is rather a linking over a stanza or more and a rhetoric of repetition of word or phrase with modulation. In 'Cynara' for example, 'last night' develops through 'yesternight' to 'all night' and 'night-long', to be rounded off in the final stanza's 'the night is thine'. In the first stanza 'Betwixt her lips and mine' is balanced against its rhyming phrase 'between the kisses and the wine'; 'I was desolate and sick of an old passion' seems to be about to be repeated, 'Yes, I was desolate and', but what follows is not another matching adjective but a verb whose falling action is matched by the rhythm. The final line, picking up the name Cynara, sums up the persistent state as opposed to the actions before, and seems something of a new start rhythmically after the realization of desolation in the shorter fifth line. In the fourth stanza Dowson repeats 'Then falls thy shadow, Cynara!' slightly changed, and returns to the word 'lips', though this time the absent lips as opposed the present lips of stanza one. Of course, the whole form of the poem with its refrain in the fourth and sixth lines of each stanza, merely elaborates the repetitions, and the pattern of each stanza too is similar – three lines of the attempt to rid his mind of

Cynara proving futile, and three lines of the desolate faithfulness, the central one of which is the shorter, bleaker line. Dowson is not just skilful with alexandrine or individual line, but in balancing lines in stanzas and in developing a pattern through a whole poem.

'*Vitae summa brevis spem nos vetat incohare longam*' is a good short example of the same thing, repeating the first four words as the first words of the second stanza, parallelling the second half of the first line with the second half of the second stanza's first line, and then moving from the first stanza's tentativeness to a simple description, itself cyclical, emphasizing the path from dream to dream by using the same word as its rhyme. Repetition of lines and half-lines is common in Dowson: the repetition of 'Little lady of my heart' in 'Ad Domnulam Suam'; 'Dark is the church' in 'Benedictio Domini'; 'I would not alter thy cold eyes' in 'Flos Lunae'; 'the [sad] waters of separation' in 'Exile'; or the 'Let us go hence' of 'A Last Word'; there are frequent examples. And of course, the use of the refrain and those forms which involve repetition like the roundel or villanelle emphasize the effect.

Even in the prose poems of *Decorations*, where he is more cynical than in most of his verse, he uses the repetition of word or phrase to structure the passage, as in 'Absinthia Taetra':

> Green changed to white, emerald to an opal: nothing was changed.
> The man let the water trickle gently into his glass, and as the green clouded, a mist fell from his mind.
> Then he drank opaline.
> Memories and terrors beset him. The past tore after him like a panther and through the blackness of the present he saw the luminous tiger eyes of the things to be.
> But he drank opaline
> And that obscure night of the soul, and the valley of humiliation, through which he stumbled were forgotten. He saw blue vistas of undiscovered countries, high prospects and a quiet, caressing sea. The past shed its perfume over him, to-day held his hand as it were a little child, and to-morrow shone like a white star: nothing was changed.
> He drank opaline.
> The man had known the obscure night of the soul, and lay even now in the valley of humiliation; and the tiger menace of the things to be was red in the skies. But for a little while he had forgotten.
> Green changed to white, emerald to an opal: nothing was changed.

Typically, he returns to his starting point, an appropriate form for a poet for whom the world is largely vanity.

The music is partially created by metrical devices and Dowson was

much concerned with form. Apart from his 14 sonnets, his five villanel-
les, and his handful of rondeaus, he experimented with a variety of lines
and stanza forms. He seldom uses a metre other than iambic or trochaic
(at least basically so) – in others he cannot escape Swinburne. His
favourite stanzas emphasize the dying fall metrically, as 'Amor
Umbratilis' with its extended third line

> I watch you pass and pass,
>   Serene and cold: I lay
> My lips upon your trodden, daisied grass,
>   And turn my life away,

which reflects the commitment turning to resignation in the short final
line. Or the obsessiveness and inescapability of a situation prolongs a
stanza from four lines to a breathless fifth:

> Beyond the need of weeping,
>   Beyond the reach of hands,
> May she be quietly sleeping,
>   In what dim nebulous lands?
> Ah, she who understands!

Dowson was fond of this stanza, sometimes without the rhyme in the
first and third lines, and fond of the way the last line quietens (one
might say at times weakens) the tone, using a version with a longer line,
and one with a shorter line:

> I was always a lover of ladies' hands!
>   Or ever mine heart came here to tryst,
> For the sake of your carved white hands' commands;
>   The tapering fingers, the dainty wrist;
>   The hands of a girl were what I kissed.

And the shorter line in:

> What land of Silence,
>   Where pale stars shine
> On apple-blossom
>   And dew-drenched vine,
>   Is yours and mine?

Many of Dowson's effects lead him to end the stanza or the poem on a
quiet note, in the meaning as well as in the rhythm. 'Venite Des-
cendamus' for example, using the stanza of 'Vitae summa . . .' and
playing an intricate game of picking up words and echoing them, is
totally engaged in this approach to quietude:

> Let be at last; give over words and sighing,
>   Vainly were all things said:

Better at last to find a place for lying,
  Only dead.

Silence were best, with songs and sighing over;
  Now be the music mute;
Now let the dead, red leaves of autumn cover
  A vain lute.

Silence is best: for ever and for ever,
  We will go down and sleep,
Somewhere beyond her ken, where she need never
  Come to weep

Let be at last: colder she grows and colder;
  Sleep and the night were best;
Lying at last where we can not behold her,
  We may rest.

Almost every poem in *Decorations* ends on a note of disillusion, reaching nothing, silence; even a notable exception like 'Carthusians' ends on a note of *unsure* hope 'Though the world fall apart, surely ye shall prevail'. The rhythm – Dowson has 'nervous rhythms that depend greatly on pauses and heard silences, a rhetoric of silence almost' – echoes the sense and syntax in reaching a calm. Dowson's endings are not hopeful; sleep and rest are more the objects of his search, certainly not the energetic goals of Henley – Dowson's soul seems eminently conquerable. Nearest both to his content and movement is Housman:

> 'Lie down, lie down, young yeoman;
>   The sun moves always west;
> The road one treads to labour
>   Will lead one home to rest,
> And that will be the best.'

But Housman both in rhythm and attitude is more energetic.

Dowson's rhythms owe something to his love of rhythmical prose, something to his experience of French and Latin verse, and something to the type of phrasing and repetition which makes passages from the Bible poetic; he uses Biblical phrases like the 'water of separation' from Numbers XIX 9 and 13. The lack of strong rhythmical beat is yet another of those reticences that make his poetry such a compilation of negatives:

> By the sad waters of separation
>   Where we have wandered by divers ways,
> I have but the shadow and imitation
>   Of the old memorial days.

This moves away from regularity to a disciplined freedom like the
Bible's, a movement which could lead to the best of Eliot and Pound,
who described what might well have been Dowson's method: 'As
regarding rhythm: to compose in the sequence of the musical phrase,
not in sequence of a metronome.'

Symons and Yeats fixed Dowson as the artist seeking innocent and
ideal perfection amid the world's vanities, and Yeats thought he could
explain the cause of Dowson's (and Johnson's) dissipation:

> What portion in the world can the artist have
> Who has awakened from the common dream
> But dissipation and despair?

Ironically in view of the objections raised to their portraits, Symons
and Yeats do seize the central core of what Dowson was trying to do in
his poems. It may be put forward as biography, but Symons's Memoir
prefaced to Dowson's *Poems* describes, and very accurately, the
making of the self, the life and the poetic achievement:

> He was not a dreamer; destiny passes by the dreamer, sparing him
> because he clamours for nothing. He was a child, clamouring for so
> many things, all impossible. . . . He sang one tune, over and over,
> and no one listened to him. He had only to form the most simple
> wish, and it was denied him. He gave way to ill-luck, not knowing
> that he was giving way to his own weakness, and he tried to escape
> from the consciousness of things as they were at the best, by volun-
> tarily choosing to accept them at their worst.

Although Symons and Yeats are faithful in their fashion, the split in
Dowson is emphasized to fit in with their view of the development of
poetry. Here is a Decadent ('that curious love of the sordid, so common
an affectation of the modern decadent, and with him so genuine', wrote
Symons) worn out by life and escaping like Peter Pan into 'a little verse
which has the pathos of things too young and too frail ever to grow old'.
Here is a man who does not know that 'In dreams begins responsibility'.
It was the Symbolists who followed who were to get back to the 'foul
rag-and-bone shop of the heart' and find their visions there by uniting
the opposite poles of characters like Dowson. He is a haunting minor
poet in his own right, but he is also emblematic of the divided sensibility
which a Symbolist poetry would triumphantly unite.

So it happens that our typical Decadent becomes a phase in the
development of Yeats's poetry. The musicality of his verse, the flavour
of sensationalist sex (largely the contribution of his most famous
poem), the successful translation and assimilation of contemporary
French poetry, the development of the 1880s' interest in complex forms
into a more subtle lyricism, the self-conscious artificiality of language

and inspiration, the wistful depiction of a sterile love and a fruitless existence, all these characteristics are modified by the fundamental sense of division. That division, not only the biographical truth, but both the subject and the style, is the Decadent Dilemma.

To make a final division: the music is so distinctively his own, his themes, images and dilemmas connect him indissolubly with the Decadence.

5 Lionel Johnson

If Dowson is the poet most frequently cited as the typical Decadent, Lionel Johnson is usually second on the list, often paired with Dowson as if they had to stand together to achieve sufficient stature for recognition. For some, as for Yeats in his poem 'In Memory of Major Robert Gregory',

> Lionel Johnson comes the first to mind,
> That loved his learning better than mankind,
> Though courteous to the worst; much falling he
> Brooded upon sanctity
> Till all his Greek and Latin learning seemed
> A long blast upon the horn that brought
> A little nearer to his thought
> A measureless consummation that he dreamed.

Johnson fits less easily than Dowson into conventional descriptions of Decadence. Nowhere in evidence is a 'beauty so bizarre and unconventional that one might feel more justified in calling it ugliness' or a poetry 'at odds with the prevailing notions of decency and morality', though I take these characteristics from the fullest and the best-informed attempt to define Decadence, that of John M. Munro; less considered definitions would offer much more strange and inappropriate features. But I do not think we have to agree with Jean Wilson's provocative view (voiced in *The Yearbook of English Studies*, 1971) that Johnson is a 'poet who has more in common with classic English traditionalists than with the "decadents" he is supposed to represent', although Johnson's sophisticated withdrawal from Decadent extremes lends her some support.

Johnson saw as clearly and described as wittily as Owen Seaman of *Punch* the ridiculous side of Decadence (they did, one should note in passing, see a Decadence to mock), and made such fun of it that it might seem difficult for him to belong to it. Take his description of the 'Cultured Faun' which elaborates the excesses of the type and makes clear its characteristics, particularly its 'double "passion" ':

He, or shall we say it? is a curious creature; tedious after a time, when you have got its habits by heart, but certainly curious on first acquaintance. You breed it in this way:

Take a young man, who had brains as a boy, and teach him to disbelieve everything that his elders believe in matters of thought, and to reject everything that seems true to himself in matters of sentiment. He need not be at all revolutionary; most clever youths for mere experience's sake will discard their natural or acquired convictions. He will then, since he is intelligent and bright, want something to replace his early notions. If Aristotle's *Poetics* are absurd, and Pope is no poet, and politics are vulgar, and Carlyle is played out, and Mr. Ruskin is tiresome, and so forth, according to the circumstances of the case, our youth will be bored to death by the nothingness of everything. You must supply him with the choicest delicacies, and feed him upon the finest rarities. And what so choice as a graceful affectation, or so fine as a surprising paradox? So you cast about for these two, and at once you see that many excellent affectations and paradoxes have had their day. A treasured melancholy of the German moonlight sort, a rapt enthusiasm in the Byronic style, a romantic eccentricity after the French fashion of 1830, a 'frank, fierce', sensuousness *a la jeunesse Swinburnienne*, our youth might flourish them in the face of society all at once, without receiving a single invitation to private views or suppers of the elect. And, in truth, it requires a positive genius for the absurd to discover a really promising affectation, a thoroughly fascinating paradox. But the last ten years have done it. And a remarkable achievement it is.

Externally, our hero should cultivate a reassuring sobriety of habit, with just a dash of the dandy. None of the wandering looks, the elaborate disorder, the sublime lunacy of his predecessor, the 'apostle of culture'. Externally, then, a precise appearance; internally, a catholic sympathy with all that exists, and 'therefore' suffers, for art's sake. Now art, at present, is not a question of the senses so much as of the nerves. Botticelli, indeed, was very precious, but Baudelaire is very nervous. Gautier was adorably sensuous, but M. Verlaine is pathetically sensitive. That is the point: exquisite appreciation of pain, exquisite thrills of anguish, exquisite adoration of suffering. Here comes in a tender patronage of Catholicism: white tapers upon a high altar, an ascetic and beautiful young priest, the great gilt monstrance, the subtle-scented and mystical incense, the old world accents of the Vulgate, of the Holy Offices; the splendour of the sacred vestments. We kneel at some hour, not too early for our convenience, repeating that solemn Latin, drinking in those Gregorian tones, with plenty of modern French sonnets in memory, should the sermon be dull. But to join the Church! Ah, no!

better to dally with the enchanting mysteries, to pass from our dreams of delirium to our dreams of sanctity with no coarse facts to jar upon us. And so these refined persons cherish a double 'passion', the sentiment of repentant yearning and the sentiment of rebellious sin.

To play the part properly a flavour of cynicism is recommended: a scientific profession of materialist dogmas, coupled – for you should forswear consistency – with gloomy chatter about 'The Will to Live'. If you can say it in German, so much the better; a gross tongue, partially redeemed by Heine, but an infallible oracle of scepticism. Jumble all these 'impressions' together, your sympathies and your sorrows, your devotion and your despair; carry them about with you in a state of fermentation, and finally conclude that life is loathsome yet that beauty is beatific. And beauty – ah, beauty is everything beautiful! Isn't that a trifle obvious, you say? That is the charm of it, it shows your perfect simplicity, your chaste and catholic innocence. Innocence of course: beauty is always innocent, ultimately. No doubt there are 'monstrous' things, terrible pains, the haggard eyes of the *absintheur*, the pallid faces of 'neurotic' sinners; but all that is the portion of our Parisian friends, such and such a 'group of artists', who meet at the Cafe So-and-So. We like people to think we are much the same, but it isn't true. We are quite harmless, we only concoct strange and subtle verse about it. And, anyway, beauty includes everything; there's another sweet saying for you from our 'impressionist' copy-books. Impressions! that is all. Life is mean and vulgar. Members of Parliament are odious, the critics are commercial pedants: we alone know Beauty, and Art, and Sorrow, and Sin. Impressions! exquisite, dainty fantasies; fiery-coloured visions; and impertinence straggling into epigram, for 'the true' criticism; *c'est adorable!* And since we are scholars and none of your penny-a-line Bohemiams, we throw in occasional doses of 'Hellenism': by which we mean the Ideal of the Cultured Faun. That is to say, a flowery Paganism, such as no 'Pagan' ever had; a mixture of 'beautiful woodland natures', and 'the perfect comeliness of the Parthenon frieze', together with the elegant languors and favourite vices of (let us parade our 'decadent' learning) the *Stratonis Epigrammata*. At this time of day we need not dilate upon the equivocal charm of everything Lesbian. And who shall assail us? – what stupid and uncultured critic, what coarse and narrow Philistine? We are the Elect of Beauty: saints and sinners, devils and devotees, Athenians and Parisians, Romans of the Empire and Italians of the Renaissance. *Fin de siècle! Fin de siècle!* Literature is a thing of beauty, blood, and nerves.

Let the Philistine critic have the last word; let him choose his words with all care, and define in his rough fashion. How would it do to call the Cultured Faun a feeble and a foolish beast?

This is a remarkably early picture of a Decadent fully-fledged – it comes from the *Anti-Jacobin* of 14 March 1891 – and demonstrates a knowledge of the largely French-derived type to which one might be expected to conform.

Such witty perceptiveness, however, does not mean that Johnson was in no way Decadent, nor that he might not take seriously what he mocks the 'Cultured Faun' for adopting as a pose. For example, he joined the Catholic Church three months after this article was published. More important, parody is a typical Decadent response to the recognition of the inevitable failure of ideals, and his traditionalism is an equally typical Decadent turning away from life to the inspiration of art. For Yeats, as he implies in the poem quoted at the beginning of this chapter, Johnson is another man who relinquished his humanity to pursue his ideal, his 'measureless consummation', creating himself in a Yeatsian way – almost in a Yeatsian mould – and choosing always the most traditional things to root himself in.

His family tradition would have had him in the army; his brothers Ralph and Hugh were in military service, and his father was a Captain of Light Infantry; but Johnson's small stature and boyish appearance – he stopped growing at the age of 16 – put that profession out of the question. He was born Lionel Pigot Johnson to give him his full name, at Broadstairs on 15 March 1867, and was educated privately until his entry, on a scholarship in 1880, to Winchester College 'Where six years, what years! were mine', as he wrote in his poem on 'Winchester'. There he won verse and prose prizes, converted the school paper under his editorship into something of a literary review, and won a scholarship to New College, Oxford, where he went in October 1886. He had already begun to write verse and criticism and to acquire a reputation for eccentricity, and both the reputation and the output of original work grew during his stay at Oxford, though his start there was inauspicious. He passed the preliminary examinations only with difficulty and help and, though he took a second in classical moderations in 1888 and a first in *literae humaniores* in 1890, he never fulfilled the expectations that his Winchester teachers had of him. The effect on him of Winchester and Oxford was profound; he retained a deep affection for both the places themselves and their associations – his poems 'Winchester', 'Winchester Close', 'Oxford', and 'Oxford Nights' show this clearly – and they gave him a great reverence for learning and tradition.

During his Oxford years he formed friendships with members of the Century Guild and, on going down in 1890, joined them at 20 Fitzroy

Street to make a serious beginning on his literary career. He was aided by Charles Kegan Paul, the publisher, to whom he had sent the manuscript of a closet drama called 'Miserabilia' in 1885. Kegan Paul had liked it but thought it was not a commerical proposition. Though he did not publish it, he proved useful in introducing Johnson to the literary world in 1890, and Johnson was soon reviewing for various papers, including the *Academy*, the *National Observer* and the *Daily Chronicle*. By the end of 1891 he had paid off substantial debts contracted by lavish spending on books and prints at Oxford, which left him more free to publish the book of poems which he had already planned. Although he wished to become known as a poet rather than as reviewer or critic, his first book to appear after two years of irritating delay, was in fact his critical work on *The Art of Thomas Hardy* (1894).

On 22 June 1891 he was received into the Roman Catholic Church, an act which marks the end of long internal debate, and indeed more open debate in his letters. It was the logical outcome of his love for tradition, his aesthetic sensibility and his spiritual longings, and the process can be glimpsed in *Some Winchester Letters* (1919), a collection of his letters from the ages of 16 to 18. He talked often of becoming a priest:

> A priest! I am to be a priest! What do you think of it? Do think of it as I put it in my first letter: I am almost decided.
>
>   Of course I don't mean a mitre in a shrine, or even a stall: but a vantage ground of my own, an enticing people under the pretence of shovel hattism, to put it openly. Oh, it is a high ideal!   (pp. 89–90)

Or more significantly:

> I will be a priest of the Church of England, as I have so often dreamed of being. . . . I can conscientiously (oh, that pestilential word) 'take orders', I love the expression. What hypocrisy is there in enrolling myself with the visible spiritualists: shall I turn my poor back on the Church because it is a medley of grotesque and divine? I may try and write something not all unworthy of being read: but that is not work altogether, and I distrust myself. I cannot bear to think of the Church simply left to drift itself hopelessly into vacuity for want of fresh steersmen: it is a live protest against materialism, and shall not die.
>   (pp. 85–6)

He was in the end too indulgent, especially in drink, to be the true ascetic he yearned to be, but he is as firmly as Dowson in the mould of Pater's Marius, for whom

> That first, early, boyish ideal of the priesthood, the sense of dedication, survived through all the distractions of the world, and when all thought of such vocation had finally passed from him, as a ministry,

in spirit at least, towards a sort of hieratic beauty and order in the conduct of life.   (*Marius the Epicurean*, chapter II)

In the early nineties the problems of over-indulgence were not controlling him and he had friends, a congenial place to live, work to do. This was the fruitful period of his poetic writing, and his reviews were remarkable for their close and discriminating criticism, having a scholarly elegance that wears well in comparison to Le Gallienne's gushy belle-lettrism. He is prone to the learned digression and, though his digressions usually serve to reveal his attitudes to the book under review, this cannot be said of his book on Hardy, where there is much acute criticism of Hardy but too much besides. Yeats thought the book on Hardy 'very wonderful' and cared

> more for his theories about literature in general than those about Hardy in particular. However his summing up of those scenic qualities of Hardy in the chapter 'Wessex' and elsewhere is very stately. I feel however that there is something wrong about praising Hardy in a style so much better than his own.   (*Letters*, p. 235)

The book established Johnson's reputation, which increased with the publication of *Poems* (1895). His second book of verse, *Ireland, with Other Poems* (1897), like Dowson's second book in that it is to a great extent made up of material rejected for the first, was a mere continuation rather than a development. The creative years were past.

His whole existence began to shrink; he left the circle of friends at Fitzroy Street and his habits became more solitary. As his drinking increased, his circle of friends decreased and, always a lover of books, he isolated himself more and more with these 'friends that fail not'. It is the period that Georg Santayana describes in *The Middle Span* (1947):

> He still looked very young, though he was thirty, but pale, haggard and trembling. He stood by the fireplace, with a tall glass of whisky and soda at his elbow, and talked wildly of persecution. The police, he said, were after him everywhere. Detectives who pretended to be friends of his friend Murphy or of his friend MacLaughlin had to be defied. Without a signed letter of introduction he could trust nobody. He had perpetually to sport his oak. As he spoke, he quivered with excitement, hatred, and imagined terrors. He seemed to be living in a dream; and when at last he found his glass empty, it was with uncertainty that his hat sat on his head as with sudden determination he made for the door, and left us without saying good night.   (p. 66)

Perhaps Johnson was not overcome so soon or so completely. His determination to be Irish despite his birth and ancestry meant much work and effort on his part, and he visited Ireland several times between 1891 and 1898 to give lectures on Irish writers to the National Literary Society. The last one, on 23 May 1898 about James Clarence Mangan, may derive from an early essay, but his reviews in general were still incisive, able, and full of that sort of humour he admired in his master Pater, a gentle undertone which occasionally reveals itself in a wittily exact phrase. There is no doubt, however, that repeated illness and insobriety strained his frail body. He had been frequently ill since childhood, and at the turn of the century a more serious illness kept him indoors for a year and temporarily crippled his hands and feet. This was probably one of a series of strokes, the last of which caused his death in St Bartholomew's Hospital on 4 October 1902. It is a less sensational end than those partial myths which have been put about: Le Gallienne's that Johnson was knocked down by a cab while drunk; H.W. Nevinson's that he collapsed at the corner of Fleet Street on the way to the offices of the *Daily Chronicle*; or that which Pound puts in the mouth of Victor Plarr, the 'Monsieur Verog' of 'Hugh Selwyn Mauberley', who tells

> how Johnson (Lionel) died
> By falling from a high stool in a pub . . .
>
> But showed no trace of alcohol
> At the autopsy, privately performed –
> Tissue preserved – the pure mind
> Arose toward Newman as the whiskey warmed.

But Pound, though sensational, captures as Yeats does the essential Johnson by placing the emotional instability and practical chaos of his life against the splendid order and ritual for which he longed and which his poems move towards (' "take orders", I love the expression'). Though passions shape his verse, a passion for Catholicism, a passion for Celticism, and a passion for the Classics, each one is a rage for order. And only when one considers his education at Winchester and Oxford and what they meant to him, his commitment to the Church, his love for Ireland, and his notion that 'life is ritual' – Johnson's favourite phrase Yeats tells us in *Autobiographies* – can one see how right Pound is to call him, as he does in the Introduction to his edition of *The Poetical Works of Lionel Johnson* (1915), a 'traditionalist of traditionalists'. Johnson, as Pound goes on to say, 'loved the speech of books and proposed to make life copy it', and like a true Decadent made his life in the image of his art.

His religion gave him restraint, an ideal, and a group of traditional symbols which admirably suited his poetic pattern. It is obviously their shared religion which makes so easy the comparison between Johnson and early Hopkins, before Hopkins's linguistic and metrical curiosity had taken him quite beyond Johnson's reach. After his decision to join the Catholic Church, Johnson wrote more specifically religious poems. The new subject matter did not always inspire him to effective statement, but it gave him a scale of values against which everything was measured, and thus is an essential part of his poetry. If at times it appears too ready made, and conventional forms and ideas take the place in his verse of his own discovery of things, it also reinforces his sense of sin which was the driving force of some of his finest work.

He was born to neither a Catholic nor a Celtic tradition, though he created them and, as Yeats saw, united them:

> Historic Catholicism, with all its councils and its dogmas, stirred his passion like the beauty of a mistress, and the unlearned parish priests who thought good literature or good criticism dangerous were in his eyes 'all heretics'. He belonged to a family that had, he told us, called itself Irish some generations back, and its English generations but enabled him to see as one single sacred tradition Irish nationality and Catholic religion.   (*Autobiographies*)

Johnson strove to be Irish, and Ireland in the end adopted him. He had been interested in his Celtic background from his Winchester days; in 1886 while walking in Wales, he had written to his friend Campbell Dodgson that Wales holds 'earthly paradises that you Saxons don't know', and by 1888 he was writing of Ireland's plight. In the nineties his second book of poems proudly waves the title of Ireland. That Ireland fits in so well with the mood of the rest of his poetry owes much to Matthew Arnold, that 'Prince of song' as Johnson calls him in 'Winchester', to whom Johnson owes many things good and bad. Arnold's *On the Study of Celtic Literature* almost created the Celtic Renaissance single handed, so much so that 'Alfred Nutt, the Celtic scholar, recorded in 1910, that in judging Eisteddfod essays dealing with the Celtic influence on English literature, he found most of the papers to be a mere elaboration of Arnold's ideas' (Frederic E. Faverty, *Matthew Arnold the Ethnologist*, Evanston, 1951, p. 114). Arnold's description of the characteristics of the Celt suited Johnson's ideas and aims much better than those of the diligent but boring Saxon: Johnson's sympathies were with the underdog and the martyr and, praising the Victor Victim in his poem 'De Profundis', he sees in Ireland the extension of himself as Victim Victor. This is in key with the Celtic genius as Arnold saw it, characterized by the epigraph to his essay, quoting from Macpherson's Ossian, 'They went forth to the war, but they always fell.' It was one of Yeats's brilliant simplifications to capture the literal and symbolic truth of Johnson's 'much falling', as sick man, as drunkard, as sinner, and as Irishman. He had seen it in Johnson himself in poems like 'Mystic and Cavalier': 'Go from me: I am one of those who fall'. This Decadence in a variety of senses echoes throughout his poems on Ireland; in 'Parnell':

> Faithful and true is she,
> The mother of us all:
> Faithful and true! may we
> Fail her not, though we fall.

Or in 'Ireland', 'Signed with the Cross, they conquered and they fell.' However much he may have become the Irishman of his own literary creation, Ireland was essential to his poetry, and he claimed loudly the right to be Irish, even in a speech before the Irish Literary Society, where he said, not too aware of the irony that 'It would be pleasant if we could persuade ourselves that a man may write, read, say, and do all manner of things uncongenial to us, yet have quite as much patriotism, and as much Irish spirit, and as many "Celtic notes", as ourselves.'

If he was Celtic in a broad sense, his Classicism was a Classicism in the broadest sense: a love, knowledge and respect not only for the writings of Greece and Rome (and a little of Ireland and Wales) but for the traditions of English literature. This too taught him restraint, and he was never to lose his respect for those 'treasured sages', always measuring contemporaries against them in the same way that Arnold had done, and as Pound was to do later when, in his essay on Johnson, he wrote that he must maintain a standard where 'one should weigh Theocritus and one's neighbour in one balance.' Johnson concentrates not so much on the creations as on the authors themselves, for whom the characters provide life; so in 'Brontë' he writes of Charlotte:

> Thou too, before whose steadfast eyes
> Thy conquering sister greatly died:
> By grace of art, that never dies,
> She lives: thou also dost abide.

> For men and women, safe from death,
> Creatures of thine, our perfect friends:
> Filled with imperishable breath,
> Give thee back life, that never ends.

In a poem that familiarly and rather charmingly goes through a roll-call of 'The Classics', the authors are much more than the names on dead books; they become the companions, the 'friends that fail not' among – one presumes – many failing friends:

> Fain to know golden things, fain to grow wise,
> Fain to achieve the secret of fair souls:

His thought, scarce other lore need solemnize,
Whom Virgil calms, whom Sophocles controls:

Whose conscience Aeschylus, a warrior voice,
Enchaunted hath with majesties of doom:
Whose melancholy mood can best rejoice,
When Horace sings, and roses bower the tomb.

What one usually means by Classical reference, the myths and legends of the ancient world, is on the whole absent from Johnson's poems. He longed to join that literary and classical fraternity and, by cutting himself off from contemporaries and living among books as he did, he began to construct his own 'artifice of eternity'.

One of Johnson's methods of giving life to the classical authors and involving himself with them is that eighteenth-century habit of assuming a phrase from a favourite author. Ian Fletcher notes many examples of this in his edition of Johnson's poems, but let me take one that he does not mention, Johnson's poem to 'Collins', himself a past master of poetic annexation. Johnson's 'mingled measure' not only remembers Collins and his work but makes gestures towards Wordsworth who had also composed a 'Remembrance of Collins'. Johnson's poem (the second stanza was dropped in the printed version) mingles his themes of literature, death, friendship and place:

Through glades and glooms! Oh, fair! Oh, sad!
The paths of song, that led through these
Thy feet, that once were free and glad
To wander beneath Winton trees!
Now in soft shades of sleep they tread
By ways and waters of the dead.

There dwell thy loving thoughts! but we,
    Who know not yet thy sacred gloom,
Who love the sunlight on the lea,
    Till death will mourn thy early doom:
And dying, hope among the dead
    To walk with thee, where poets tread.

There tender Otway walks with thee,
And Browne, not strange among the dead:
By solemn sounding waters ye,
By willow vallies, gently led,
Think on old memories of her,
Courtly and cloistral Winchester.

So memory's mingled measure flows,
In shadowy dream and twilight trance:

> Past death, to dawn of manhood, goes
> Thy spirit's unforgetting glance;
> Through glades and glooms! And hails at last
> The lovely scenes long past: long past.

Johnson picks up the 'Through glades and glooms!' of the first line and the 'mingled measure' of the last stanza from line 64 of Collins's 'The Passions: an Ode for Music': 'Through glades and glooms the mingled measure stole.' Aptly for Johnson, the line describes the music made by 'Pale Melancholy'. The music of Hope suggests a phrase for the last lines of Johnson's poem; Collins asks:

> But thou, O Hope, with eyes so fair,
> What was thy delightful measure?
> Still it whispered promised pleasure,
> And bade the lovely scenes at distance hail!

In the cancelled second stanza, lines from Collins's 'Ode Occasioned by the Death of Mr. Thomson' are echoed, as indeed is its ring effect:

> The genial meads, assigned to bless
> Thy life, shall mourn thy early doom.

Equally, 'tender Otway' may be a reminder of 'gentlest Otway' of line 20 of Collins's 'Ode to Pity'; and more words and ideas, like the 'solemn sounding waters' or the twilight, remind one of Collins. The whole poem, as often in Johnson, is a subtle set of variations on his own familiar themes set with quotations or gentle echoes designed to call up the past and establish the decorous tradition in which he works. It is a dangerous practice in poetry, a characteristic of the gracious rather than the great, but it has a charm which Johnson noted in another of his scholarly delights, the use of a word with a consciousness of its derivation. He wrote of Pater's 'courtesy towards language' in *Post Liminium*:

> Strangeness, a stirring of pleased surprise, the charm of an admiring wonder felt without disturbance, yet with something of a thrill, are elements, in all the finest art: and, as language loses its 'uncharted freedom,' becoming fixed and formal, literary artists are increasingly forced to this 'strangeness,' which is to be had far less by a *bizarre* vocabulary than by a sensitiveness to the value, the precise value, of common words in their precise signification. *Mystery, economy, pagan, gracious, cordial, mortified* – to use such words, with just a hint of their first meanings, is for the scholarly writer and reader a delicate pleasure, heightening the vivid interest of a phrase.
> (p. 31)

Both in his use of individual words and in quotation, Johnson seems to aim for this delicate pleasure.

The three traditions I have mentioned – Celticism, Catholicism and the Classics – are the subject and part of the nature of many of his best poems, and they are his props when inspiration fails. If at times the poems read like hollow exercises, they are never less than skilful, and at his best his work rises to an austere perfection. The purity of this perfection lies to a large extent in Johnson's abandoning argument for sound, preferring what Yeats calls 'pure poetry' to a poetry of discursiveness and argument about history and politics. When Yeats describes in *Autobiographies* how Johnson and Horne 'imposed their personalities' on the Rhymers' Club, he makes a comment that is echoed more than once in his work: 'I saw . . . that Swinburne in one way, Browning in another, and Tennyson in a third, had filled their work with what I called 'impurities,' curiosities about politics, about science, about history, about religion; and that we must create once more the pure work.' Johnson uses the same antithesis in his impressive speech on 'Poetry and Patriotism in Ireland' which is printed in *Post Liminium* (1911); the poet

> writes, let us say, dreams and all manner of imaginative things, in plaintive, lovely cadences, about the faeries, or about the mysteries of the world, birth and life and death, writing out of the depths of his own nature; and lo! instead of being grateful, we abuse him for not writing historical ballads, valiant and national, upon Patrick Sarsfield or Owen Roe.

It is his own poetry that he is describing.

Other writers escaped 'impurities' and 'curiosities' in impressionistic visual detail. Indeed when Pound wrote that Johnson could not be shown to be 'in accord with our present [1915] doctrines and ambitions' he admitted that 'no one has written purer Imagisme than he has in the line "Clear lie the fields, and fade into blue air".' But the colour of such lines, or indeed whole poems like 'In England' with its

> Red wreckage of the rose
> Over a gusty lawn:
> While in the orchard close,
> Fruits redden to their dawn,

is not what we come to expect from Johnson; he evokes a mood and a music, and if it is colourless and cold it is because he restrains his use of description, limits to a small range his similes and metaphors, and concerns himself with music both as subject and principle of construction. When Johnson writes of Byron, another essay from *Post*

Liminium, he prefers Byron the satirist as many modern critics do, but denies that the satire is poetry.

> Byron could shout magnificently, laugh splendidly, thunder tumultuously; but he could not sing. There was something in him of Achilles, nothing whatever of Apollo. Think only of these mighty masters of passion, Aeschylus, Lucretius, Dante, Milton, Hugo; what sweetness proceeding from what strength! They are filled with a lyrical loveliness, the very magic of music, the beauty almost unbearable. By the side of these Byron is but a brazen noise.

'Pure poetry' and music are obviously the same thing, though there is more than a touch of Arnold's influence in the selection for comment of lines of wistful defeat when Johnson writes of *Childe Harold* that

> In that long and elaborate work there are precisely two lines of pure poetry, the lines on the Dying Gladiator:
> 'He heard it, but he heeded not: his eyes
> Were with his heart, and that was far away.'
> That and perhaps a score of other lines in Byron, have an enduring freshness and fragrance of thought and word.

Johnson makes another contrast of the architectural power of design in Hardy's novels with the music which is more proper to poetry: 'music is wont to leave but a vague sense of airy charm. That flying, elusive delight has its place in literature: but only, I think, in verse' (p. 41).

It is of course no surprise that Johnson should aim for the pure poetry of music; he knew his contemporary French poetry and Verlaine's demand for 'De la musique avant toute chose' and more important for such a disciple, he knew his Pater and the claim that 'All art constantly aspires towards the condition of music.' But it is his first and foremost interest. When in 'The Dark Angel' Johnson finds that because of his sinister enemy 'no thought, no thing/Abides for me undesecrate', the first thing he mentions is the bringing down of the uncontaminated quality of music to a sensual level:

> When music sounds, then changest thou
> Its silvery to a sultry fire.

'The Last Music' is a good example of Johnson's practice of capturing the vague charm and elusive delight, creating the decorous and sorrowful music rather than describing it. It is a poem which again has another poem behind it, this time Robert Bridges's 'Elegy on a Lady whom Grief for the Death of her Betrothed Killed', of which Johnson had written in the *Century Guild Hobby Horse* for 1891 that 'Arnold, we find, is not the only poet of our day, who without a specious resemblance can use the ancient symbols and imageries for the stately expression of sorrow'.

But where Bridges's poem has descriptive detail and a narrative line which seem to cry out for illustration by some late Pre-Raphaelite, Johnson has no narrative and his indefinite epithets merely create a mood, almost totally unpictorial.

> Calmly, breathe calmly all your music, maids!
> Breathe a calm music over my dead queen.
> All your lives long, you have nor heard, nor seen,
> Fairer than she, whose hair in sombre braids
>   With beauty overshades
>   Her brow, broad and serene.
>
> Surely she hath lain so an hundred years:
> Peace is upon her, old as the world's heart.
> Breathe gently, music! Music done, depart:
> And leave me in her presence to my tears,
>   With music in mine ears;
>   For sorrow hath its art.
>
> Music, more music, sad and slow! she lies
> Dead: and more beautiful, than early morn.
> Discrowned am I, and of her looks forlorn:
> Alone vain memories immortalize
>   The way of her soft eyes,
>   Her musical voice low-borne.
>
> The balm of gracious death now laps her round,
> As once life gave her grace beyond her peers.
> Strange! that I loved this lady of the spheres,
> To sleep by her at last in common ground:
>   When kindly sleep hath bound
>   Mine eyes, and sealed mine ears.
>
> Maidens! make a low music: merely make
> Silence a melody, no more. This day,
> She travels down a pale and lonely way:
> Now for a gentle comfort, let her take
>   Such music, for her sake,
>   As mourning love can play.
>
> Holy my queen lies in the arms of death;
> Music moves over her still face, and I
> Lean breathing love over her. She will lie
> In earth thus calmly, under the wind's breath:
>   The twilight wind, that saith:
>   *Rest! worthy found, to die.*

This is no narrative: it expands the call for music, which becomes a symbol of artistic and eternal perfection. The lady seems to assume the permanence of Pater's *La Gioconda*, that symbol of pure poetry which Yeats placed at the beginning of the *Oxford Book of Modern Verse*, and achieves permanence in the same way, by uniting life and death. The poetry moves by an intertwining of two sets of ideas, that of music, breath, wind, and life, with that of silence, calm, and death, and achieves a balance between them not by a paradoxical reconciliation but by a continued acceptance of the restfulness of death and a vocabulary which animates the dead woman. She rests and sleeps, just as Bridges's lady goes to her lover. The whole effect is a gentle melancholy of reverence.

From his younger days when in *Some Winchester Letters* he wrote that 'I would give immortality to be a music-god' (p. 161), Johnson aimed deliberately for this type of combination of statement and subject. He was deliberate and careful in all aspects of his art. On punctuation, for example, he wrote to Richard Le Gallienne ' "Casual commas": I thank you; no, you are right, my commas, Heaven be praised, are *not* casual. What right has anything, in any work of art, however slight, to be casual? Oh, for the scholarly graces of Addison and Goldsmith' (*The Romantic '90s*, 1926, p. 145). He claimed that a good review had more permanence than a bad book and should be given the same care as a book in writing, and this serious care, what Yeats called his 'conscious, deliberate, craft', lies behind that characteristic device of his poetry, repetition, and modulation. Perhaps it was this which so attracted him to Bridges's poem 'Elegy on a Lady whom Grief for the Death of her Betrothed Killed', where it is much in evidence:

> Assemble, all ye maidens, at the door,
> And all ye loves, assemble: far and wide
> Proclaim the bridal, that proclaimed before
> Has been deferred to this late eventide:
>   For on this night the bride,
>   The days of her betrothal over,
> Leaves the parental hearth for evermore;
> Tonight the bride goes forth to meet her lover.

Johnson is fond of such things as the movement from 'bridal' to 'bride', and the cross movement and repetition that is evident here. A glance at his own first stanza shows a modulation of sound in the words 'breathe', 'braid', 'brow', 'broad', a careful repetition of 'calmly' and 'breathe' which return in the last stanza, and a tight rhyme scheme, and the whole poem revolves around the idea of music which grows nearer and nearer to silence.

Repetition is the most noticeable feature of many of Johnson's poems, his 'By the Statue of King Charles at Charing Cross', 'To

Morfydd', or 'The Church of a Dream', for example. Take the last poem:

> Sadly the dead leaves rustle in the whistling wind,
> Around the weather-worn, gray church, low down the vale:
> The Saints in golden vesture shake before the gale;
> The glorious windows shake, where still they dwell enshrined;
> Old Saints by long dead, shrivelled hands, long since designed;
> There still, although the world autumnal be, and pale,
> Still in their golden vesture the old saints prevail;
> Alone with Christ, desolate else, left by mankind.
>
> Only one ancient Priest offers the Sacrifice,
> Murmuring holy Latin immemorial:
> Swaying with tremulous hands the old censer full of spice,
> In gray, sweet incense clouds; blue sweet clouds mystical:
> To him, in place of men, for he is old, suffice
> Melancholy remembrances and vesperal.

Not only do we have the repetition of words, the 'Saints', 'long', 'golden vesture', 'clouds' and so on, but also a repetitive syntax that builds up the picture out of small sections some adding to, some modifying what has gone before: 'In gray, sweet incense clouds; blue sweet clouds mystical'. The effect is in a way Biblical, or at least ritualistic, not inappropriate both for the subject and for the writer who was to be for the Rhymers' Club, says Yeats, 'our critic, and above all our theologian' (*Autobiographies*, p. 221). Indeed, Johnson's poems are sometimes cast in the form of prayers, poems like 'Guardian Angels', 'Friends', the third 'Cadgwith' poem, or the poem 'To Leo XIII' which strikingly recalls Hopkins's prayers for the return of England to Rome; and Johnson was in the habit of writing Latin prayers in his copies of books that had some connection with his friends. Clearly he could have been influenced by Biblical and ecclesiastical repetitions, and he could also have found examples in the medieval Latin lyrics that he knew, since his nine Latin poems show the same marked rhymes and balanced construction.

More important even than this repetition of words or motifs within the framework of a poem is his repetition of words or concepts throughout his work. One needs no concordance to see which words are frequently and deliberately repeated: death (or dead), silence, star, moon, white, rose, music, wind, water, sea, sky, sun, dream, night, calm, fire, flame, earth, light, and soul. One can perhaps best see the importance of these words by looking at 'The Dark Angel' and noting in what things he delights, how they are tainted and how Johnson overcomes the tempter in a heroic renunciation (more hoped for than achieved) which is firmly founded on Revelation:

Dark Angel, with thine aching lust
To rid the world of penitence:
Malicious Angel, who still dost
My soul such subtile violence!

Because of thee, no thought, no thing,
Abides for me undesecrate:
Dark Angel, ever on the wing,
Who never reachest me too late!

When music sounds, then changest thou
Its silvery to a sultry fire:
Nor will thine envious heart allow
Delight untortured by desire.

Through thee, the gracious Muses turn
To Furies, O mine Enemy!
And all the things of beauty burn
With flames of evil ecstasy.

Because of thee, the land of dreams
Becomes a gathering place of fears:
Until tormented slumber seems
One vehemence of useless tears.

When sunlight glows upon the flowers,
Or ripples down the dancing sea:
Thou, with thy troop of passionate powers,
Beleaguerest, bewilderest, me.

Within the breath of autumn woods,
Within the winter silences:
Thy venemous spirit stirs and broods,
O Master of impieties!

The ardour of red flame is thine,
And thine the steely soul of ice:
Thou poisonest the fair design
Of nature, with unfair device.

Apples of ashes, golden bright;
Waters of bitterness, how sweet!
O banquet of a foul delight,
Prepared by thee, dark Paraclete!

Thou art the whisper in the gloom,
The hinting tone, the haunting laugh:
Thou art the adorner of my tomb,
The minstrel of mine epitaph.

I fight thee, in the Holy Name!
Yet what thou dost, is what God saith:
Tempter! should I escape thy flame,
Thou wilt have helped my soul from Death:

The second Death, that never dies,
That cannot die, when time is dead:
Live Death, wherein the lost soul cries,
Eternally uncomforted.

Dark Angel, with thine aching lust
Of two defeats, of two despairs:
Less dread, a change to drifting dust,
Than thine eternity of cares.

Do what thou wilt, thou shalt not so,
Dark Angel! triumph over me:
Lonely, unto the Lone I go;
Divine, to the Divinity.

There is a finely grandiloquent ascetic idealism here, balancing the fear of worldly corruption; and Johnson's favourite words fall fairly neatly into the two sides of the Decadent dilemma, worldly things and eternal things, with words like 'music' mediating between the two. Some of the words having a place in both groups, worldly in their literal sense, eternal in a symbolic one.

The things which stand for earthly life are traditionally those natural delights which are also changeable, emphasizing the mutability of things, sea, wind, night and day, weathers and seasons. Johnson took a great delight in the natural world in his younger days, as one can see from his description of sunrise and sunset seen from the top of Snowdon, though even there his habit of mind is to connect the night with the old myths of battle in the heavens; but nature is more a symbol than a vividly realized subject. At times nature is a consoling influence; as in the first 'Cadgwith' poem:

Winds rush and waters roll:
Their strength, their beauty, brings
Into mine heart the whole
Magnificence of things:

That men are counted worth
A part upon this sea,
A part upon this earth,
Exalts and heartens me.

But the opposite is usually the case, where things eternal scorn (to use Yeats's phrase) common bird and petal, and Johnson laments the gulf between the world and one's ideals. Writing more typically of elemental

forces rather than tangible objects, Johnson contrasts the impermanence of winds and waters to the stability of the stars, and sees the moon
and stars relieving the blackness of night and all darkness, real and
symbolic.

The moon and the stars, 'the fires of God' as Johnson calls them in one
poem with a hint of Hopkins which merely emphasizes the difference
between the exactly-focussing Jesuit and the Decadent who turns away
from the world, mark the point where the first group of words merges
into the second, where earthly becomes heavenly and spiritual. Death,
as with Dowson, always hurrying near Johnson's mind, also marks the
change from worldly delights to those white pure things to which he is
drawn in his finest moments, where he sees the soul, perfected and
made white, living eternally in the radiance of God; though the difficulties and dangers of the getting there are as important as the arrival for
his verse.

Let us take 'Pax Christi' as an example of the way in which Johnson
works these obsessive themes into a poem with typical patterns of
repetition, voicing the exultant side of the Decadent Dilemma. Dated
the day of his reception into the Roman Catholic Church (aptly St
Alban's) it indicates the place that religion had in his scheme of things.

> Night has her Stars, and Day his Sun: they pass,
> Stars of the Night! it fades, Sun of the Day!
> Soft rose leaves lie upon the beaten grass,
> Till the wind whirl them, with itself, away.
>
> Eyes have their fill of light: in every voice
> Lives its own music: but the dear light pales,
> The golden music perishes. What choice,
> What choice is ours, but tears? For the world fails.
>
> O Sun and Stars! O glory of the rose!
> O eyes of light, voices of music! I
> Have mourned, because all beauty fails, and goes
> Quickly away: and the whole world must die.
>
> Yet, Sun and Stars! Yet, glory of the rose!
> Yet, eyes of light, voices of music! I
> Know, that from mortal to immortal goes
> Beauty: in triumph can the whole world die.

This perhaps lacks the restraint of his best work, and indicates how
repetition can defeat its own ends, but it shows him attempting to stress
the transfer from mortal to immortal beauty so that the stars can
become both temporal and permanent. But unlike Hopkins, who tends
to *create* that transition, Johnson merely asserts it and, although the
stressing of 'I know' is effectively done by the placing at the line break, it

is imaginatively insufficient to bear the weight of the argument. Johnson, by the way, could well have read some Hopkins, though I am not suggesting any influence; Johnson wrote the article on 'Michael Field' in Alfred H. Miles's *The Poets and Poetry of the Century* (1893), which published nine poems by Hopkins and two fragments.

An awareness of Johnson's typical themes and movement is a great help in understanding all his poetry, but particularly those more mysterious poems which he does so well, where a vague but powerful sense of sin and threat radiates from some haunted face. 'A Stranger' and 'Quisque Suos Manes' are two such, which in fact clarify each other, and there are interesting comparisons to be made with Dowson's poems of division, particularly 'To One in Bedlam'. Johnson's stranger is somehow wilder and more separate than Dowson's madman:

> Her face was like sad things: was like the lights
> Of a great city, seen from far off fields,
> Or seen from sea: sad things, as are the fires
> Lit in a land of furnaces by night:
> Sad things, as are the reaches of a stream
> Flowing beneath a golden moon alone.
> And her clear voice, full of remembrances,
> Came like faint music down the distant air.
> As though she had a spirit of dead joy
> About her, looked the sorrow of her ways:
> If light there be, the dark hills are to climb
> First: and if calm, far over the long sea.
> Fallen from all the world apart she seemed,
> Into a silence and a memory.
> What had the thin hands done, that now they strained
> Together in such passion? And those eyes,
> What saw they long ago, that now they dreamed
> Along the busy streets, blind but to dreams?
> Her white lips mocked the world, and all therein:
> She had known more than this; who wanted not
> This, who had known the past so great a thing.
> Moving about our ways, herself she moved
> In things done, years remembered, places gone.
> Lonely, amid the living crowds, as dead,
> She walked with wonderful and sad regard:
> With us, her passing image: but herself
> Far over the dark hills and the long sea.

There is none of the calm, sad security of Dowson's nuns, much more the haunted isolation of Johnson himself as he separates the passing image from the essence and concentrates, with varying degrees of success, on the essence, which lives in the 'measureless consummation that he dreamed'.

'Quisque Suos Manes' is somewhat clearer with that poem in mind, though here Johnson concentrates on the nature of the vision rather than on the apartness of the stranger:

> What have you seen, eyes of strange fire! What have you seen,
> Far off, how far away! long since, so long ago!
> To fill you with this jewel flame, this frozen glow:
> Haunted and hard, still eyes, malignant and serene?
> In what wild place of fear, what Pan's wood, have you been,
> That struck your lustrous rays into a burning snow?
> What agonies were yours? What never equalled woe?
> Eyes of strange fire, strange eyes of fire! on what dread scene?
> Smitten and purged, you saw the red deeps of your sin:
> You saw there death in life; you will see life in death.
> The sunlight shrank away, the moon came wan and thin,
> Among those summer trees the sweet winds held their breath.
> Now those celestial lights, which you can never win,
> Haunt you, and pierce, and blind. The Will of God so saith.

The eyes, burning rather ironically with a hard gem-like flame, have gazed on some other-worldly vision, which has both purged and smitten the character who 'can never win' the haunting and mocking 'celestial lights'. One can see the poem as addressed to a shade; the title from the sixth book of the *Aeneid* (line 743) refers to suffering as a shade for misdeeds, and Johnson in 'Visions' almost translates the line

> Each suffers in the ghost
> The sorrows of the flesh.

It is very close to Yeats's vision of the shade in 'Byzantium':

> Before me floats an image, man or shade,
> Shade more than man, more image than a shade;
> For Hades' bobbin bound in mummy-cloth
> May unwind the winding path;
> A mouth that has no moisture and no breath
> Breathless mouths may summon;
> I hail the superhuman;
> I call it death-in-life and life-in-death.

But the poem may be addressed to a more specific shade, the avenging angel from those who torment Ireland in the poem of that name:

> Swift at the word of the Eternal Will,
> Upon thee the malign armed Angels came.

Flame was their winging, flame that laps thee still;
And in the anger of their eyes was flame.
One was the Angel of the field of blood,
   And one of lonelier death:
One saddened exiles on the ocean flood,
And famine followed on another's breath.
Angels of evil, with incessant sword,
   Smote thee, O land adored!
And yet smite: for the Will of God so saith.

Or the subject may be the Dark Angel himself ('what thou dost, is what God saith') who certainly can never win the lights eternal. The poem remains powerful because it remains mysterious, yet at the same time its effect rests on an understanding of Johnson's familiar antithesis.

Again, the basic pattern of permanence against impermanence lies behind poems like 'To Morfydd', whose music has been praised, but whose meaning has been ignored:

A voice on the winds,
A voice by the waters,
   Wanders and cries:
Oh! what are the winds?
And what are the waters?
   Mine are your eyes!

Western the winds are,
And western the waters,
   Where the light lies:
Oh! what are the winds?
And what are the waters?
   Mine are your eyes!

Cold, cold, grow the winds,
And wild grow the waters,
   Where the sun dies:
Oh! what are the winds?
And what are the waters?
   Mine are your eyes!

And down the night winds,
And down the night waters
   The music flies:
Oh! what are the winds?
And what are the waters?
Cold be the winds,
And wild be the waters,
   So mine be your eyes!

What Yeats called 'his only love song, his incomparable *Morfydd'* (*Autobiographies*) is in fact no more a conventional love song than any other of Johnson's poems. It is a sort of Celtic 'Cynara', longing for the eyes past change beyond the changeful world, and hearing hints of eternal music across the 'estranging sea' which also kept Arnold conscious of being alone. The companion poems of three and four years later, 'To Morfydd Dead', long for death to join him to her so that they can 'wander through the night, / Star and star', but the complex cross rhyming and sound patterning – perhaps imitated from Welsh verse – the formal and inverted syntax which provide the elegant charm of the poems, and the passionate decorum of their idealism is more in evidence than any tangible Morfydd.

The tension between real and ideal can at times be resolved with what seems a too easy choice, but in poems like 'Magic' the choice seems not only difficult but also heroic and right:

> They wrong with ignorance a royal choice,
> Who cavil at my loneliness and labour:
> For them, the luring wonder of a voice,
> The viol's cry for them, the harp and tabour:
>   For me divine austerity,
>   And voices of philosophy.
>
> Ah! light imaginations, that discern
> No passion in the citadel of passion:
> Their fancies lie on flowers; but my thoughts turn
> To thoughts and things of an eternal fashion:
>   The majesty and dignity
>   Of everlasting verity.
>
> Mine is the sultry sunset, when the skies
> Tremble with strange, intolerable thunder:
> And at the dead of an hushed night, these eyes
> Draw down the soaring oracles winged with wonder:
>   From the four winds they come to me,
>   The Angels of Eternity.
>
> Men pity me; poor men, who pity me!
> Poor, charitable, scornful souls of pity!
> I choose laborious loneliness; and ye
> Lead Love in triumph through the dancing city:
>   While death and darkness girdle me,
>   I grope for immortality.

The choice of images is not based on their pictorial quality but on their significance; the viol, the harp, the tabour, are not parts of a procession which we visualize but shorthand for a state of mind; 'Their fancies lie on flowers' does not ask for a literal imagining, and although the scornful 'ye / Lead Love in triumph through the dancing city' is clear, it is not pictorial. A comparison with Dowson's 'Cynara' reveals the same antitheses and indicates the more tangible physical realities in Dowson, but even in Dowson's poem the kisses, the wine, the dancing, the roses are much more disembodied than they might at first appear. Johnson's poem stands up well to such a comparison, since it is phrased with a fine delicacy of touch, balancing long and short words, long line against short line, developed argument against brief assertion, in musical and stately cadences. It was perhaps this poem that Yeats remembered in 'The Grey Rock' when he addressed his 'Companions of the Cheshire Cheese':

> you may think I waste my breath
> Pretending that there can be passion
> That has more life in it than death.

Johnson did indeed have a passionate yearning for eternity.

It would be a mistake to leave Johnson seeming quite as detached as I have suggested. He had, among his unworldly passions, other loves, as he wrote in 'To the Saints':

> Here upon earth a many loves I know, –
> Of friends, and of a country wed to woe;
> Of the high Muses; of wild wind, pure snow;
> Of heartening sun, exhilarating sea.

To his love of literature, Ireland and nature, one must add therefore his love of friends, for he had something of Yeats's genius for friendship and his consciousness that 'my glory was I had such friends'. His two poems called 'A Friend', his poems 'In Memory' of Malise Archibald Cunningham-Grahame, his 'To a Spanish Friend', his 'To a Belgian Friend' with its echo of the syntax and form of Dowson's 'Nuns', his 'Counsel', 'To Certain Friends', 'Friends', the over-protesting 'De Amicitia', and all those collected and uncollected prayers for his friends and dedicatory verses he was in the habit of making, as well as the dedications of individual poems, all these testify to the importance friendship had for Johnson, and his increasing conviction of its eternity. As he says at the end of 'Friends', 'Heaven were no Heaven, my friends away'; and his hatred is reserved for one, perhaps Wilde to whom he had introduced Lord Alfred Douglas, who had taken not only his friend but his friend's purity, creating yet another of Johnson's haunted sinners:

> I hate you with a necessary hate.
> First, I sought patience: passionate was she:

My patience turned in very scorn of me,
That I should dare forgive a sin so great,
As this, through which I sit disconsolate;
Mourning for that live soul, I used to see;
Soul of a saint, whose friend I used to be:
Till you came by! a cold, corrupting, fate.

Why come you now? You, whom I cannot cease
With pure and perfect hate to hate? Go, ring
The death-bell with a deep, triumphant toll!
Say you, my friend sits by me still? Ah, peace!
Call you this thing my friend? this nameless thing?
This living body, hiding its dead soul?

Perhaps Johnson was conscious of his own tendencies here, but friendship extends through all his other affections and beliefs and welds them into a whole.

'Why should men', asks Yeats after a passage about Johnson, 'live lives of such disorder and seek to rediscover in verse the syntax of impulsive common life? Was it that we lived in what is called "an age of transition" and so lacked coherence, or did we but pursue antithesis?' (*Autobiographies*, p. 304). Whatever the reason, it was certainly in verse that Johnson discovered the syntax; Celticism gave him a tradition of failure in battle with the compensation of serving a lofty cause, Catholicism gave him a religion which reconciled the aesthetic and the moral, literature gave him a tradition which reincarnated the dead authors into their own and he hoped his eternity, and friendship gave this disturbingly solitary man his link with his fellows. He urges friends, admired authors, saints and patriots, all towards his own ideal of white perfection won from struggle, and is haunted by his failure to achieve it. His lines in memory of Ernest Dowson, undistinguished though they are, bring together many of the different strands: he refers to Dowson's short story 'The Dying of Francis Donne' by quoting its epigraph, he remembers the ceremonial and ritual appropriate to his Church and his fellow Catholic, and he sees death as powerless against friendship, as it had always been against faith, love, literature, and music. His passionate ideal and the struggle against himself to realize it are both the cause and subject of his best work.

How is it then that an unsensational, rather scholarly poet who is at times visionary, at times occasional, should come to be considered not only as a Decadent but as characteristic of the period? It is surely that he has that longing for the ideal, and the sadness at its impossibility, that love which is powerful but also sterile, that assumption that eternity is gained by being assumed into art, that consciousness of technique, that awareness of artistic inspiration rather than the inspiration of life, that leaning towards music as technique and image, that feeling for formality and tradition, his Catholicism – 'that too was a tradition' says Yeats in *The Oxford Book of Modern Verse*. Perhaps most important of all he could fit with little adaptation into the myth of the period, the myth of failure where poets were defeated in their desire to resolve the conflicting elements of their Decadent dilemma. Yeats is right to leave us with a picture of him moving towards that 'measureless consummation that he dreamed.'

Johnson was not a narrow traditionalist in theory nor out of key with his time. In his book on Hardy, he wrote that

> the supreme duties of the artist towards his art, as of all workmen toward their work, are two in number, but of one kind: a duty of reverence, of fidelity, of understanding, toward the old, great masters; and a duty of reverence, of fidelity, of understanding, toward the living age and the living artists. (p. 5)

Yet it is harder to find things about contemporary poetry that he admired than to find things he disliked. His critical eye was too keen to let him fall in unwittingly with any school of writing. Comparing the authors of the past with a modern in 'Friends that Fail Not', Johnson mocks the modern who would 'compose a "lyrical note" upon "world-weariness," and an "aquarelle" or "pastel" upon "Pimlico at twilight" ', adding a little later that 'He has caught the gray and vanishing soul of a tragic impression. If my friend is not of this pallid school, he will probably belong to the school of fresh and vigorous Blood.' He likewise mocked the Aesthetic school, saying of the phrase 'Art for Art's sake' that 'I have spent years in trying to understand what is meant by that imbecile phrase.'

With an intimacy with the literary styles of his day and an eye acute enough to parody them, he remained aloof from their extremes. His poetry lacks the colour of his impressionist contemporaries, as it lacks romantic colour. It endures for its music, clarity, and intellectual hardness, its self-conscious literariness and its order. The strength and tragedy of some of his best poetry lie in the eternal battle of desire and indulgence. He said in *The Art of Thomas Hardy* that

> It is in the conflict of will with will, and of force with force, that Tragedy finds a voice: men battling with the winds and waves, or with the passions and desires; men played upon by the powers of nature, or by the powers known to science, or with the powers known to conscience: an eternal warfare, and no illusion of battles in the clouds. (p. 265)

Out of this he created his image.

6 Arthur Symons

I have said enough in earlier pages to suggest that Arthur Symons had an important part to play in the Decadence, not only by his poetic practice but also by his critical theory and his creative flair. Like Wilde, he revelled in public discussion and knew the value of being known, for whatever reason. He made himself the chief spokesman of Decadence, and was one of its most characteristic examples. As Max Beerbohm remarked of Wilde and Beauty, it had existed long before but it was Arthur Symons 'who first trotted her round'.

Ironically enough, or there may be some logic of the subconscious in it, Arthur Symons was from a solid religious background. He was born at Milford Haven on 21 February 1865, the son of a Methodist minister, and his childhood was marked by that repeated uprooting which is the lot of the families of ministers of that denomination; he was always, he claimed, a wanderer. He started reading late, but this was balanced by a precocious literary talent which crystallized into a profound desire for a literary life. He plunged into that life with enormous enthusiasm; luck was with him in his friendships with those who could help further his aspirations, and in 1885 he took on the task of editing the first Quarto of *Venus and Adonis*, a job that Symons, not yet out of his teens, had somewhat miraculously secured from F.J. Furnivall, with whom he had come into contact in the context of the Browning Society. It was Browning who was the subject of Symons's first important book, *An Introduction of the Study of Browning* (1885), the first part of which is still worth reading. Symons's early adoration of the work of Walter Pater − 'the most exquisite critic of our day' − and his absorption of its ideas and its style were to have a significant part in shaping his later career; and his correspondence with Pater from 1886 combined with their subsequent meeting and friendship firmly fixed the debt. He acknowledged it frequently in his writings, earliest perhaps in the dedication of his first book of poems, *Days and Nights* (1889). This book was received publicly and privately with enough praise from people as important to Symons as Pater and Meredith to offset the private dislike he found in other of his friends; all however seemed to agree that he was well on the path to becoming a writer of note. The single most important thing that Symons had by that time not done, he did in 1889; he went to Paris.

This first visit to France, and the second and more lengthy stay of the spring of 1890, helped to confirm Symons in his characteristic interest in French, and indeed European, literature. Symons armed with letters of introduction and Havelock Ellis organizing the broad outlines of the trip, the two young men succeeded in meeting many notables of the French artistic scene, including Rodin and Verlaine, Mallarmé and Huysmans. As if confirmed by the trip and having, like Havelock Ellis, finished in France his 'apprenticeship to life', Symons returned to London where he was to become a central figure in the movements of the nineties.

This representative figure, whose *Silhouettes* (1892, 2nd edn 1896) and *London Nights* (1895, 2nd edn 1897) are central to the Decadent period, is characterized by both authors of recent book-length studies of him as torn apart by the opposing natures of his upbringing and his enthusiasms. Lhombreaud in his useful and careless biography writes that:

> Brought up in a family of rigorous religious devotion, Symons lost his faith, and gained his emancipation, without violence; his education was in a sense incomplete, often interrupted, yet at twenty-four he was an accomplished linguist and a scholar of note. After spending the whole of his youth and adolescence in the country or in small towns, he fell passionately in love with the great city and the London crowds. The country lad counted among his advisers and friends men of letters at the height of their fame, ready, at the right moment, to encourage him, to come forward and take him by the hand.
>
> Thus was formed the genius of Arthur Symons, before and during that emancipation. The reason for many contradictions and later themes, as well, perhaps, as for his illness in 1908, lay in this tragic duality by which he was rent. (p. 57)

While John. M. Munro says:

> he came to look upon sex and evil as synonymous. This conjunction of physical passion and sinfulness remained with Symons beyond adolescence, and it is perhaps not too much to say that his inability to recognize that enjoyment did not necessarily mean damnation was an important factor in his subsequent mental breakdown.
>
> (*Arthur Symons*, New York, 1969, p. 27)

Symons was another of those conscious of an artistic ideal and yet committed to life, taught by Pater to 'walk upon a rope tightly stretched through serene air, and . . . left to keep our feet upon a swaying rope in a storm.' As Karl Beckson points out in the introduction to his edition of *The Memoirs of Arthur Symons* (1977), Symons saw in the French Decadent Hugues Rebell his own struggle:

> On one side was nature, instinct, the universal attraction of the Sexes: on the other side, pure imagination; nor did he ever fix his gaze upon the brilliant face of this double Image without the other appearing to him a sinister and exciting altar of repose. As he rendered homage to Woman and to her Sex he seems to have fought the inevitable battle between the Flesh and the Spirit which is part of our inevitable Destiny. (p. 149)

However obsessed with moral guilt he may have been up to his breakdown in 1908, in the nineties Symons's most obvious characteristics are his delight in the world of experience, sensation and impression, and his concentration upon style. I have followed earlier some of the changing views of this most important theorist of the Decadence, and now intend to look at this in relation to his poetry.

He did not begin his career with a noticeably Decadent volume. *Days and Nights* (1889) was written in those years before Symons knew France, and its two most important influences are Pater and Browning. It is dedicated to the former, and his preceding book had been about the latter. Although it does not seem Decadent, there are suggestions of his later practice in this book. 'Prologue' sounds bravely the determination of the author to concern himself with all experience, observing rather than judging, and yet inclining more to troubles and death. Art is no longer withdrawn from man, he says; she

> stands amidst the tumult, and is calm;
> She reads the hearts self-closed against the light;
> She probes an ancient wound, yet brings no balm;
> She is ruthless, yet she doeth all things right.
> . . .
> With equal feet she treads an equal path,
> Nor recks the goings of the sons of men;
> She hath for sin no scorn, for wrong no wrath,
> No praise for virtue, and no tears for pain.
> . . .
> The winter of the world is in her soul,
> The pity of the little lives we lead,
> And the long slumber and the certain goal,
> And after us our own rebellious seed.
> Therefore the notes are blended in her breath,
> And nights and days one equal song unites;

Yet, since of man with trouble born to death
She sings, her song is less of Days than Nights.

The penultimate stanza has a ring of Dowson, though less elegantly
phrased, and the penultimate line of the poem, with its reference to Job
v.7, suggests Symons's background and reminds us of an ever-present
Hound of Heaven. The whole poem gives us Pater's theory without
Pater's detachment from the crowd, and in its place has a concern with
life that perhaps comes from Browning. Primarily Art here is observer.

The concerns of the whole book are characteristically Brown-
ingesque, the minds of individuals at work on various problems
highlighting their lives. So 'A Revenge', one of the poems he sent to
Pater for his verdict – a cross between 'Andrea del Sarto' and 'My Last
Duchess', with the form and arrogance of the latter and the coolness of
the former – deals as much with the speaker as with the tale he tells.
'Red Bredbury's End' is in the same vein, suggesting the Kiplingesque
development of the dramatic monologue. 'A Vigil in Lent' again
reminds one of 'Andrea del Sarto' and works more effectively than most
of the others, although Symons has not got Browning's skill in
incorporating the actions around the character within the speech of the
character herself. Symons can be comically imperceptive about his
effects, as in the unfortunate 'A Café-Singer', and there are poems
where he fails to carry through his effect to the end, in particular in
'The Knife-Thrower', which builds up well before a tritely moralistic
end.

There is something of what Symons would later amplify, and hints of
the way in which he developed Pater. 'A Vigil in Lent' chooses life and
love instead of the hard 'stones / That pave the sacred floors', and 'Vale,
Flos Florum' advises 'Live in to-day'. The 'Scènes de la Vie de Bohème'
strike that somewhat languid cynical note that Wratislaw was to
imitate so well, and open a subject which was to be one of Symons's
favourites. The first of them, 'Episode of a Night of May', is very like
Gray's version of Rimbaud's 'Charleville' while the third smacks of
Verlaine. In fact most of the poems recall some literary source, and
some of them work by animating a pictorial source.

It is in the dozen or so sonnets in the volume that Symons comes
nearest to his later style, forced by the form into that clarity of observation of the setting or event which he later developed and refined; for
example, in 'A Winter Night', with its anticipation of Yeats's line in 'The
Sorrow of Love'. In the 1902 *Poems*, sonnets make up five of the nine
pieces he kept from the whole of *Days and Nights*. One of the remaining
four will show the change to his next volume. This is 'The Fisher's
Widow' From *Days and Nights*:

> The boats go out and the boats come in
>   Under the wintry sky;
> And the rain and foam are white in the wind,
>   And the white gulls cry.
>
> She sees the sea when the wind is wild
>   Swept by the windy rain;
> And her heart's a-weary of sea and land
>   As the long days wane.
>
> She sees the torn sails fly in the foam,
>   Broad on the sky-line gray;
> And the boats go out and the boats come in,
>   But there's one away.

The title gives away the central interest here, and relates the poem to the observer. The details are very obviously parts of her mood, and a reader able to tackle Tennyson's 'Mariana' would have no difficulty in appreciating this poem and making out of it a picture; like 'Mariana' it could well be the subject of a Pre-Raphaelite study. In contrast, character and event have been purged from the accurately-titled *Silhouettes* (1892); the paintings that they bring to mind are Sickert's sombre impressions:

> The sea lies quieted beneath
>   The after-sunset flush
> That leaves upon the heaped grey clouds
>   The grape's faint purple blush.
>
> Pale, from a little space in heaven
>   Of delicate ivory,
> The sickle-moon and one gold star
>   Look down upon the sea.

The elaborately set-up situation with its life-and-death issues is abandoned for the brief flash of the perhaps significant moment, a much more Paterian moment than in the earlier poems, much more in accord with Pater's view in the Conclusion to the *Renaissance* that 'Every moment some form grows perfect in hand or face; some tone of the hills or the sea is choicer than the rest; some mood of passion or insight or intellectual excitement is irresistibly real and attractive to us, – for that moment only.' For Browning's way of seizing the moment in the actions and reactions of people, Symons has learned to substitute a precise detailing of externals, seizing the moment with things.

This concentration on objects places Symons obviously among those of whom Yeats is thinking in the Introduction to the *Oxford Book of Modern Verse*:

The revolt against Victorianism meant to the young poet a revolt against irrelevant descriptions of nature, the scientific and moral discursiveness of *In Memoriam* – 'When he should have been broken-hearted,' said Verlaine, 'he had many reminiscences' – the political eloquence of Swinburne, the psychological curiosity of Browning, and the poetical diction of everybody. Poets said to one another over their black coffee – a recently imported fashion – 'We must purify poetry of all that is not poetry', and by poetry they meant poetry as it had been written by Catullus, a great name at that time, by the Jacobean writers, by Verlaine, by Baudelaire.   (p. ix)

Symons is well on his way towards the sort of poetry which forms the ideal of the Imagists and culminates in Pound's 'Petals on a wet black bough'. In 'Pastel' for example, only the connection with the writer in the words 'I know' at the end of the second stanza, and the implied judgments in 'grace' and 'lyric' of the third give any touch of situation:

> The light of our cigarettes
>   Went and came in the gloom:
>   It was dark in the little room.
>
> Dark, and then, in the dark,
>   Sudden, a flash, a glow,
>   And a hand and a ring I know.
>
> And then, through the dark, a flush
>   Ruddy and vague, the grace –
>   A rose – of her lyric face.

Much more important are the properties, the dark, the room, the hand, the ring, the face, and the cigarette, brought into poetry by Symons as a new and somewhat shocking gesture, just as Wilde was to bring it into his provocative remarks about his play after the performance of *Lady Windermere's Fan* in February 1892. All is possible story and situation, but nothing but the visible is there. There is no comment, no psychological curiosity. Instead there is a conscious aspiration towards music and the condition of music, a playing with repetitions and modulations, from 'light' to 'little' and from 'flash' to 'flush', to add pattern to the rhymes.

Symons defended his poetry of observation in the preface to the second edition of *Silhouettes*, dated from London in 1896, where the earlier edition is dedicated from Paris in 1892; the scene of battle after the Wilde trial had shifted.

I need not, therefore, on this occasion, concern myself with more than the curious fallacy by which there is supposed to be something inherently wrong in artistic work which deals frankly and lightly with the very real charm of the lighter emotions and the more fleeting sensations.

I do not wish to assert that the kind of verse which happened to reflect certain moods of mine at a certain period of my life, is the best kind of verse in itself, or is likely to seem to me, in other years, when other moods have made me their own, the best kind of verse for my expression of myself. Nor do I affect to doubt that the creation of the supreme emotion is a higher form of art than the reflection of the most exquisite sensation, the evocation of the most magical impression. I claim only an equal liberty for the rendering of every mood of that variable and inexplicable and contradictory creature which we call ourselves, of every aspect under which we are gifted or condemned to apprehend the beauty and strangeness and curiosity of the visible world.   (p. xiv)

Most of the lyrics in the book illustrate this impressionism, reflecting the excitement of one for whom, as Yeats says in *Autobiographies* (p. 335), 'the visible world existed'.

> The train through the night of the town,
>   Through a blackness broken in twain
>   By the sudden finger of streets;
> Lights, red, yellow, and brown,
>   From curtain and window-pane,
>   The flashing eyes of the streets.
>
> Night, and the rush of the train,
>   A cloud of smoke through the town,
>   Scaring the life of the streets;
> And the leap of the heart again,
>   Out into the night, and down
>   The dazzling vista of streets!

In that poem, 'London Nights: I – Going to Hammersmith', there is nothing save the fleeting sensation, and even in the other poems where there is some small narrative content, usually concerned with love in one form or another, the simple realization of the nature of the sensation is preferred to the explanation of it or theorizing about it. There are many impressions: 'At Burgos', 'On the Bridge', the brilliantly casual 'At the Cavour' (added in 1896), or 'Impression' (added in 1896), where Symons seems to reverse Dowson's 'Benedictio Domini', looking for the miracle in the world instead of in the church. Lionel Johnson, in one of those flashing summaries he wrote for Katharine Tynan, catches Symons's impressionism delightfully:

A singular power of technique, and a certain imaginativeness of conception, mostly wasted upon insincere obscenities. Baudelaire and Verlaine generally ring true, and their horrors and squalors and miseries and audacities have the value and virtue of touching the reader to something of compassion or meditation. Symons no more does that than a teapot. 'This girl met me in the Haymarket, with a straw hat and a brown paper parcel, and the rest was a delirious delight: that girl I met outside a music hall, we had champagne, and the rest was an ecstasy of shame.' That is Symons. And this sort of thing in cadences of remarkable cleverness and delicacy! He can be pleasant and cleanly when he chooses: has written things of power and things of charm. But is a slave to impressionism, whether the impression be precious or no. A London fog, the blurred, tawny lamplights, the red omnibus, the dreary rain, the depressing mud, the glaring gin-shop, the slatternly shivering women: three dexterous stanzas, telling you that and nothing more. And in nearly every poem, one line or phrase of absolutely pure and fine imagination. If he would wash and be clean, he might be of the elect.

(Dublin Review, October 1907, p. 337)

It was not solely impressionism which characterized *Silhouettes* and made it a central Decadent book, nor was it the sole, or even the main, subject of Symons's Preface. The subtitle of that Preface 'Being a Word on Behalf of Patchouli' represents Symons's determination to defend the 'artificially charming', and shows Symons with a malicious wit justifying artifice in a way he may well have learnt from his favourite French authors. Symons is not as outrageous as Gautier and Baudelaire, allowing as he does for higher forms of art than his impressions, and allowing other subjects, but he is nonetheless provoking. Gautier had argued in the Introduction to *Albertus* (1832) that 'In general, when a thing becomes useful, it ceases to be beautiful.' Symons in both theory and practice seeks out the artificial:

An ingenuous reviewer once described some verses of mine as 'unwholesome', because, he said, they had, 'a faint smell of Patchouli about them.' I am a little sorry he chose Patchouli, for that is not a particularly favourite scent with me. If he had only chosen Peau d'Espagne, which has a subtle meaning, or Lily of the Valley, with which I have associations! But Patchouli will serve. Let me ask, then, in republishing, with additions, a collection of little pieces, many of which have been objected to, at one time or another, as being somewhat deliberately frivolous, why art should not, if it please, concern itself with the artificially charming, which, I suppose, is what my critic means by Patchouli? All art, surely, is a form of artifice, and thus, to the truly devout mind, condemned already, if not as actively noxious, at all events as needless. That is a point of view which I quite understand, and its conclusion I hold to be absolutely logical. I have the utmost respect for the people who refuse to read a novel, to go to the theatre, or to learn dancing. That is to have convictions and to live up to them. I understand also the point of view from which a work of art is tolerated in so far as it is actually militant on behalf of a religious or a moral idea. But what I fail to understand are those delicate, invisible degrees by which a distinction is drawn between this form of art and that: the hesitations, and compromises, and timorous advances, and shocked retreats, of the Puritan conscience once emancipated, and yet afraid of liberty. However you may try to convince yourself to the contrary, a work of art can be judged only from two standpoints: the standpoint from which its art is measured entirely by its morality, and the standpoint from which its morality is measured entirely by its art.   (pp. xiii-xiv)

The artificial is probably most effectively summed up in the poem with a title that might have suggested the argument of the Preface, 'Perfume', where the 'priceless hour of love' goes and yet the perfume still occupies the vacant place. There is no story or comment, nothing but the delight of the memory; and the same formula is repeated in 'White Heliotrope' in *London Nights*. Moral considerations are out of the question; the artificial becomes the ideal, the permanent, the lasting, when human lives and values are shifting. So a photograph too becomes the centre of a poem in 'To a Portrait'.

As with Baudelaire, an important aspect of the superiority of the artificial is make-up, cosmetics, and Symons's poem 'Maquillage', admitting its ancestry in its title, deliberately sets up this contrast of real and artificial:

> The charm of rouge on fragile cheeks,
>   Pearl-powder, and, about the eyes,
>   The dark and lustrous Eastern dyes;
> A floating odour that bespeaks
> A scented boudoir and the doubtful night
> Of alcoves curtained close against the light.
>
> Gracile and creamy white and rose,
>   Complexioned like the flower of dawn,
> Her fleeting colours are as those
>   That, from an April sky withdrawn,
> Fade in a fragrant mist of tears away
> When weeping noon leads on the altered day.

The stress is on the fragility of the cheeks, the fact that the day alters, that night is 'doubtful', while the artificial fragility has a perfection like the pearl. The figure here has that combination of the ambiguous charm

of youthful innocence and cynical sophistication and disdain that
occurs in some of Beardsley's drawings.

An interest in art and make-up combine in Symons's love of the
theatre, an interest that he so regretted Dowson did not share:

> It was at the time when one or two of us sincerely worshipped the
> ballet; Dowson, alas! never. I could never get him to see that charm
> in harmonious and coloured movement, like bright shadows seen
> through the floating gauze of the music, which held me night after
> night at the two theatres which alone seemed to me to give an
> amazing colour to one's dreams.
>
> *(The Poems of Ernest Dowson*, 1905, p. x)

This indicates how he would come to use the theatre in his poems, as
one way of groping towards the reality behind the surface of things. He
had not yet in *Silhouettes* reached that stage when he could expound
this fully, and the poems which centre on this idea are much more
characteristic of *London Nights*. 'Impression' and 'Javanese Dancers'
however indicate the start of the movement towards that stage.

Nor in *Silhouettes* is woman yet the symbol she is to become. Instead
Symons sings the passing charms of flirtation, brief loves and cynical
and sometimes romantic observations, concentrating in poem after
poem on single features, face, smile, eyes, rather as Eliot was to do in his
'Preludes', and again like Eliot within a city situation. It is worth thinking of the Eliot of 'Portrait of a Lady' (what a nineties combination of
the literary and pictorial is that title!) in poems like 'The Last Exit':

> But now the love that once was half in play
>   Has come to be this grave and piteous thing.
>   Why did you leave me all the suffering
> For all your memory when you went away?
>
> You might have played the play out, O my friend,
>   Closing upon a kiss our comedy.
>   Or is it, then, a fault of taste in me,
> Who like no tragic exit at the end?

The self-doubt, the self-dramatization, the insecurity, the questioning
of the appropriate rôle, all seem to be features also of the Eliot who
could make his young man wonder 'should I have the right to smile?' or
Prufrock ask 'would it have been worth it, after all?'

London is of course the most obvious of man's gestures to create his
environment in a way not nature's, and is thus a central concern of the
artist committed to praising man's creation of perfection. This will
obviously be central to *London Nights*; but in *Silhouettes* there are
poems concentrating on urban scenes and details: 'In an Omnibus',

'Emmy at the Eldorado', 'At the Cavour' (added for the second edition), 'In the Haymarket', 'At the Lyceum', 'In Kensington Gardens', 'In the Temple', 'In Fountain Court'. The Preface, written nearly four years after the first edition, sees clearly the way in which artificiality is at the core of the poems:

> Is there any 'reason in nature' why we should write exclusively about the natural blush, if the delicately acquired blush of rouge has any attraction for us? Both exist; both, I think, are charming in their way; and the latter, as a subject, has, at all events, more novelty. If you prefer your 'new-mown hay' in the hayfield, and I, it may be, in a scent-bottle, why may not my individual caprice be allowed to find expression as well as yours? Probably I enjoy the hayfield as much as you do; but I enjoy quite other scents and sensations as well, and I take the former for granted, and write my poem, for a change, about the latter. There is no necessary difference between a good poem about a flower in the hedge and a good poem about the scent in a sachet. I am always charmed to read beautiful poems about nature in the country. Only, personally, I prefer town to country; and in the town we have to find for ourselves, as best we may, the *décor* which is the town equivalent of the great natural *décor* of fields and hills. Here it is that artificiality comes in; and if anyone sees no beauty in the effects of artificial light, in all the variable, most human, and yet most factitious town landscape, I can only pity him, and go on my own way.
>
> That is, if he will let me. But he tells me that one thing is right and the other is wrong; that one is good art and the other is bad; and I listen in amazement, sometimes not without impatience, wondering why an estimable personal prejudice should thus be exalted into a dogma, and uttered in the name of art. For in art there can be no prejudices, only results. If we are to save people's souls by the writing of verses, well and good. But if not, there is no choice but to admit an absolute freedom of choice.   (pp. xiv-xv)

As with Wilde, his practice does not always fit his theory, and there is some obvious social comment in two of the sonnets, poems that stick out from their company and fit rather with Henley's *London Types* or his hospital sonnets, with Dowson's 'To One in Bedlam' and Johnson's 'In a Workhouse'. Even 'At the Lyceum' bears comparison with Henley's 'Staff-Nurse: New Style' as well as with Symons's own 'At the Cavour'. So the arch-Decadent Symons in one of his two books of the early nineties writes this elegant version of the anti-Decadent Henley:

> His fourscore years have bent a back of oak,
>   His earth-brown cheeks are full of hollow pits;

His gnarled hands wander idly as he sits
Bending above the hearthstone's feeble smoke.
Threescore and ten slow years he tilled the land [;]
   He wrung his bread from out the stubborn soil;
   He saw his masters flourish through his toil,
He held their substance in his horny hand.

Now he is old: he asks for daily bread:
   He who has sowed the bread he may not taste
     Begs for the crumbs: he would do no man wrong.
The Parish Guardians, when his case is read,
   Will grant him (yet with no unseemly haste)
     Just seventeen pence to starve on, seven days long.

There are hints of a larger meaning in the reference to 'daily bread' but, in general, this has the same tone as Henley's 'Lady-Probationer' or 'Staff-Nurse: New Style' of which this is the sestet:

She talks BEETHOVEN; frowns disapprobation
At BALZAC's name, sighs it at 'poor GEORGE SAND'S';
Knows that she has exceeding pretty hands;
Speaks Latin with a right accentuation;
And gives at need (as one who understands)
Draught, counsel, diagnosis, exhortation.
                   (*A Book of Verses*, 1888, p. 16)

There is no clear debt, but the detailing of the scene is similar, and in particular in the case I quote the movement of the next to the last line bears comparison. It may well be that Symons admired these poems of Henley enough to imitate them, as he imitated other of his contemporaries. Certainly he praised Henley in 'The Decadent Movement in Literature' because

In *A Book of Verses* and *The Song of the Sword* he has brought into the traditional conventionalities of modern English verse the note of a new personality, the touch of a new method. The poetry of impressionism can go no further, in one direction, than that series of rhymes and rhythms named *In Hospital*.
      (*Harper's New Monthly Magazine LXXXVII*, 1893, p. 867)

Symons perferred the rhymed poems in Henley's book to the rhymeless experiments, and may well have been drawn to the sonnets; and, although one would not expect to find Symons learning his Decadent style in 'The Absinthe-Drinker' from Henley, I would suggest that he is aware of Henley's 'After'.

Committed as it is to impression, *Silhouettes* seems always conscious of time, and the Absinthe-Drinker, like 'The Opium-Smoker' of the earlier book, escapes from the flood of observations pressing themselves upon him, but only temporarily; as for Dowson's drinker in 'Absinthia Taetra', 'nothing was changed'. The theme of the futility of dream is explicit in 'In Bohemia':

> Drawn blinds and flaring gas within,
>   And wine, and women, and cigars;
> Without, the city's heedless din;
>   Above, the white unheeding stars.
>
> And we, alike from each remote,
>   The world that works, the heaven that waits,
> Con our brief pleasures o'er by rote,
>   The favourite pastime of the Fates.
>
> We smoke, to fancy that we dream,
>   And drink, a moment's joy to prove,
> And fain would love, and only seem
>   To live because we cannot love.
>
> Draw back the blinds, put out the light:
>   'Tis morning, let the daylight come.
> God! how the women's cheeks are white,
>   And how the sunlight strikes me dumb!

Stranded between an external world with which he finds no connection and an eternal world which he cannot reach, like Arnold between two worlds, he has nothing in which to root his belief. The world only reveals its horrors, there is not an escape in the ecstasy of love, and the artificial world behind the blinds has been left. Most of the loves, and he is Pierrot committed to love, are wistful and sad, conscious of ending like the last poem in the volume, 'For a Picture of Watteau':

> Your dancing feet are faint,
> Lovers: the air recedes
> Into a sighing plaint,
> Faint, as your loves are faint.
>
> It is the end, the end,
> The dance of love's decease,
> Feign no more now, fair friend,
> It is the end, the end.

London Nights (1895) called down on Symons's head much more criticism than his previous book, and this response is Dowson's reason for foreseeing in 1896 (see his *Letters*, p. 372) that he would 'dispute the honour with you of being the most abused versifier in England'. The response of the critics to *London Nights* is not particularly surprising, considering the date of publication, which was soon after the date of the

dedication to Paul Verlaine, 6 May 1895. On 7 May Wilde was released
on bail after the jury had failed to agree on a verdict, to be found guilty
and sentenced to two years' hard labour on 25 May. In the circumstances when a moral fervour rose against all that Wilde stood for,
when Beardsley was implicated by a mere rumour, what else could be
expected? Symons tells it clearly in the Preface to the second edition of
London Nights:

> The publication of this book was received by the English press with a
> singular unanimity of abuse. In some cases the abuse was ignoble;
> for the most part it was no more than unintelligent. Scarcely any
> critic did himself the credit of considering with any care the intention
> or the execution of what offended him by its substance or its subject.
> I had expected opposition, I was prepared for a reasonable amount
> of prejudice; but I must confess to some surprise at the nature of the
> opposition, the extent of the prejudice, which it was my fortune to
> encounter. Happening to be in France at the time, I reflected, with
> scarcely the natural satisfaction of the Englishman, that such a recep-
> tion of a work of art would have been possible in no country but
> England. . . .
> I have been attacked, then, on the ground of morality, and by
> people who, in condemning my book, not because it is bad art, but
> because they think it bad morality, forget that they are confusing
> moral and artistic judgments, and limiting art without aiding
> morality. I contend on behalf of the liberty of art, and I deny that
> morals have any right of jurisdiction over it. Art may be served by
> morality, it can never be its servant.   (pp. xiii-xiv)

Symons goes on to explain and rather to labour the point that morality
is shifting in its standards while he claims that art is constant. The basic
point of the remainder of the Preface, apart from its stylistic and occasionally verbal nods in the direction of Walter Pater, is that whatever
passes has the right to become the subject of art.

> If it be objected [he concludes] to me that some of them were moods I
> had better never have felt, I am ready to answer, Possibly; but I must
> add, What of that? They have existed; and whatever has existed has
> achieved the right of artistic existence.   (p. xv)

One comment, however, in the centre of the Preface shows that
Symons is going in a different direction from before, perhaps explained
by the location for the writing of the Preface, Rosses Point. It was from
Sligo that he wrote his 'Causerie from a Castle in Ireland' for the *Savoy*
of October 1896, where he saw the temptations of the idealists of the
Celtic Renaissance:

If I lived here too long I should forget that I am a Londoner and remember that I am a Cornishman. And that would so sadly embarrass my friends of the Celtic Renaissance! No, decidedly I have no part among these remote idealists: for I have perceived the insidious danger of idealism ever since I came into these ascetic regions.

(*Savoy VI*, p. 95)

In his Preface to *London Nights* he writes:

The whole visible world itself, we are told, is but a symbol, made visible in order that we may apprehend ourselves, and not be blown hither and thither like a flame in the night.   (p. xiv)

Yeats is behind Symons, suggesting he look further than the surfaces, and Symons is on the way to the position he took in the Introduction to *The Symbolist Movement in Literature*.

The movement from impressionism to symbolism is not as far as it might seem. The moment, the impression, the sensation, realized distinctly at its most intense, might well be the occasion when one could *transcend* the real. 'Only through time time is conquered', Eliot reminds us at the end of the second section of *Burnt Norton*. The moment may be Browning's 'moment one and infinite' or Eliot's 'point of intersection of the timeless / With time', and it might be that Symons was near to this before; but it was in and after *London Nights* that he moved more positively and more consciously towards it.

There are still the poems of artifice, in fact many more specifically on the subject. When Symons reprinted the poems in 1902 he added the 'Prologue: Before the Curtain', which sees all life as a play, but more completely than 'The Last Exit' had done:

> We are the puppets of a shadow-play,
> We dream the plot is woven of our hearts,
> Passionately we play the self-same parts
> Our fathers have played passionately yesterday,
> And our sons play to-morrow. There's no speech
> In all desire, nor any idle word,
> Men have not said and women have not heard;
> And when we lean and whisper each to each
> Until the silence quickens to a kiss,
> Even so the actor and the actress played
> The lovers yesterday when the lights fade
> Before our feet, and the obscure abyss
> Opens, and darkness falls about our eyes,
> 'Tis only that some momentary rage
> Or rapture blinds us to forget the stage,
> Like the wise actor, most in this thing wise.

> We pass, and have our gesture; love and pain
> And hope and apprehension and regret
> Weave ordered lines into a pattern set
> Not for our pleasure, and for us in vain.
> The gesture is eternal; we who pass
> Pass on the gesture; we, who pass, pass on
> One after one into oblivion,
> As shadows dim and vanish from a glass.

The pattern of the last section here reminds us of Symons's interest in sound and also reflects the monotonous inevitabilities of the subject. The poem merely emphasizes the theme which was there in the earlier editions in the original 'Prologue', which tackles the subject in a more personal way:

> My life is like a music-hall,
>   Where, in the impotence of rage,
> Chained by enchantment to my stall,
>   I see myself upon the stage
> Dance to amuse a music-hall.

Again Symons uses the repetition to reflect the mirroring of the situation; not just the repetition of words or the repetition of sounds, but the use of the same word as rhyme, which creates its own sense of futility, of circularity, of lack of progression. Artifice is taken further along the road des Esseintes took when Symons in 'Lilian: I. Proem' finds the simplest and most natural thing the most artificial:

> Yet here, in this spice-laden atmosphere,
>   Where only nature is a thing unreal,
> I found in just a violet, planted here,
>   The artificial flower of my ideal.

Of course, London, which figures in the title, is important as a symbol of artifice, and there is a sense of design about the volume, as if Symons, like Yeats, thought of the book as a whole. The design is much clearer in the original editions, which show three sections of 'London Nights' broken by an 'Intermezzo: Pastoral' and an 'Intermezzo: Venetian Nights'. London is more of a setting and a declaration of enthusiasm than a subject, since there are few poems which treat it, and none as completely as Henley's *London Voluntaries*. Most of the theatres and music-halls might as well be Paris as London, and some specifically are, like 'La Mélinite: Moulin Rouge' which is later dated Paris, 22 May 1892, or 'At the Ambassadeurs' later dated Paris, 19 June 1894. The 'Intermezzo: Pastoral' is the other side of the coin from the

London sections and recalls the rejected 'A Retreat' from *Silhouettes* (1892), being what it says, a pastoral, which shows Symons leaning towards some ideal away from London. In 'At Carbis Bay' the stars reveal the 'peace of the sky' as opposed to the 'terror by night' of the sea and 'The menace of land', while 'In the Vale of Llangollen' rather crudely finds some unspecified statement in nature:

> In the fields and the lanes again!
> There's a bird that sings in my ear
> Messages, messages;
> The green cool song that I long to hear.
>
> It pipes to me out of a tree
> Messages, messages;
> This is the voice of the sunshine,
> This is the voice of the grass and the trees.
>
> It is the joy of Earth
> Out of the heaven of the trees:
> The voice of a bird in the sunshine singing me
> Messages, messages.

Wales and Ireland seemed to call up something in Symons's mind that he related in his *Savoy* article to his Cornish blood, yet the 'insidious danger of idealism' had not found its place fully yet. Nonetheless, there is a specific rebuke for the artificial world which Symons very self-consciously erects in 'In the Meadows at Mantua':

> But to have lain upon the grass
>   One perfect day, one perfect hour,
> Beholding all things mortal pass
> Into the quiet of green grass;
>
> But to have lain and loved the sun,
>   Under the shadow of the trees,
> To have been found in unison,
> Once only, with the blessed sun;
>
> Ah, in these flaring London nights,
>   Where midnight withers into morn,
> How blissful a rebuke it writes
> Across the sky of London nights!
>
> Upon the grass at Mantua
>   These London nights were all forgot.
> They wake for me again: but ah,
> The meadow-grass at Mantua!

Perhaps if the critics had read the book as a whole they would not have found it lacking in the complete view. Even the 'Intermezzo: Venetian Nights' yearns for the stars, or for the moon, like a Pierrot. The comparison with Dowson which that calls to mind is even closer in that combination of Dowson and Baudelaire which is the second part of 'To One in Alienation'.

Love, as in that last poem, is the central subject of the book. As Symons wrote in the Preface to the second edition of *Silhouettes*,

> In connection with these 'Silhouettes', I have not, if my recollection serves me, been accused of actual immorality. I am but a fair way along the 'primrose path', not yet within singeing distance of the 'everlasting bonfire'. In other words, I have not yet written 'London Nights', which, it appears (I can scarcely realize it, in my innocent abstraction in aesthetical matters), has no very salutary reputation among the blameless moralists of the press. (p. xiv)

The reputation that Symons acquired for his poems about light and often dubious loves is an important part of the picture of Decadence given by its critics. In Dowson's work there is little after 'Cynara' to shock the most sensitive 'blameless moralist'; perhaps the cavalier aspect of 'To his Mistress', 'Rondeau', or the rather silly *'Soli Cantare Periti Arcades'*. In Johnson there is little or nothing. In both Dowson and Johnson, the type of material one might class as 'London Nights' type is there to be rejected. Symons lingers on it and, although he justifies his right to any subject, he does concentrate on the particularly shocking (at least to a Victorian sensibility). Even 'To a Dancer', which has the footlights between observed and observer, contrives to be a sexual encounter moving to a climax and repose:

> And oh, intoxicatingly,
> When, at the magic moment's close,
> She dies into the rapture of repose,
> Her eyes that gleam for me!

Symons could, however, manage a blatant directness about his loves which could not help but shock a public which had previously had its literary sex spiritualized or concealed in metaphor.

> Why is it I remember yet
> You, of all women one has met
> In random wayfare, as one meets
> The chance romances of the streets,
> The Juliet of a night? I know
> Your heart holds many a Romeo.

Even more blatantly, without the Shakespearean allusion, Symons examines his commitment to sensation in 'Idealism':

> I know the woman has no soul, I know
>   The woman has no possibilities
>   Of soul or mind or heart, but merely is
> The masterpiece of flesh: well, be it so.
> It is her flesh that I adore; I go
>   Thirsting afresh to drain her empty kiss.
> I know she cannot love: it is not this
> My vanquished heart implores in overthrow.
> Tyrannously I crave, I crave alone,
>   Her perfect body, Earth's most eloquent
>   Music, divinest human harmony;
>   Her body now a silent instrument,
>   That 'neath my touch shall wake and make for me
> The strains I have but dreamed of, never known.

The simple impressionistic description of making love, a description
without lengthy moral comment (although one must admit that there is
often a suggested moral attitude) is in itself shocking. The descriptions
in 'Stella Maris' for example must have helped substantially to form the
caricature of the *Yellow Book* — even Symons was to write to Verlaine
that he was sending a copy of the first volume of that periodical 'où il y
aura un poème de moi, un peu osé pour une revue anglaise, dont
j'espère bien que vous serez content' (quoted in Roger Lhombreaud's
Arthur Symons, p. 112) — and those in 'Leves Amores' have a cynicism
and a worldliness new to the nineteenth century. Even Rossetti in
'Jenny' did not have this brutal accuracy:

> And still beside me, through the heat
>   Of this September night, I feel
>   Her body's warmth upon the sheet
> Burn through my limbs from head to heel.
>
> And still I see her profile lift
>   Its tiresome line above the hair,
>   That streams, a dark and tumbled drift
> Across the pillow that I share.

Again it is to Eliot that we must go for the comparison, *The Waste
Land's* typist and the house agent's clerk:

> The time is now propitious, as he guesses,
> The meal is ended, she is bored and tired,
> Endeavours to engage her in caresses
> Which still are unreproved, if undesired.
> Flushed and decided, he assaults at once;
> Exploring hands encounter no defence;

His vanity requires no response,
And makes a welcome of indifference.

Jenny had been transformed into 'A Danaë for a moment' while Symons, using the same form as Rossetti had done, has the indecency of accuracy in 'Stella Maris' about his lack of involvement, a mode which Eliot was to use with greater effect by giving it a larger context. Nonetheless, Eliot could well have learnt the intense realization of indifferent sex from the Symons of *London Nights*.

If there are poems of make-up, artifice, London, love and sex in this book, there is also a movement towards investing these things with a significance, most obviously in the image of the dance. There is a danger in criticism of Symons to dwell on the dance because of its fundamental thematic significance and its central place in the matter of technique, as has been pointed out by Frank Kermode and Ian Fletcher, and subsequently by Edward Baugh and John M. Munro, but it is by no means his only subject. Nonetheless it must be mentioned, so I propose to glance at the progression of Symons's thought on this matter.

'Javanese Dancers', dated October–December 1889 and published in *Silhouettes*, is the first poem on this subject, and as early as this suggests something of the later use of the image in its last lines:

> The little amber-coloured dancers move,
> Like little painted figures on a screen,
> Or phantom-dancers haply seen
> Among the shadows of a magic grove.

That is the version in *Silhouettes*. How much more precise Symons became in his use of the image can be seen in his revision for the 1902 *Poems*:

> . . . spectral hands that thrill
>
> In measure while the gnats of music whirr,
> The little amber-coloured dancers move,
> Like painted idols seen to stir
> By the idolaters in a magic grove.
>
> (I, p. 39)

By this time it has become much more a trembling of the veil, much more a religious vision; the viewer has become involved in worshipping the image. The pictorial detail of the 'figures on a screen' is cut out so that one is not distracted from the one important simile of the moving idols. Symons had revised after he had discovered a way of moving through appearance to essence. 'Nora on the Pavement' moves in just this way; as Edward Baugh says in his 'Arthur Symons, Poet: A Centenary Tribute' (*Review of English Literature*, July 1965, pp. 72–3), moving 'from an impressionistic to a symbolic conception of the dancer, who undergoes a transfiguration into what Symons would call "a living symbol"; we see her transcending the merely spectacular, becoming truly individual, achieving self-fulfilment, no longer just a dash of colour in the pattern woven by the *corps de ballet*.'

> As Nora on the pavement
> Dances, and she entrances the grey hour
> Into the laughing circle of her power,
> The magic circle of her glances,
> As Nora dances on the midnight pavement;
>
> Petulant and bewildered,
> Thronging desires and longing looks recur,
> And memorably re-incarnate her,
> As I remember that old longing,
> A footlight fancy, petulant and bewildered;
>
> There where the ballet circles,
> See her, but ah! not free her from the race
> Of glittering lines that link and interlace;
> This colour now, now that, may be her,
> In the bright web of those harmonious circles.
>
> But what are these dance-measures,
> Leaping and joyous, keeping time alone
> With Life's capricious rhythm, and all her own,
> Life's rhythm and hers, long sleeping,
> That wakes, and knows not why, in these dance-measures?
>
> It is the very Nora;
> Child, and most blithe, and wild as any elf,
> And innocently spendthrift of herself,
> And guileless and most unbeguiled,
> Herself at last, leaps free the very Nora.
>
> It is the soul of Nora,
> Living at last, and giving forth to the night,
> Bird-like, the burden of its own delight,
> All its desires, and all the joy of living,
> In that blithe madness of the soul of Nora.

This movement to symbol is not fully worked out in *London Nights*, and is as yet more a tendency than a realized method. There are various poems moving towards an ecstasy of love, where he may reach some only dreamed-of state:

> Her body now a silent instrument,

> That 'neath my touch shall wake and make for me
> The strains I have but dreamed of, never known.

And there are suggestions of some world other than that of impressions: the 'visionary violets' of 'In the Temple'; the vision in 'Rosa Mundi' when he debates with the 'angel of pale desire':

> Then I saw that the rose was fair,
>   And the mystical rose afar,
>   A glimmering shadow of light,
>   Paled to a star in the night.

Particularly important are the breakthroughs in the series 'Décor de Théâtre'. Here the 'radiant moment' on the stage is 'The footlights' immortality' in 'Behind the Scenes: Empire', where the dancers are both shivering and sad girls and 'angels' and 'creatures of the air'. There is a reaching for 'enchantment' and 'Wizard music' in 'The Primrose Dance: Tivoli', where the dancer is a dancing flower magically appearing where flower and bird 'might never be'. Most emphatically in 'La Mélinite: Moulin Rouge', Symons puts together his images of roses, music, shadow, light, dream, dancer, and circles, into a poem with a sense of mystery behind the surface:

> Olivier Metra's Waltz of Roses
>   Sheds in a rhythmic shower
>   The very petals of the flower;
> And all is roses,
>   The rouge of petals in a shower.
>
> Down the long hall the dance returning
>   Rounds the full circle, rounds
>   The perfect rose of lights and sounds,
> The rose returning
>   Into the circle of its rounds.
>
> Alone, apart, one dancer watches
>   Her mirrored, morbid grace;
>   Before the mirror, face to face,
> Alone she watches
>   Her morbid, vague, ambiguous grace.
>
> Before the mirror's dance of shadows
>   She dances in a dream,
>   And she and they together seem
> A dance of shadows;
>   Alike the shadows of a dream.
>
> The orange-rosy lamps are trembling
>   Between the robes that turn;

In ruddy flowers of flame that burn
The lights are trembling:
The shadows and the dancers turn.

And, enigmatically smiling,
In the mysterious night,
She dances for her own delight,
A shadow smiling
Back to a shadow in the night.

New as this is, it nonetheless recalls again Symons's first poetic master, Browning, in the latter's rather uncharacteristic 'Women and Roses' which Symons had passed by in his *Introduction to the Study of Browning* with a comment on its 'rich and marvellously modulated music, the glowing colour, vivid and passionate fancy' (p. 114).

Before leaving *London Nights* to glance at the development of the dancer in that very different book *Images of Good and Evil* (1899), one must look at the manner of these poems up to and including *London Nights*. Edward Baugh has said, and I think accurately, that 'His most remarkable and distinctive verse is to be found mainly in *Silhouettes* (1892) and *London Nights* (1895). These volumes are also the ones in which he preserves most fully the flavour of "the Beardsley period" ' (p. 72). Symons had written in the Introduction to *The Symbolist Movement in Literature* that the term Decadence 'is in its place only when applied to style'.

The first characteristic, the seeking after the precise detail, the impression, whatever the subject, has already been implied. In diction Symons achieves his distinctiveness by a deliberate simplicity and a use of contemporary detail, unlike Johnson who looked backward for his diction, tying himself to tradition even in his vocabulary and his punctuation. Very nearly those things which Johnson listed in his notes on Symons – London, footlights, cigarettes, gaslight, a photograph, a train – give Symons's poems a characteristic urban flavour. There is no evidence of 'le style tacheté et faisandé' that Huysmans notes in the Goncourts, and Symons notes in Huysmans; rather there is a 'revolt from the ready-made of language' in order to seize precisely the unique moments of experience. It is the revolt that all good writing must make from the constricting traditions of its predecessors, and Symons sought natural speech as an essential element of his work. He is, again unlike Johnson, a most un-literary poet. Where Johnson seeks for a tradition to which to belong and connects himself to it by making it the subject of his poems, Symons uses another kind of artifice; and quotation from or reference to earlier writers is infrequent. This does not mean that Symons is unaware of other writers, but that he is more likely to borrow from his contemporaries than from poets of an earlier period.

Dowson, who must have impressed him, is a source for 'Mundi Victima', Symons's 'Heart's Desire' is a pendant to 'Cynara', while the second 'To One in Alienation' owes something to both Dowson and Baudelaire. I have noted Symons's debt to Henley. 'Hesterna Rosa' may owe something to the Song from *The Tragic Mary* by 'Michael Field'; 'Peace at Noon' may have something to do with Lionel Johnson's 'Nihilism'; 'At the Ambassadeurs' seems to derive from a poem of André Raffalovich. But Symons in general tends to recreate rather than imitate slavishly. This is another facet of that skill which Yeats remarked in Symons (*Autobiographies*, p. 319): 'Arthur Symons, more than any man I have ever known, could slip as it were into the mind of another', and indeed this is probably at the root of his considerable abilities as a translator, especially of contemporaries.

Of great significance for the Symons of these years is his mastery of form. Yeats, in a letter to Rhoda Symons in 1908, wrote

> I do not believe it possible that Arthur Symons made a bad rhyme. If there is a mistake I will do my best to put it right, but a mistake is very unlikely. Your husband has always been most masterly in all his uses of rhyme and rhythm.   (Lhombreaud, p. 292)

This is not merely comfort for Symons's wife after his critical illness, since Yeats asked Symons in a letter of September 1905, 'if you have in your memory any misdoings of mine, please tell me of them that I may put them right' (*Letters*, p. 460). Perhaps most distinctive and characteristic of Symons's verse is a five-line stanza, closely rhymed, and very often repeating a rhyme-word rather than finding a different rhyme. One sees it in *Days and Nights* in 'A Woman', and the subject is interestingly indicative of Symons's development:

> Dowered with all beauty bodily,
>   Her soul she meshed in her own snare;
> Beyond herself she might not see,
>   Infantine-idly unaware
>   Of any end but being fair.
>
> Therefore being dead she is but dust,
>   And being but dust she shall not rise
> With souls the grave hath kept in trust.
>   Soulless, her body, dying, dies,
>   Cast out of hell and paradise.

Compare this with 'Nora on the Pavement'; although the infant quality is still there in the subject, and the self-contemplation, there is the new element in the later poem of the inner and more true self which 'leaps free' from what had been in the earlier poem mere dust. A typical use of the five-line stanza, varying the length of the third line, is in 'Morbidezza':

> White girl, your flesh is lilies,
> Grown 'neath a frozen moon,
> So still is
> The rapture of your swoon
> Of whiteness, snow or lilies.
>
> The virginal revealment
> Of the black gown's thin slope –
> Concealment,
> 'Neath fainting heliotrope,
> Of whitest white's revealment –
>
> Is like a bed of lilies,
> A jealous-guarded row,
> Whose will is
> Simply chaste dreams; – but oh,
> The alluring scent of lilies!

The music of that poem is not in a single line, or a single stanza, but runs through the whole and achieves that characteristic circling movement that aptly fits into the dance theme later on. Symons almost certainly derived the stanza from Verlaine, who used it in poems like 'A Poor Young Shepherd':

> J'ai peur d'un baiser
> Comme d'une abeille.
> Je souffre et je veille
> Sans me reposer.
> J'ai peur d'un baiser!

Verlaine's influence seems likely, but Symons made the stanza his own; varying subtly its line lengths or its rhyme scheme to express hesitancy and reluctance and abortive departures from some haunting theme. In these five-line stanzas, particularly in 'Nora on the Pavement' and 'La Mélinite: Moulin Rouge', dance, introspection, turning, reflection, the movement between reality, shadow, image, and dream, are all woven into a pattern of words which is the image of the statement. Surely these are among the poems that made Yeats call him 'most masterly in all his uses of rhyme and rhythm'.

Symons uses longer lines for his more serious, thoughtful poems, where theory takes over from observation, yet he manages a longer line with less skill than Dowson or Johnson. His shorter lines fit the brief staccato of his impressions, building up a scene out of fragments as he builds books out of single poems, most clearly seen in *Amoris Victima*

(1897). His hypnotic rhythms and reiterations create a lyrical music which he never recaptured, certainly never with that cool detachment which marked the poems of the middle nineties. His longer line sometimes achieved an imposing solemnity, as in that poem which ends *London Nights* still on the note of involvement with life as it passes:

> Each, in himself, his hour to be and cease
>   Endures alone, but who of men shall dare,
>   Sole with himself, his single burden bear.
> All the long day until the night's release?

> Yet, ere night falls, and the last shadows close,
>   This labour of himself is each man's lot;
>   All he has gained of earth shall be forgot,
> Himself he leaves behind him when he goes.

> If he has any valiancy within,
>   If he has made his life his very own,
>   If he has loved or laboured, and has known
> A strenuous virtue, or a strenuous sin;

> Then, being dead, his life was not all vain,
>   For he has saved what most desire to lose,
>   And he has chosen what the few must choose,
> Since life, once lived, shall not return again.

> For of our time we lose so large a part
>   In serious trifles, and so oft let slip
>   The wine of every moment, at the lip
> Its moment, and the moment of the heart.

> We are awake so little on the earth,
>   And we shall sleep so long, and rise so late,
>   If there is any knocking at that gate
> Which is the gate of death, the gate of birth.

Amoris Victima (1897) is chiefly remarkable for its form. It was designed, he writes in the prefatory note 'to be read as a single poem, not as a collection of miscellaneous pieces. . . . Each poem is, I hope, able to stand alone, but no poem has been included without reference to the general scheme of the book, the general psychology of the imaginary hero.' Symons varies the method of Meredith's *Modern Love* (which had provided the epigraph for his *Days and Nights*) by varying the form of the individual lyrics instead of keeping to one form as Meredith did, the 16-line 'sonnet'. The love on which the poetry here was based was Symons's involvement with Lydia and, despite the mention of an 'imaginary' hero, the poems seem too close to experience for Symons's detached technique to function as it had; one's camera should not be involved in the picture. The poems are most successful

when most like the earlier work: in the impressionist simplicity of
'Twilight' for example, with its darkness behaving rather like a
Prufrockian fog:

> The pale grey sea crawls stealthily
>   Up the pale lilac of the beach;
>   A bluer grey, the waters reach
> To where the horizon ends the sea.
>
> Flushed with a tinge of dusky rose,
>   The clouds, a twilit lavender,
>   Flood the low sky, and duskier
> The mist comes flooding in, and flows
>
> Into the twilight of the land,
>   And darkness, coming softly down,
>   Rustles across the fading sand
> And folds its arms about the town.

The poem is dated from Dieppe, which perhaps explains its similarity to
the earlier 'At Dieppe: I. After Sunset' and 'Colour Studies: I. At
Dieppe'. 'Amor Triumphans: I. Envoi' and 'II. Why?' recapture the old
cynical tone, and 'Amoris Exsul: XII. In Saint-Jacques' regrets the
inability to see the vision available to the old woman in the chapel. As
always, he is the outsider, unable to take Pater's escape through Anglo-
Catholic ritual:

> Here, in the shadowy chapel, where I stand,
>   An alien, at the door, and see within
> Bent head and benediction of the hand,
>   And may not, though I long to, enter in.
>
> Sightless, she sees the angels thronging her,
>   She sees descending on her from above
> The Blessed Vision for her comforter:
>   But I can see no vision, only Love.
>
> I have believed in Love, and Love's untrue:
>   Bid me believe, and bring me to your saint,
> Woman! and let me come and kneel with you . . .
>   But I should only see the wax and paint.

His escape through love, which had been fairly adequate solace before,
is proving impossible in this volume, and as painful as the world itself.
Love, which had been part of his London scene, becomes separate; as in
'Munda Victima', the final section of which Yeats called 'a long ecstasy
of sorrow, a long revery of that bitter wisdom which comes only to
those who have a certain emotional distinction' (*Bookman*, April 1897,
p. 16):

> love whose intent
> Is from the world to be in banishment,
> Love that admits but fealty to one,
> Love that is ever in rebellion.
> The world is made for dutiful restraint,
> Its martyrs are the lover and the saint,
> All whom a fine and solitary rage
> Urges on some ecstatic pilgrimage
> In search of any Holy Sepulchre.

More profoundly, it becomes the 'redeeming mystery of love'. The 'fine and solitary rage' is Yeatsian, but the power of the final poem is a mixture of the grand and the over-dramatic in its precipitous plunge into the senses for oblivion.

> Finally I commend myself to you,
> Multitudinous senses: carry me
> Upon your beating wings where I may see
> The world and all the glory of the world,
> And bid my soul from lust to lust be hurled,
> Endlessly, precipitously, on.
> Only in you there is oblivion,
> Multitudinous senses; in your fire
> I light and I exterminate desire.
> Though it cry all night long, shall I not steep
> My sorrow in the fever of your sleep?
> Where, if no phantom with faint fingers pale
> Beckon to me, wildly, across the veil
> Of the dim wavering of her sorcerous hair,
> I may yet find your very peace, despair!

There is a noticeable change in this book away from the precise detail of surroundings and towards a more philosophic examination of mood, away from things to thoughts, away from the impressionist interior of the theatre to the symbolist landscape of the mind. It has become more difficult to visualize his poems, since he has moved away from the pictorial.

Amoris Victima is an interesting experiment, but it does not get Symons very far; *Images of Good and Evil* (1899) is a much more positive change. Where in *Amoris Victima* 'The Dance' had been merely the ecstasy of love:

> For an immortal moment we endured the whole
> Rapture of intolerable immortality,

it becomes religious in the later book, but perhaps because he had been able to reject that earlier love. In *Images of Good and Evil*, and especially in 'The Dance of the Daughters of Herodias',

> Symons's dancers are transfigured: he passes from the Music Hall or simple spectacle of the ritual dance. We now have an ambitious attempt to present the Dance as a composite image: of the poet's situation; of the predicament of a society which had rejected his wisdom; of the dancer as at once fascinating and terrible; warning and epiphany at once.
> (Ian Fletcher in 'Explorations and Recoveries – II: Symons, Yeats and the Demonic Dance', *The London Magazine* VII, June 1963 p. 57)

The image of the dancer can be followed at more length in Frank Kermode's *Romantic Image*, in Ian Fletcher's essay quoted above, and in Edward Baugh's dissertation; but that development can be paralleled or rather augmented by other developments, for example Symons's concentration on ideas like mysticism and the dream. As if to deny the commitment to sensation announced at the end of *Amoris Victima*, the opening poem of *Images of Good and Evil* is 'The Dance of the Seven Sins'. There both the body and the soul reject the sins: 'Dancers, I tire of you,' they both say, but the soul remembers a dream:

> I, who seem
> To have some memory of a dream,
> I know not when, I know not where,
> Dream not, remember, and despair.

This increasing mysticism is the result of the association with Yeats that proved so fruitful for Yeats and obviously changed Symons. On Rosses Point Symons wrote 'By the Pool at the Third Rosses', where the magical and supernatural elements of the place prompted his Cornish blood:

> I heard the sighing of the reeds:
> At noontide and at evening,
> And some old dream I had forgotten
> I seemed to be remembering.

> I hear the sighing of the reeds:
> Is it in vain, is it in vain
> That some old peace I had forgotten
> Is crying to come back again?

Symons says specifically in the Dedication to *The Symbolist Movement in Literature* that it was Yeats who introduced the Mysticism to him:

I speak often in this book of Mysticism, and that I, of all people, should venture to speak, not quite as an outsider, of such things, will probably be a surprise to many. It will be no surprise to you, for you have seen me gradually finding my say, uncertainly but inevitably, in that direction which has always been to you your natural direction. (p. vi)

But as Symons implies in the Introduction, the development to Symbolism is a development away from Decadence. The reaching 'through beautiful things to the eternal beauty' which is Symbolism is a development from that 'literature of form' where

> form aimed above all things at being precise, at saying rather than suggesting, at saying what they had to say so completely that nothing remained over, which it might be the business of the reader to divine. And so they have expressed, finally, a certain aspect of the world; and some of them have carried style to a point beyond which the style that says, rather than suggests, cannot go. (pp. 5–6)

One can gain some other notions of Decadence in the description of Symbolism as 'a literature in which the visible world is no longer a reality, and the unseen world no longer a dream' (p. 4). Symons, in his exploration of the dance and his discussion with Yeats did a great deal to map out the new territory of Symbolism, and to show other poets how the surface might be made to show the soul; but his own greatest and in a sense most typical achievements are mostly in the style that he rejects in the Introduction.

In the period before he moved on to Symbolist theories, he captured certain moments in deft and precise lyrics, singing the praises of love and art and artifice. As he says of Flaubert, he was a poet 'of a world in which art, formal art, was the only escape from the burden of reality' (p. 5). It is then that London is at the heart of his poems as it never is again. He captures the visible world in brief, musical lines, but never forgets completely the dream, or perhaps the nightmare, of an unseen world. His most characteristic and lasting successes are those Decadent poems of artificial or transient pleasure, but his critical achievement, as translator and disseminator of ideas, is obviously greater. His energy lies at the heart of the development of Symbolism in England. It may be, as Beardsley perhaps flippantly maintained in the epistle dedicatory to *The Story of Venus and Tannhäuser*, that the 'critical faculty is more rare than the inventive'; certainly it is important, as T.S. Eliot would have agreed. For Eliot develops both as a poet and as a critic on ground prepared by Symons. Prufrock inhabits Symons's London, the 'Preludes' are played there, and Eliot's 'impersonality' surely develops from Symons's 'disembodied voice, yet the voice of a human soul'. Eliot could reject Symons's style of criticism, but there is no doubt that he had read it, and noted it.

For Symons, as for literature, Decadence was only a passing phase. He typified it, described it, and outgrew it; but he also helped to make possible that method of seeing and understanding by which its dilemma was solved, by which the ideal and the real were seen together within the one symbol, at once life and art, real and ideal, timeless and in time.

7 W.B. Yeats

It would require a complete book to do justice to Yeats's involvement with the Decadence, but three things can usefully be put forward here. First that Yeats was associated with the movement at the time both by others and by himself; second that he shared important themes with his Decadent contemporaries, and developed those themes in his subsequent poetry; third that the idea of Decadence is an integral part of his theories.

There is no need to dwell on the first. Yeats in the nineties was continually in search of some group to which he could belong or some idea in which he could believe, and because of this he seems to belong to many groups, the Decadents among others. Yeats tells in his *Autobiographies* how Henley sent a copy of Yeats's 'The Man Who Dreamed of Faeryland' to a friend with the comment: 'See what a fine thing has been written by one of my lads' (p. 129); and that Morris had told him that 'The Wanderings of Oisin' was 'my sort of poetry' (p. 146). Yeats helped found and was one of the enthusiastic members of the Rhymers' Club, often taken as an example of a Decadent group. He contributed to a number of periodicals associated with other writers called Decadent, and writes of his part in the *Savoy* with a sense of involvement; 'We might have survived but for our association with Beardsley' (p. 323). It was after all an illustration to Yeats's article on Blake which was the excuse for W.H. Smith to refuse to sell the *Savoy*, an important contributory factor in its death. And when the magazine had closed and Decadence was not the popular thing it had been, Ernest Rhys, friend, fellow Rhymer and fellow editor, said in the *Literary Year-Book* for 1897:

> As for the 'Decadence', some of the younger men who have been most freely displaying its colours during the year, as, in the derelict *Savoy*, Mr. Symons and (I fear) Mr. Yeats, are gone south only to return, let us hope, under a crescent star! The century's end, then, need not prove quite fatal. (p. 28)

Whatever else Yeats was, and he was many things, he was also a Decadent.

It is evident that his poems shared important themes with those of his friends. To begin with those poems of the nineties. Where Yeats's later poems work on a scheme of oppositions resolved in a higher truth, the early poems characteristically feature an unresolved opposition, often the cause of sadness. The epigraph to the title poem of his first book repeats that division which I have remarked in Dowson and Johnson:

> Give me the world if Thou wilt, but grant me an asylum for my affections.

Of course Yeats later saw the way he had refused life for dream in that poem, when he enumerated this as one of his old themes in 'The Circus Animals' Desertion':

> First that sea-rider Oisin led by the nose
> Through three enchanted islands, allegorical dreams,
> Vain gaiety, vain battle, vain repose,
> Themes of the embittered heart, or so it seems,
> That might adorn old songs or courtly shows;
> But what cared I that set him on to ride,
> I, starved for the bosom of his faery bride?

For Yeats, unlike Arthur Symons, it was not a question of getting away from the world to the land of the ideal, but rather of getting away from the land of the ideal to reality.

Yeats realized this early. In a letter to Katharine Tynan of 14 March 1888 he expressed very clearly that subject matter which dominated his contemporaries:

> I have noticed some things about my poetry I did not know before, in this process of correction; for instance, that it is almost all a flight into fairyland from the real world, and a summons to that flight. The Chorus to the 'Stolen Child' sums it up – that it is not the poetry of insight and knowledge, but of longing and complaint – the cry of the heart against necessity. I hope some day to alter that and write poetry of insight and knowledge.   (*Letters*, p. 63)

This perceptive summary shows a fruitful way in which we may connect Yeats with his fellows of the nineties, for this is not an analysis which he later rejects. A movement from exploration to discovery marks his Preface to *Poems* (1895):

> He [the poet] has printed the ballads and lyrics from the same volume as *The Wanderings of Usheen*, and two ballads written at the same time, though published later, in a section named *Crossways*, because in them he tried many pathways; and those from the same volume as *The Countess Cathleen* in a section named *The Rose*, for

in them he has found, he believes, the only pathway whereon he can hope to see with his own eyes the Eternal Rose of Beauty and of Peace.

Even in the introductory poem to the *Rose* section of the book, however, he sees but cannot grasp the ideal. He begs the rose to come near:

> Come near, that no more blinded by man's fate,
> I find under the boughs of love and hate,
> In all poor foolish things that live a day,
> Eternal beauty wandering on her way.

But when it seems he wishes them to be united, the poem turns away from unification to a plea for separateness:

> Come near, come near, come near, – Ah, leave me still
> A little space for the rose-breath to fill!
> Lest I no more hear common things that crave;

and so on with a list of the ordinary things he must have, to prevent him from becoming too distant from men. He is faithful to the rose in his fashion, but there is still that aching space between.

The legends of Ireland are drilled into service on like topics. 'Fergus and the Druid' shows a king given a 'bag of dreams' which makes him 'nothing, being all' since he has to share in the 'loss or victory' of human life. 'Cuchulain's Fight with the Sea' ends in the early versions with Cuchulain's death:

> For four days warred he with the bitter tide;
> And the waves flowed above him, and he died.

Despite Bloom's preference for the earlier version, the revised version expresses more clearly the inevitable and continued struggle with reality:

> Cuchulain stirred,
> Stared on the horses of the sea, and heard
> The cars of battle and his own name cried;
> And fought with the invulnerable tide.

Whatever magic Yeats may introduce into his poems, whatever reverberations he manages to include that make his poems even at this period so much richer than those of most of his contemporaries, he is still a man torn between this world and the next. It is clear in 'The Man who Dreamed of Faeryland'; each stanza begins with some involvement with the world and earth, and each stanza, changing direction in its fifth line, places against that world an island without change, almost a Byzantium, though unlike Byzantium in that it does not contain the resolution of opposites. When that resolution comes, when God burns up Nature with a kiss, it is no source of comfort for the dreamer. The consciousness of the inadequacy of the physical world of poems like 'The Lamentation of the Old Pensioner' in its first and very different version, the longing for the idealized and dreamy kingdoms of 'The Lake Isle of Innisfree' and 'The White Birds', provide the opposites of which many other poets were writing, and have a similar tone to many other poems of the period. Even 'When you are old', which has the hint from Ronsard to gather the roses of life, escapes into the mountains and stars.

Old age becomes for Yeats one of those forms under which he sees the physical world and its pains, and the theme runs through all his poetry, as he remembered in a letter of 30 June 1932:

> My first denunciation of old age I made in *The Wanderings of Usheen* (end of part 1) before I was twenty and the same denunciation comes in the last pages of the book. The swordsman throughout repudiates the saint, but not without vacillation. Is that perhaps the sole theme – Usheen and Patrick . . .?   (*Letters*, p. 798)

His 'A Prayer for Old Age' is for a resolution of the opposites of body and mind, one of those resolutions he is persistently seeking:

> God guard me from those thoughts men think
> In the mind alone;
> He that sings a lasting song
> Thinks in a marrow-bone.

This topic has its antecedents and echoes in poems other than Decadent, of course, but there are other Decadent themes clearly in Yeats. The dancer, who begins her career as observed impression, ends it as 'incorporation visuelle de l'idée', though I shall refer the reader to those works mentioned in the discussion of Symons and the dancer. She helps to resolve the tensions so painfully unresolved by the Decadents.

The season, the colours, the mood of 'The Falling of the Leaves' make it a typically Decadent love-lyric, as with Eternal Beauty in 'To The Rose Upon the Rood of Time', more concerned to retire than to grasp,

> Autumn is over the long leaves that love us,
> And over the mice in the barley sheaves;
> Yellow the leaves of the rowan above us,
> And yellow the wet wild-strawberry leaves.

> The hour of the waning of love has beset us,
> And weary and worn are our sad souls now;
> Let us part, ere the season of passion forget us,
> With a kiss and a tear on thy drooping brow,

This is the mood of Dowson:

> So shall we not part at the end of day
>   Who have loved and lingered a little while,
> Join lips for the last time, go our way,
>   With a sigh, a smile?

And it is more common in the 'Crossways' section of Yeats's poems than elsewhere in his work, though still in *The Wind Among the Reeds* (1899) in 'The Hosting of the Sidhe' there is the sense of division. The Sidhe, which Yeats links to the dance of the daughters of Herodias in a note on this poem, act rather as the shadow in 'Cynara' since

> *if any gaze on our rushing band,*
> *We come between him and the deed of his hand,*
> *We come between him and the hope of his heart.*

And the Secret Rose, 'Far-off, most secret, and inviolate Rose', retains its distant power, available only to mystics and heroes and sought through wine or religion.

One of the most specifically Decadent poems is 'Into the Twilight', which had first appeared in the *National Observer* on 29 July 1893, with the title 'The Celtic Twilight'. Its opening lines 'Outworn heart in a time outworn' and its fifth line 'Your mother Eire is always young' must obviously be connected with Yeats's article on 'The Rhymers' Club' in *The Boston Pilot* of 23 April 1892, reprinted in *Letters to the New Island* (Harvard, 1934), which ends:

> the literature of Ireland is still young, and on all sides of this road is Celtic tradition and Celtic passion crying for singers to give them voice. England is old and her poets must scrape up the crumbs of an almost finished banquet, but Ireland has still full tables.

For Yeats, it is not so much the falling Ireland that was dear to Johnson, though it is connected with the twilight; Celtic twilight becomes Celtic Renaissance.

Many of the most fruitful uses of Decadent themes, however, come in the poems of later date. The full working out of the idea of the dancer, of the idea of the city, the exploration of the implications of the artificial, the extension of the idea of the mask, come in his work in the twentieth century. He had gained a good deal in the way of example in the Decadent period. As Harold Bloom says of Yeats's contemporaries, in his study of *Yeats* (New York, 1970),

> their influence upon him as examples, rather than as accomplishments, was to remain constant. There are more echoes of their poetry in the middle and later Yeats than are generally realized, but

> their principal effect upon him was in the style of their lives, and
> their stance as poets, rather than in their actual work.   (p. 28)

Yeats will not be remembered for his Decadent poetry. But his poetry
and indeed his poetic theory found necessary food in those friends
whom he helped to remake in his *Autobiographies*.

That Yeats's theories involved a Decadence, indeed many
decadences, hardly needs to be mentioned, such a commonplace is it.
His theory of gyres demands a Decadence, though not quite coin-
cidental with the nineties:

> the end of an age, which always receives the revelation of the
> character of the next age, is represented by the coming of one gyre to
> its place of greatest expansion and of the other to that of its greatest
> contraction. At the present moment the life gyre is sweeping out-
> ward, unlike that before the birth of Christ which was narrowing,
> and has almost reached its greatest expansion.
>
> (*Variorum Yeats*, pp. 824–5)

A letter of 24 July 1934 to Olivia Shakespear describes his division of
history into four ages of which the last two are:

> The Air = From the Renaissance to the end of the 19th Century
> The Fire = The purging away of our civilization by our hatred
>
> (*Letters*, p. 825)

It is striking that the quarter into which Yeats sees the age moving is a
time of conflict 'against the Soul', and he explains that 'The conflict is to
restore the body'.

Yeats's transformation of Decadent motifs in his poems shows how
he could build upon what seems to some critics a dead end. Kermode,
on the other hand, writing in *Puzzles and Epiphanies* (1962), sees the
Decadence as essential:

> His love of the Decadence – of Moreau, for example – his habit of
> categorizing men he admired in terms of which the Decadence would
> have approved – Robert Gregory, for instance – is unintelligible if
> one does not see that in some ways the period was more closely
> related to our own than its habitual themes suggest; for that reason a
> great poet was able at least to give them a place in modern art. (p. 63)

Yeats's use of his Decadent friends in his *Autobiographies* and other
writings shows how he grew by using and creating them. And all the
force of Decadent writers lies behind this extract from *A Vision* (1925),
which begins with Beerbohm and ends with that vision of Unity at
which the Decadence never arrived:

> A decadence will descend, by perpetual moral improvement, upon a

community which may seem like some woman of New York or Paris who has renounced her rouge pot to lose her figure and grow coarse of skin and dull of brain, feeding her calves and babies somewhere on the edge of the wilderness. The decadence of the Greco-Roman world with its violent soldiers and its mahogany dark young athletes was as great, but that suggested the bubbles of life turned into marbles, whereas what awaits us, being democratic and *primary*, may suggest bubbles in a frozen pond – mathematical Babylonian starlight.

When the new era comes bringing its stream of irrational force it will, as did Christianity, find its philosophy already impressed upon the minority who have, true to phase, turned away at the last gyre from the *Physical Primary*. And it must awake into life, not Dürer's, not Blake's, not Milton's human form divine – nor yet Nietzsche's superman, nor Patmore's catholic, boasting 'a tongue that's dead' – the brood of the Sistine Chapel – but organic groups, *covens* of physical or intellectual kin melted out of the frozen mass. I imagine new races, as it were, seeking domination, a world resembling but for its own immensity that of the Greek tribes – each with its own Daimon or ancestral hero – the brood of Leda, War and Love; history grown symbolic, the biography changed into a myth. Above all I imagine everywhere the opposites, no mere alternation between nothing and something like the Christian brute and ascetic, but true opposites, each living the other's death, dying the other's life. (pp. 213–14)

Decadence itself could never get to this inclusive view of opposites within Unity; when it did it was no longer Decadence.

8 Aubrey Beardsley

If Dowson and Johnson are the typical poets of the English Decadence, Symons its most articulate critic, and Yeats the most important writer to feel its influence, Beardsley is without doubt its great artist. There are few contenders. One might mention Sickert, whose gloomy but glowing impressions of music-halls often illustrated *The Yellow Book*; but he was never a close associate of the movement nor the butt of its critics that Beardsley was. One might mention Charles Conder, a still underrated artist, whose delicate paintings on silk capture the period's wispy charm in a manner like that of Constantine Guys, and whose fans epitomize the ephemeral coquetry of the poems of Wratislaw or Symons; in fact Symons wrote a poem called 'Faint Love' for a Conder fan. One might mention William Rothenstein, who managed to sketch in his crisp if pale and academic way many of the period's interesting figures, but he observes the participants rather than creates the mood of the period. Or one might mention a range of excellent illustrators, poster-designers or craftsmen, or architect-designers like Mackintosh, for it is in the applied and plastic arts that one finds those objects which declare themselves immediately of the period. Or finally Max Beerbohm, who shares Beardsley's economy though not always his elegance of line, and represents both in word and line that literary and self-mocking note that is an essential part of Decadent work; but Beerbohm acknowledged Beardsley's pride of place and suggested his significance when he wrote that 'I belong to the Beardsley period'. Beardsley created, almost single-handed, Decadent art, and conforms in both his life and writings to the notion of the Decadent artist.

There is no doubt that his contemporaries considered Beardsley Decadent in his life and his art. His dismissal from *The Yellow Book* demonstrates the power of the hostility against him, and he has been regarded as a Decadent ever since. Holbrook Jackson, for example:

> He was as necessary a corner-stone of the Temple of the Perverse as Oscar Wilde, but, unlike that great literary figure of the decadence in England, his singularity makes him a prisoner for ever in those Eighteen Nineties of which he was so inevitable an expression.

And Annette Lavers in a lively consideration of 'Aubrey Beardsley, Man of Letters' says of his wish to be known as a writer that 'the little that survives of this great ambition . . . has nonetheless imposed an image of Beardsley as the epitome of "decadence" in literature as well as art'.

Despite the implication with Wilde, and despite Beardsley's own admission to Yeats that 'I look like a Sodomite', Beardsley was not homosexual, and even at times took pains to let the world know the fact. But his life fits readily into the pattern which Yeats and Symons saw in other of their contemporaries, battling against nature artistically if not sexually, drawing by candlelight in a curtained room, and fighting a lonely battle for idealism and artistic integrity against mocking criticism and an unhealthy body. Beardsley's death from consumption at the age of 25 seemed to symbolize, as it did with Dowson, who died of the same disease, more than mere physical unfitness for this world. Yeats places him with Dowson at the thirteenth Phase, and in a tentative explanation in *Autobiographies* makes Beardsley a victim:

> French psychical research has offered evidence to support the historical proofs that such saints as Lydwine of Achiedam, whose life suggested to Paul Claudel his *L'Annonce faite à Marie*, did really cure disease by taking it upon themselves. As disease was considered the consequence of sin, to take it upon themselves was to copy Christ. All my proof that mind flows into mind, and that we cannot separate mind and body, drives me to accept the thought of victimage in many complex forms, and I ask myself if I cannot so explain the strange, precocious genius of Beardsley. He was in my Lunar metaphor a man of the thirteenth Phase, his nature on the edge of Unity of Being, the understanding of that Unity by the intellect his one overmastering purpose; . . . and so being all subjective he would take upon himself not the consequences but the knowledge of sin.
> (pp. 330–1)

It is an explanation that recalls Huysmans's willing pain, or Wilde's self-destroying resolution to stay in England and face the charges against him when he might easily have fled, or Lionel Johnson's looking with pleasure on the prospect of a penniless and shabby future. The artist is not looking on sin as new territory to explore, but as a means of enshrining the guilt of his age.

The movement between the erotic and the ascetic in Beardsley's life is aptly represented by his letters on the one hand to André Raffalovich and on the other to Leonard Smithers, which come to a dramatic conclusion in the final letter to Smithers imploring him to destroy all the obscene drawings. Annette Lavers brings out the same division in her comment on the 'toilette' scenes:

Beauty, the equivocal substitute of the ultimate good, passively appears as a victim on whom the desires of all converge and who offers a strong contrast with the motley crowd which surrounds her. She abandons herself to the care of the officiant, one of the corrupt, but whose experience gives an impression of security because it suggests a bottomless and properly maternal indulgence. Both live together in a symbiotic relationship which seems obscurely to express the fundamental ambiguity of life; which is at the same time experience (and therefore corruption or qualified morals at least) and ideal, faceless depth and brilliant surface.

(*Romantic Mythologies*, pp. 258–9)

It is a division found in the story of Venus and Tannhaüser, and the division is implied in the illustrations for both *The Rape of the Lock* and *Volpone*, where Beardsley chooses to depict a man worshipping at a false altar, both the Baron and Volpone setting up in their love, lust and greed an attractive worldly rather than a spiritual god.

Beardsley became a Roman Catholic, joining that faith which united him with Wilde and Dowson, with Johnson and Gray, a faith which is always conscious of traditions, of the strength of symbols, of significance beyond the visible. Perhaps it is this that allowed him to see his religion as part of his artistic thought:

Heine certainly cuts a poor figure beside Pascal. If Heine is the great warning, Pascal is the great example to all artists and thinkers. He understood that to become a Christian the man of letters must sacrifice his gifts, just as Magdalen must sacrifice her beauty.

For the artist far more than the man of letters, the visible world is important, but it was this world of appearance which Beardsley felt obliged to reject. It is much more difficult to make a picture out of that rejection of the world than it is to make a poem as Dowson and Johnson did; but Beardsley seldom drew the real world. His topical drawings for the *Pall Mall Budget* are mostly unsuccessful, and his reply to a friend of Symons who asked whether he saw visions was 'No, I do not allow myself to see them except on paper.' Symons, again conscious of division, saw Beardsley working between nature and artifice, and his essay on the artist ends with a view of Beardsley resolving the two, reaching his final synthesis:

And thus in his last work, done under the very shadow of death, we find new possibilities for an art, conceived as pure line, conducted through mere pattern, which, after many hesitations, has resolved finally upon the great compromise, that compromise which the greatest artists have made, between the mind's outline and the outline of visible things.

Nobody dies of an artistic theory, but Beardsley certainly lived with a consciousness of the struggle between life and art, and his friends and commentators see him clearly in its light.

Beardsley's written work is small in compass, three poems and his prose piece, *The Story of Venus and Tannhäuser*, which even in its cut and altered version in the *Savoy* as *Under the Hill* increased Beardsley's reputation for Decadence. Mario Praz in *The Romantic Agony* (1960) considered that 'The essence of the English Decadent school is contained in the forty-odd pages of Aubrey Beardsley's "romantic novel" *Under the Hill*' (p. 376).

The poems are surprisingly accomplished for one whose work is so limited, two original poems and a translation in verse. The translation is from Catullus, one of the poets whom Yeats lists in the Introduction to *The Oxford Book of Modern Verse* (1936) as writing the sort of poetry that the poets of the period wished to write. In his seventh and eighth lines Beardsley deviates from the Latin, introducing 'heirlooms' which gives a different impression from the custom which the Latin mentions, and adding 'thy coffin shell'; he complicates here what is in the Latin fairly straightforward. But his translation does its job neatly for the most part, and contrives in the process to resemble Dowson and Johnson in its style and its dignified and resigned sadness. The other two poems, 'The Ballad of a Barber' and 'The Three Musicians', are much gayer in tone, a gaiety not out of keeping with the latter subject, but rather odd for the former, where the sinister story is given an added twist of the macabre by its ingenuous style, in the manner of Browning's 'Porphyria's Lover'. Its subject links it not only with Gray's poem 'The Barber' but also with all those drawings of toilet scenes of which Beardsley was so fond. He illustrated this ballad with another, 'The Coiffing', which R.A. Walker in *The Best of Beardsley* considers 'possibly the finest'. It is indeed a fine drawing, constructed like many of Beardsley's designs on the skeleton of that very sparse design used as the cover of Dowson's *Verses*, though it is not as strikingly dramatic as some of his earlier designs. The poem however has a mystery absent in the drawing, although the mother and child in the background might provide some useful hints for understanding it. The barber has several things in common with Cosmé in *Venus and Tannhäuser*, not surprising since the works are close in date and Beardsley intended to use the poem as chapter IX of *Under the Hill*. He is the uncommitted artist, he lives in Meridian Street and 'nobody had seen him show/A preference for either sex'. His skill was sufficient to perform acts of creation:

> Such was his art he could with ease
> Curl wit into the dullest face;
> Or to a goddess of old Greece
> Add a new wonder and a grace.

2. Beardsley's 'The Coiffing' from *The Savoy*, No. 3 (July 1896).

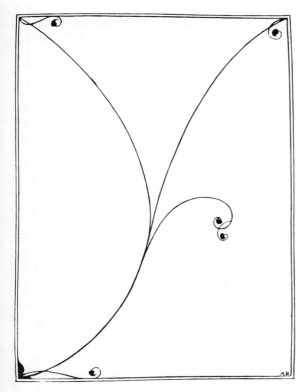

3. Design for the cover of Dowson's *Verses* (1896), a skeleton (sometimes reversed) of many of Beardsley's designs.

His art, like a good aesthete's, was for the sake of art; his 'daily task was all he loved'. There is no reason given why he should kill the Princess, but one can make an attempt to explain. There is nothing that he can add to her perfections, he can only curl a lock and straighten it again pointlessly:

> His fingers lost their cunning quite,
> His ivory combs obeyed no more;
> Something or other dimmed his sight,
> And moved mysteriously the floor.
>
> He leant upon the toilet table,
> His fingers fumbled in his breast;
> He felt as foolish as a fable,
> And feeble as a pointless jest.

He is becoming a work of art – foolish as a fable – while she, 'thirteen years old, or thereabout', the age of Dowson's Adelaide, has a perfection that art cannot improve and the world only mar. The combination of innocence, violent death and victimage that are suggested in the drawing by the Christ figure again recall 'Porphyria's Lover', seeking permanence for the necessarily transient. Carrousel, the genius of *maquillage*, makes and destroys his final masterpiece. Jerome H. Buckley just misses the point when he writes in *The Victorian Temper* (1952) that the poem 'was surely intended to convey a complete allegory of Decadence itself through the tale of the artist–barber Carrousel, whose amoral art for art's sake crumbled forever on the intrusion of insane desire' (p. 236). It was not a crumbling but a final resolution of life and art in death. This is the way that Decadence *must* go, and the reason that Carrousel was 'smiling that things had gone so well'.

'The Three Musicians' is a less fascinating piece, almost an exercise in bourgeois-shocking. It too takes artists as its subject-matter and, equally typical of the period and of Beardsley himself, is fascinated by clothes and music – Beardsley's designs are full of inventive and fantastic costume and his musical talent was evident before his talent with the pen. There is a curious simplicity about this poem too because, although the stanza form is complex, the grammar is simple, and the whole poem is full of lists, just like *Venus and Tannhäuser* of which Annette Lavers writes that 'The most typical feature, frequent enumerations in the text (of decorations, shoes, masks, names, and habits, etc.), reflects an attempt to grasp reality by the means of saturation and excess' (*Romantic Mythologies*, p. 256).

> Along the path that skirts the wood,
>   The three musicians wend their way,
> Pleased with their thoughts, each other's mood,
>   Franz Himmel's latest roundelay,
> The morning's work, a new-found theme, their breakfast
>   and the summer day.

It is this rather detached listing that provides the irony, juxtaposing like Pope the serious and the frivolous. Certainly the 'tweeded tourist' who scorns Gluck provides a pattern for bourgeois response, bewailing the degeneration of France. Beardsley may well have chosen Gluck deliberately because of an earlier argument. His title-page ornament for the *Yellow Book*, volume I, depicted a woman playing a piano in a field, and Beardsley had to write to the editor of the *Pall Mall Budget* in the following way:

SIR, – So much exception had been taken, both by the Press and by

4. Beardsley's title-page design for *The Yellow Book*, vol. 1 (1894).

private persons, to my title-page of 'The Yellow Book', that I must plead for space in your valuable paper to enlighten those who profess to find my picture unintelligible. It represents a lady playing a piano in the middle of a field. Unpardonable affectation! cry the critics. But let us listen to Bomvet. 'Christopher Willibald Ritter von Glück, in order to warm his imagination and to transport himself to Aulis or Sparta, was accustomed to place himself in the middle of a field. In this situation, with his piano before him, and a bottle of champagne on each side, he wrote in the open air his two "Iphigenias", his "Orpheus", and some other works.' I tremble to think what critics would say had I included those bottles of champagne. And yet we do not call Glück a decadent.

(Quoted in *Under the Hill and Other Essays in Prose and Verse*, p. 69)

They obviously did call Beardsley Decadent, and the flirtatious encounter of the last stanza of the poem would do nothing but harden their opinion.

The Story of Venus and Tannhäuser would also have that effect. Either of the two versions would do it; for there are basically two, not counting the versions completed by other writers. The one published earlier in the *Savoy* and republished by Lane in *Under the Hill and Other Essays in Prose and Verse* (1904 [1903]) is an altered and cut version of the more elaborate and more daring version not published until 1907, when it was printed for private circulation by Leonard Smithers under the title *The Story of Venus and Tannhäuser*. The proliferation of footnotes of a learned, lengthy and elaborate nature make *Under the Hill* much nearer to the eighteenth century than the other version. My comments on the style and theme refer to the *Venus and Tannhäuser* version, although much is to be learnt of the climate of censorship by the response to the other, and from the tactics which Beardsley used to avoid the overtly sexual. On this last point it is worth digressing to note that odd feature of Beardsley criticism – a curious willingness to see the sinister and sexual in drawings where it is far from evident and yet to defend the prose against those who might think it too sinister and sexual; yet both are part of Beardsley's restless curiosity. See the tendency, for example, of Derek Stanford's *Aubrey Beardsley's Erotic Universe* (1967), and Brigid Brophy's hothouse prose in *Black and White: a Portrait of Aubrey Beardsley* (1968). For example in the latter: 'He must be . . . the most intensely and electrically erotic artist in the world' (p. 11).

The story of *Venus and Tannhäuser* as far as we have it is an escape into enchantment and dream, just as the style is an escape into artifice. The whole of the first chapter emphasizes this, having the Chevalier Tannhäuser pick his moment:

> It was taper-time; when the tired earth puts on its cloak of mists and shadows, when the enchanted woods are stirred with light footfalls and slender voices of the fairies, when all the air is full of delicate influences, and even the beaux, seated at their dressing-tables, dream a little.
>
> A delicious moment, though Tannhäuser, to slip into exile.

Once out of nature, Tannhäuser meets all extravagance of artifice, but takes with him one touch of nature that clings to him when he has just bid farewell to the moon/Madonna:

> A wild rose had caught upon the trimmings of his muff, and in the first flush of displeasure he would have struck it brusquely away, and most severely punished the offending flower. But the ruffled mood lasted only a moment, for there was something so deliciously incongruous in the hardy petal's invasion of so delicate a thing, that Tannhäuser withheld the finger of resentment, and vowed that the wild rose should stay where it had clung – a passport, as it were, from the upper to the underworld.
>
> 'The very excess and violence of the fault,' he said, 'will be its excuse.'

His piece is to be a sort of erotic 'The Wanderings of Oisin'. As Peter Ure says in his little book on Yeats in the 'Writers and Critics' series (1903), after noting that the thought of wandering hand in hand with a dream mistress is an ideal of Shelley and Morris, 'But for Oisin this thought is also a kind of exile; although all the islands compose a long love-adventure, all become insipid in the end because he longs for the real world of war and hunting and companions' (p. 21). Perhaps this is how Beardsley's book would have ended, as *A Rebours* ended, with a return to the real world for the protagonist, and a choice between the muzzle of a pistol or the foot of the cross for its author. Beardsley was soon to meet both death and the cross.

The style of *Venus and Tannhäuser* comes curiously close to the descriptions of Decadent styles in Huysmans, Pater, Wilde and Symons. It is almost ideally a style with an 'intense self-consciousness, a restless curiosity in research, an over-subtilizing refinement upon refinement, a spiritual and moral perversity', as Symons described that style in his article on 'The Decadent Movement in Literature' (p. 858). It is above all artificial, just the sort of thing that would shock a public prepared to find Decadent a piano in a field. Life in the book always moves towards artifice, books, refinements of civilization. Natural things are seen in terms of the artificial: 'His hand, slim and gracious as La Marquise du Deffand's in the drawing by Carmontelle, played nervously about the gold hair that fell upon his shoulders like a finely curled peruke.' This is the first paragraph of the first chapter. The first lines of the second chapter compare Venus's toilet to 'the altar of Notre Dame des Victoires'. And the sinister lake in the ninth chapter is a veritable 'artifice of eternity', frightening, attractive, but 'Perhaps the lake was only painted, after all.' Even love is music, and when Beardsley writes of Tannhäuser 'tuning her [Venus's] body as a violinist tunes his instrument before he plays upon it', one remembers both Symons's 'Idealism' with its 'Her body now a silent instrument' and Lionel Johnson's parody with its 'Her body music is'. Live butterflies are used as fans; and Beardsley's style seems exactly 'high-flavoured and spotted with corruption' as Symons describes a Decadent style, when he writes of 'veils that seemed to stain the skin with some exquisite and august disease', or of 'black silhouettes painted upon the legs, and which showed through a white silk stocking like a sumptuous bruise.' Disease is connected explicitly with a Decadent style in the last chapter, when Rossini's 'Stabat Mater' is called a 'delicious *démodé pièce de décadence*. There is a subtle quality about the music, like the unhealthy bloom upon wax fruit, that both orchestra and singer contrived to emphasize with consummate delicacy.' As Annette Lavers well puts it, 'the experience of life is constantly born from the experience of books.' The vocabulary is affected (Beardsley is once said to have remarked that even his lungs were affected), mainly leaning towards French, and using words like 'ombre', 'fardeuse,' 'escalier', 'papillons', and 'triste' when there are for most of them easy English equivalents. The observed details of the place are all part of the complex of artificiality; the masks, the make-up, the clothes, the perversions, all impose a new order on nature. The women 'put on delightful little moustaches' and Tannhäuser, who began with his hands compared to a woman's, ends dressed as a woman and looking like a Goddess. Even the usual formula which anticipates the barbarian attack on the declining civilization is reversed when the 'dandies and smart women' of Sporion's entourage in the ballet of chapter V leave the town 'and had invaded the Arcadian valley hoping to experience a new *frisson* in the destruction of some shepherd's or some satyr's naïveté, and the infusion of their venom among the dwellers of the woods.'

It may be interesting to speculate how *Venus and Tannhäuser* might have ended; but what can be said for certain is that it deals rather obsessively and at times wittily with detail of erotic, artificial and perverse ideas to the exclusion of any contrast, just as some of its illustrations lack contrast (I am thinking of 'The Chevalier Tannhäuser' and 'The Fruit Bearers' rather than 'The Return of Tannhäuser', with 'The Toilet of Venus' nearly going over the edge). All the available space is drawn and overdrawn until the design is a uniform grey, lacking the power of some of the earlier work. Both the drawings and the novel as it stands represent something of a surfeit of things, physical things and physical love, a subject almost designed to please his co-editor of the *Savoy*, Arthur Symons. One feels that Beardsley is trying to push experience to its extreme or to break out through excess, recognizing as he does the dangers of satiety. His Venus's breasts 'were full of the irritation of loveliness that can never be entirely comprehended or ever enjoyed to the utmost'. One is inescapably reminded of Wilde's comment in Lord Henry's statement in chapter 6 of *Dorian Gray*: 'A cigarette is the perfect type of a perfect pleasure. It is exquisite, and it leaves one unsatisfied.' Physical pleasure, as Keats knew, could never satisfy the ache within, and the Decadent, thrown into a world of sensation, longed even more for the unending.

Despite the sense of excess there is a general sense of control, a mockery which sets the bounds, and an eighteenth-century novelist's consciousness of the conventions he is working in. This creates the pastiche dedication and epistle dedicatory, the accuracy of the references to other authors, like the allusion to pages 72 and 73 of Delvau's dictionary, which duly reveal a list of appropriate vices. It creates the apologies for not being able to go as far as he could: 'I am afraid that an enforced silence here and there would leave such numerous gaps in the picture that it had better not be begun than left unfinished'; and the mock-heroic of

It is, I know, the custom of all romancers to paint heroes who can give a lady proof of their dalliance at least twenty times a night. Now

Tannhäuser had no such Gargantuan facility, and was rather relieved when, an hour later, Priapusa and Doricourt and some others burst drunkenly into the room and claimed Venus for themselves.

Perhaps the most interesting self-mockery is in the description of the prints in Tannhäuser's bedroom, a description *à la* Huysmans:

> Within the delicate, curved frames lived the corrupt and gracious creatures of Dorat and his school; slim children in masque and domino, smiling horribly, exquisite lechers leaning over the shoulders of smooth doll-like ladies, and doing nothing particular, terrible little pierrots posing as mulierasts, or pointing at something outside the picture, and unearthly fops and strange woman mingling in some rococo room lighted mysteriously by the flicker of a dying fire that throws huge shadows upon wall and ceiling.

Beardsley has added another twist to the relationship of art and life by using his own drawings as subject.

Central to Beardsley's art is its colourlessness, its dependence on the simple polarity of black and white. Matched with this is a second opposition which the starkness of the colour range forces on to the viewer, the opposition between representation and design. One of the disquieting things about Beardsley's art, quite apart from the looks on the faces of the people and the associations of various images, is a purely technical one, the movement between representation and decoration, between the object and the design based on that object and the lines that make up the design. H.C. Marillier misses this point when he asserts in the Prefatory Note to *The Early Work of Aubrey Beardsley* that 'No trace of "naturalism" ever creeps in to mar the set convention of his work.' There is of course little pictorial art which does not gain from this tension, but Beardsley emphasizes it and makes it a central issue in a way which still fascinates and was in its day sufficiently new to shock. As Brian Reade writes in his splendid *Beardsley* (1967) of the *Salomé* drawings:

> They were novel at the time and still have the power to amaze by their qualities, largely because as abstract patterns the compositions are individual, because the short cuts and evasions defy all the law and order of descriptive drawing as understood at that time.
>
> (pp. 16–17)

The drawing 'Of a Neophyte, and how the Black Art was Revealed unto Him' for example places recognizable faces and figures in a swirl of ambiguous wings, feathers, crescents, and shapes, which become at the base of the picture parts of a much more abstract design or mere lines on

5. Beardsley's 'Of a Neophyte and How the Black Art was Revealed to Him' from *The Pall Mall Magazine*, vol. 1 (June 1893).

the page. Always in the more effective drawings he leaves large areas of black or white or both to allow line to contrast with mass, and to carry the suggestions of the lines into the imagination working on unspecified areas. This magic is lost in the over-specific detail of some *Venus and Tannhäuser* drawings. Perhaps he learned the need for space in the necessity of his earlier commission on *Le Morte Darthur* to have space for the text, and his sense of contrast would have been intensified by the need to imitate the wood-blocks of Morris's books. At the same time the drawings for the *Bon-Mots* books which belong to that period helped to emphasize the absolute autocracy of line − if a line is made to represent the impossible it can demonstrate a superiority of art over nature and at the same time disturb convention and complacency.

Reaction to, and often against, Beardsley's drawing was on these technical as well as on thematic grounds, but in content he is as disturbing in his art as he was in his prose. In the first place he demands the right to depict hitherto forbidden things. Brian Reade again, in an excellent introduction to the Victoria and Albert Museum's Large Picture Book No. 32, *Aubrey Beardsley* (1966), writes that

> Certain drawings for *Salomé* had to be turned down because of erotic details, and it must be admitted that some of the series as finally printed include more details of this sort than were ever seen before in an openly published book in England. (p. 6)

Beardsley was of course aware of this shocking element, as one can see in his whimsical verse on the proofs of the first state of 'Enter Herodias' as well as in his habit of smuggling sexual and other detail into the intricacies of his design. The erotic detail of the *Lysistrata* drawings is of course a different thing since they were not published openly. But even if the specific detail were not depicted, Beardsley could shock by the attitude that seems to be expressed by his people. Trained in reading pictures as clues to a story, the public read Beardsley, and the story they found in those almost invariably frowning brows and strange mouths was sinister. When 'Michael Field' first saw the window of Lane and Mathews in Vigo Street full of copies of the first volume of the *Yellow Book*, the reaction was astonishment and horror.

> . . . we found the whole frontage a hot background of orange-colour to sly, roistering heads, silhouetted against it and half-hiding behind masks. The window seemed to be gibbering, our eyes to be filled with incurable jaundice. *La Réclame*, hideous beyond Duessa or any Witch ever seen by the mind's eyes, stood up before us as a shop where contemporary literature is sold. One felt as one does when now and then a wholly lost woman stands flaming on the pavement with the ghastly laugh of the ribald crowd in the air round her. One hates one's eyes for seeing! (B.M.Add.MS.46782, f. 70)

But one cannot get rid of something by closing one's eyes, and the shock at artistic licence combined with the familiarity of the 'wholly lost woman' highlights the period's double morality. It is difficult to recapture the sense of shock at that cover; the flat design intrigues, but the slant eyes have lost their sinister threat.

They do however have their masks, declaring unmistakably their author's intention to be artificial, restressed in the title-page ornament of the lady at the piano in the field. Artificiality is the central element in the designs, as one might expect in an artist owing much to Burne-Jones and Morris, the greatest two-dimensional designers among Victorian artists; but Beardsley's artificiality is recognized, admitted, paraded as a virtue. So we have that concentration on costume, that decoration of humanity which helped the Houyhnhnms to distinguish Gulliver from a Yahoo; so the concentration on theatrical elements in, for example, the 'Comedy-Ballet of Marionettes' drawings, 'The Scarlet Pastorale', 'Isolde', the two designs for the *Savoy* prospectus, the title-page of the first two numbers of the *Savoy*, and 'Enter Herodias' from *Salomé*; so too the frequency of masks, of make-up, and of combinations of these in the toilet scenes.

There are few other elements to stress about Beardsley's work. One must however notice its derivativeness (which is not to deny its striking originality) both from earlier artists and significantly from literature, to which he devoted a great deal of his rather limited time. His drawings are full of quotation from Watteau, Japanese prints, Burne-Jones, Brighton Pavilion, and a hundred other sources, and a glance at his drawings from life suggest that the use of real models rather than artistic sources tended to spoil rather than improve his designs. The drawings are often related to books, either because they are to appear on them, or illustrate them, or include them in the design, like the cover of the Prospectus for the *Yellow Book*, the unused design for a *Yellow Book* cover, or the two designs for 'The Toilet of Salomé'. The drawings typically depict artifice-orientated people, in an artifical manner, often showing them before a mirror, as if illustrating Symons's 'La Mélinite: Moulin Rouge':

> Alone, apart, one dancer watches
> Her mirrored, morbid grace;
> Before the mirror, face to face,
> Alone she watches
> Her morbid, vague, ambiguous grace

Often watching what goes on, apart from the ideal ladies and equally apart from the frightening grotesques, between beauty and the beast, is the Pierrot figure, whose death Beardsley depicts in a drawing in the *Savoy* No. 6, a drawing curiously prophetic of his own death. The relationship of his life and art became so close that they were the same. 'His life' says Brian Reade 'became transposed into work.'

Brian Reade writes in the Foreword to the V. and A. *Catalogue* that 'With the rise of doctrinaire formalism however his art was dismissed by connoisseurs in the recent past as artificial, morbid and "literary" ' (p. [5]). The description is accurate; only the dismissal is undiscriminating. Out of the intensity of his life and work he made his image of the struggle of the temporal with the eternal, his crystallization of the Decadent myth. As usual, the solution was left in doubt, as one can infer from the text to 'The Death of Pierrot':

> As the dawn broke, Pierrot fell into his last sleep. Then upon tip-toe, silently up the stair, noiselessly into the room, came the comedians Arlecchino, Pantaleone, il Dottore, and Columbina, who with much love carried away on their shoulders, the white frocked clown of Bergamo; whither we know not.   (*Savoy*, No. 6, p. 32)

9 The Literature of Failure

Decadent literature is a literature of failure: of a failure to provide a literary synthesis for the disintegration of life; of an expression of that disintegration and failure in elegant cadences; of a fleeing into an artificial world or an ideal world to escape from the consciousness and consequences of that disintegration; of a somewhat indulgent melancholy at the contemplation of that failure; and of a wistfully gay self-mockery at the beauty and vanity of the attempt to escape that failure. Attempts to define Decadence, like Decadence itself, must end in failure. Only partial and necessarily flawed definitions can be made of a movement which was so amorphous that some would question whether it was a movement at all. But there are varying degrees of accuracy and interest, and we ought to be aware of what has been and what can be said.

Karl Caton Kopp, the writer of a dissertation on *The Origin and Characteristics of 'Decadence' in British Literature of the 1890s* (Berkeley, 1963), was doomed from the start because he fell into the simple linguistic trap of taking the term literally. His prime question was 'How and when does literature begin to "fall away" from a previous, established state of achievement', and so he was led to see British Decadence as 'a falling away from an artistic standard set by the writers of *l'art pour l'art* in England and France'. Kopp listed four aims, which indicate the general drift of much criticism of Decadence: three of these aims

> may be taken as characteristics of literary decadence of the 1890s, and the fourth as an underlying belief of the decadent artist.
> 1. Decadent art by deliberately calling attention to the conventionally immoral nature of its subject matter invites moral censure or ridicule.
> 2. In decadent art content is emphasized at the expense of form, at the expense of 'harmony'.
> 3. The elaborate artificial and self-conscious style of decadent art is emphasized at the expense of form and content.
> 4. Life itself is an art if one lives sinfully. (p. 94)

The inadequacy of the approach is shown up by the conclusion that, although *The Picture of Dorian Gray* and *Under the Hill* reveal the characteristics of literary Decadence, Dowson's poems do not. We ought to fit the definition to the movement, not the movement to the definition.

A conference on the topic, reported by Helmut E. Gerber, takes us further and on more interesting lines, but it is of mixed value:

> a) Decadence and aestheticism, whatever precisely they are, were a reaction against or a rejection of values expressed in the subject matter of the literature and in the forms and structure of the works, the values and artistic techniques, that the aesthetes and decadents associated with Victorianism.
> b) Generally, although not necessarily and especially not in some specific works, decadence entails a falling off in quality, perhaps because decadent fiction and poetry sometimes serve only the end of shocking the public and not artistic ends: sometimes they involve a fragmentation process which destroys artistic unity.
> c) Although there was some disagreement on the matter, the possibility was suggested that the term aestheticism might be applied to technical characteristics of the works, whereas the term decadence might be better applied to the subject matter, to attitudes in the works. Historically at least, those who used the word aestheticism commonly concerned themselves with specific elements of style, whereas those who used the word decadence concerned themselves with values, moral positions, subject matter.

('The Editor's Fence', *English Literature in Transition* VI, 1963, No. 1,
p. iv)

I am not sure what value they placed on the central contemporary theorist of Decadence, Arthur Symons, for whom Decadence 'is only in its place when applied to style' (*The Symbolist Movement in Literature*, 1899, p. 6).

Those are merely the two most extended of recent discussions of the term before the most comprehensive and in many ways the most satisfactory, John M. Munro's book-length study of *The Decadent Poetry of the Eighteen-Nineties* (Beirut, 1970). His summary has a great deal more behind it:

> Apart from defining what the English Decadence was, there is, then, another problem in deciding whether it deserves to be taken seriously as a definite, if somewhat ill-defined, literary movement, or simply as an amusing interlude of no real literary or historical value. Neither problem admits of an easy solution. In general terms, however, we may say that the English Decadence, as defined by

contemporaries, was concerned with the exploration of abnormal psychology; it professed to be concerned with Beauty, but with a beauty so bizarre and unconventional that one might feel more justified in calling it ugliness; it was self-conscious to the point of artificiality; it was generally at odds with the prevailing morality; it was somewhat precious and formal in style, sometimes betraying more concern with expression than subject matter; it was contemptuous of popular movements and attitudes; and it was imbued with a tone of lassitude and regret. Furthermore, it was associated with the young and was sometimes regarded as symptomatic of the age, but unlike the Imagist Movement of a decade or so later, it had no definite program and, apart from Symons in his *Harpers' Magazine* article, no real spokesman. For some it was an intensely serious affair, while for others, usually those who stood outside the movement, it was a rather distasteful exhibition of misguided intelligence. In short, it is only in the most general terms that we can speak of a 'Decadent Movement'. Even then we should be cautious of ascribing to it precisely determined characteristics.   (pp. 7–8)

It is worth remembering this warning when offering general comments on movements in the 1890s, just as it is worth recognizing provocative views that the period had no coherence at all. Jean Wilson concluded an article on 'The "Nineties" Movement in Poetry: Myth or Reality' (*The Yearbook of English Studies* I, 1971, pp. 160–74) with the assertion that 'though Symons and Dowson conform closely to the popular concept of "Nineties" poets, they are exceptions among the outstanding writers of the period and two poets can scarcely be said to constitute a movement.'

Let me then elaborate on my assertion that Decadence is a literature of failure, and a record of a wistful mood of inadequacy in confronting man's impermanence in a world of appearances. Science, materialism, and positivism had driven man to this position.

> What happened in the late century was that reason became narrowed, hardened, crystallized out into a single, vigorously disciplined faculty – crystallized out, in short, into the scientific method as the sole source of 'a sound view of the world'. Little wonder then that as human reason was thus trimmed down to such a constricted and efficient method, it should have been felt more and more that spiritual aspirations fell 'quite outside the province of rational belief'.

So says John A. Lester in his stimulating book *Journey Through Despair 1880–1914* (Princeton, 1968, p. 26), seeing as a result of this development a split:

the needs of the aspiring imagination were frontally thwarted by a triumphant scientific method and a bleak ultimate reality – a conflict rendered none the more pleasant by its being a war not between good and evil, but between two goods, man's spiritual and imaginative life and 'the truth'.   (p. 27)

Decadent writers were not alone in following the dual paths that were shown to them, the path of scientific method and scientific truth, and the path of imaginative, creative and created truth.

Some fundamental arguments of Decadent writing depended on the scientific argument. Hume's statement in *A Treatise on Human Nature* that man is 'nothing but a bundle or collection of different perceptions which succeed each other with an inconceivable rapidity and are in a perpetual flux and movement' (book 1, part 4, section 6) was developed by Pater, who ended the Conclusion to the *Renaissance* with the comment that 'art comes to you, proposing frankly to give nothing but the highest quality to your moments as they pass, and simply for those moments' sake.' This seemingly simple desire for freedom of observation of subject matter whatever it might be was fundamental to many arguments on the irrelevance of morality to art. So for Wilde in a letter to the Editor of the *St James's Gazette*: 'To art belong all things that are and all things that are not, and even the editor of a London paper has no right to restrain the freedom of art in the selection of subject-matter' (*The Letters of Oscar Wilde*, p. 261). It is a frequent part of Wilde's critical repertoire, and he backs himself up in a letter to the *Scots Observer* with a reference to Keats's claim that 'What shocks the virtuous philosopher delights the cameleon poet' (p. 266). Richard Le Gallienne claimed in *The Book-Bills of Narcissus* (1892) that 'it is all blossom with us moderns, good or bad alike, and purity or putrescence are all one to us, so that they shine' (pp. 80–1). Arthur Symons argued for freedom of choice of subject matter in the Preface to the second edition of *Silhouettes*, and Yeats, remembering in *Autobiographies*, argued specifically from the scientific case:

> I think that had we been challenged we might have argued something after this fashion: 'Science through much ridicule and some persecution has won its right to explore whatever passes before its corporeal eye, and merely because it passes, to set as it were upon an equality the beetle and the whale, though Ben Jonson could find no justification for the entomologist in *The New Inn*, but that he had been crossed in love. Literature now demands the same right of exploration of all that passes before the mind's eye, and merely because it passes'.   (pp. 325–6)

The conservative case against freedom of expression was couched in the same sort of terms. Arthur Waugh, given the task of arguing about 'Reticence in Literature' for the first volume of *The Yellow Book*, claimed that

> The writers and critics of contemporary literature have, it would seem, alike lost their heads; they have gone out into the highways and byways and hedges in search of the new thing, and have brought into the study and subjected to the microscope mean objects of the roadside, whose analysis may be of value to science but is absolutely foreign to art. (p. 212)

Hubert Crackanthorpe, who replied to Waugh's article in the second volume, summed up the case for literary freedom in a speech delivered at the Royalty Theatre and reported in the *Daily Chronicle*, asserting that 'Before long the battle for literary freedom would be won' (13 February 1894). On the ninth of the previous month his letter in the same paper urged writers to band together in the matter of literary freedom:

> Still, there has been a very considerable advance in public opinion since the prosecution of Mr Vizetelly – even Mr Robert Buchanan and Mr Frank Harris would, I suppose, admit that.
>   Now there is one excellent way in which the extent of this advance could be determined, and, at the same time, a decisive manifestation in the favour of the cause of literary freedom achieved – namely, by fighting the same battle over again, but this time with the best weapons procurable.

The writers did not band together and the weapons were chosen by the opposing forces; the trial of Oscar Wilde set back that cause of literary freedom – he was sentenced in May 1895 – and Crackanthorpe drowned himself (over quite another matter) in the Seine in 1896.

The path of scientific method and scientific truth had an attraction for certain realistic writers (particularly the short-story writers), but it also had an influence on the recording of momentary impressions and in the range of subject matter.

On the other hand, spiritually and imaginatively unsatisfied by this, the writers followed the path of imaginative or created truth and escaped into dream or ideal. 'When you come to forms of belief', wrote Dowson, ' – there is only Pessimism & Catholicism. They are the only respectable "isms". Theism strikes me as about the worst kind of balderdash that I have yet come across except perhaps Positivism' (*The Letters of Ernest Dowson*, p. 81). For Lionel Johnson too the Church was 'a live protest against materialism, and shall not die' (*Some Winchester Letters*, p. 86). Here comes in that fundamental Decadent love of the Catholic Church, and of artifice. If the world is unsatisfactory, satisfaction may be sought in its opposite. Writers no longer sought to reflect nature, or asked for an appeal to nature. When Dowson attempted the light-hearted pastoral of 'Soli cantare periti Arcades', the result was banal, though the country life he depicts there is as artificial as any of his more spectral and spiritual retreats. Like Yeats, artists repeated to themselves that 'Art is art because it is not nature' (*Autobiographies*, p. 279), and the way out of nature was towards artifice and/or towards God. Beerbohm wrote in the first volume of *The Yellow Book* that

> the era of rouge is upon us, and as only in an elaborate era can man by the tangled accrescency of his own pleasures and emotions reach that refinement which is his highest excellence, and by making himself, so to say, independent of Nature, come nearest to God, so only in an elaborate era is woman perfect. Artifice is the strength of the world.

Beerbohm is of course deriving, as so many of his contemporaries would derive, from Baudelaire, who equated religion and artifice in his 'Le peintre de la vie moderne':

> It is this infallible nature which has created the parricide, the cannibal, and a thousand other abominations which modesty and delicacy forbid us to name. It is philosophy (good philosophy that is), it is religion which commands us to succour poor and sick parents. Nature (which is none other than the voice of self-interest) tells us to kill them. Consider, analyse everything natural, all the actions and desires of the simple natural man, and you will find nothing but what is frightful. Everything which is beautiful and noble is the result of reason and calculation. Crime, for which the human animal has derived a taste in the womb, is natural in origin. Virtue on the other hand is *artificial*, above the natural, since there has always been in all nations a need for gods and prophets to teach it to bestial humanity, and since man, on his own, would have been incapable of discovering it. Evil is done without effort, *naturally*, fatally; good is always the product of some art.
>
> (*Oeuvres complètes de Charles Baudelaire: l'Art Romantique*, Paris, 1925, pp. 96–7; my translation)

With what is almost a formula for a poem by Dowson, Baudelaire goes on to say that 'Fashion must therefore be considered as a symptom of the taste for the ideal swimming in the human brain above everything coarse, worldly and filthy that natural life stores up there'. Yeats's early diary contains ideas which derive from these: 'If we cannot imagine ourselves as different from what we are, and try to assume that second self, we cannot impose a discipline upon ourselves though we may accept one from others. Active virtue, as distinguished from the passive acceptance of a code, is therefore theatrical, consciously dramatic, the wearing of a mask' (*Mythologies*, 1962, p. 334). The thrust is then from the unworldly, to the anti-worldly, to the anti-natural, to the artificial, to the unnatural.

Art achieves a permanence denied to the natural. Gautier had phrased it many years before in his influential poem 'L'Art':

> Tout passe. – L'art robuste
> Seul a l'éternité:
> Le buste
> Survit à la cité.

And it is clearly this that Symons is thinking of rather than Shakespeare or Horace when he wrote his 'Venus of Melos':

> All passes; – sceptre, sword and throne,
>   Laws and the might whereby they swayed,
> And creed and conquests. Art alone,
>   Changeless among the changing made,
>   Lasts ever, and her workmen build
>   On sites that fallen temples filled.

This additional development of art as replacement for religion which had been adumbrated by Arnold is clearly seen also in Lionel Johnson as an artifice of eternity in *The Art of Thomas Hardy*: 'Art the preserver! Art, gathering up the wonders and the powers, no longer living of themselves; but henceforth to live only in Art: which has a natural office of piety towards the past' (p. 83).

The preserving ability of art, giving life to things no longer living of themselves, explains that curious relationship between people and works of art which comes fairly often into works of the period, that Pygmalion situation in which the artist is involved in a new relationship with his work of art. Symons calls des Esseintes 'partly the father, partly the offspring, of the perverse art that he adores' (*Harper's Magazine* LXXXVII, p. 866), and the love of statues is not unknown in English and other foreign literatures. Olive Custance, for example, wrote in 'The White Statue' that

> I love you, silent statue! for your sake
> My songs in prayer upreach
> Frail hands of flame-like speech
> That some mauve-silver twilight you may wake!
>
> I love you more than swallows love the south,
> As sunflowers turn and turn

Towards the sun, I yearn
To press warm lips against your cold white mouth!

This echoes much later in Yeats's 'The Statues' with its lines:

And pressed at midnight in some public place
Live lips upon a plummet-measured face.

Yeats has of course developed the image but the prose draft suggests the links with the nineties: 'only forms in marble, empty faces, measure Pythagorean perfection[;] only that which is incapable of show is infinite in passion. Only passion sees God' (A.N. Jeffares, *A Commentary on the Collected Poems of W.B. Yeats*, 1968, p. 490). Beardsley in *Venus and Tannhäuser* is cruder, but there may be more than mere vulgarity in the actions in the land of artifice of 'little Rosalie, perched like a postilion upon the painted phallus of the god of all gardens', like an illustration from Félicien Rops. Wilde involves a man and his picture in a strange identity in *The Picture of Dorian Gray*, while Beerbohm has a man grow into his mask in *The Happy Hypocrite*. Stories of dolls coming to life (*Pinnochio* was written in 1886) or characters created by an artist as in *Trilby* (1894) seem to express the interest. Even Shaw wrote *Pygmalion*.

Thus the artificial is at the base of a construction of associated ideas which reach from morality and religion, to the theatre (one thinks of Headlam's rather grotesque Church and Stage Guild), ballet, make-up, the mask, dance, the creation of the self, and the relationship of man and art. The images end as both artificial and vital, 'Those images that yet / Fresh images beget', as Yeats has it in 'Byzantium'. Johnson's gathering of himself into literary tradition, Dowson's love of a child who was 'spontaneously dramatic', a love which was almost invented by Pater, Symons's love of the theatre and the artificial, Yeats's and Beardsley's masks, all come from the same tradition and reach for that 'artifice of eternity' which seemed granted only to Yeats.

Decadent writers then pushed their desire for new subject matter, and their depiction of the moment as it passed, into areas which, if not new to literature, were new and shocking to the Victorians; but if they sought everything in life, they either opposed it with or tried to form it into something which was not life. Impression may represent a truth to 'one's impression as in itself it really is' as Pater had called for, but the natural phrase is moulded into a self-consciously artificial form whose artificiality is part of the gesture 'out of nature'.

Behind all this is always the consciousness of the impossibility of the task. They knew as well as Keats that 'the fancy cannot cheat so well. As she is famed to do,' and the result was occasionally delightful comedy and self-parody. There are no better analyses of the impos-

6

6–9 Burne-Jones's Pygmalion series, whose rhymed titles are respectively 'Th
Heart Desires', 'The Hand Refrains', 'The Godhead Fires', 'The Soul Attain
(completed 1878). They express the yearning for involvement in art which
mocked in his sketches (see p. 26) and almost achieved in his final 'Sleep of Kin
Arthur in Avalon'. *Reproduced by kind permission of Birmingham City A
Gallery.*

8

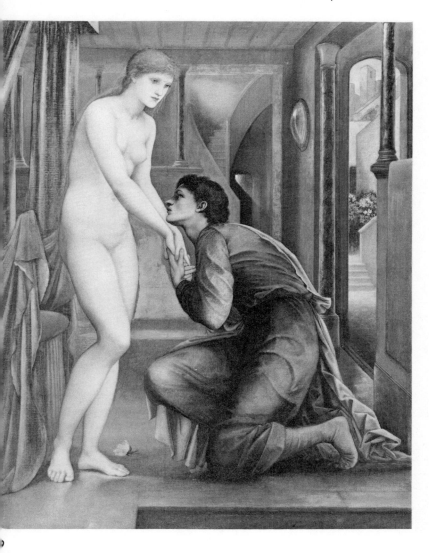

sibility of the Decadent ideal nor more perceptive and witty smiles at its failure than those written by Decadent writers themselves: Huysmans, Max Beerbohm, Lionel Johnson; and it seems an essential part of Decadent writing. Just as essential is that failure to bring together the real and the ideal, both temptingly attractive, which results in the Decadent dilemma, seeing no possibility of reaching that Unity of Being which was, as Harold Bloom reminds us in his book on *Yeats*, the 'goal of the Paterian quest' (p. 51).

When Symbolism solved that dilemma and could demonstrate that real and ideal were not separate, but united in the symbol, Decadence was at an end. The opposites of self and soul, mind and body, impression and dream, were one and the same. Writers at the turn of the century and after were striving to find ways of uniting the 'prose with the poetry' and, to quote John A. Lester again, 'the use and origin of the symbol lay partially in the very dichotomy that inspired the mask motif in this period' (p. 143). A poet of Yeats's genius became conscious of the dualism of the world and the art which described it, he discovered how to make use of the opposites of reality and ideality in creating a new whole, he discovered the dance, the mask, the symbol, already a part of Decadent vocabulary, and finally used them to solve the Decadent dilemma.

Symons had called Decadence 'half a mock-interlude'; but it was half-serious too, and it is of interest not only for its own type of sad impressionism but also for its place in literary history in its nurturing of Symbolism. As Symons summed it up in the Introduction to *The Symbolist Movement in Poetry*, words which recall Yeats's Preface to *Poems* (1895),

> That something more serious has crystallised, for the time, under the form of Symbolism, in which art returns to the one pathway, leading through beautiful things to the eternal beauty.   (p. 7)

Bibliography

This is a selective list from the large number of books either on Decadence or including some account of it or writers associated with it. It is nonetheless still so large that it seemed worthwhile marking with an asterisk the more select few which I consider make good starting points for a study of Decadence or its authors. The student should also note the useful annual bibliographies in *Victorian Studies* and the continued interest in the period 1880–1920 in *English Literature in Transition*.

Bibliography
Linda C. Dowling, *Aestheticism and Decadence* (1977).
Frederic E. Faverty, ed., *The Victorian Poets* (2nd edn, Cambridge, Mass., 1968).

Anthologies
*Karl Beckson, ed., *Aesthetes and Decadents of the 1890s* (New York, 1966; reprinted Chicago, 1981).
Helmut E. Gerber, ed., *The English Short Story in Transition 1880–1920* (New York, 1967).
John M. Munro, ed., *English Poetry in Transition 1880–1920* (New York, 1968).
Martin Secker, ed., *The Eighteen-Nineties: A Period Anthology in Prose and Verse* (1948).
Derek Stanford, ed., *Writing of the 'Nineties* (1971)
——*Three Poets of the Rhymers' Club* (1974).
A.J.A. Symons, ed., *An Anthology of 'Nineties' Verse* (1928).
R.K.R. Thornton, ed., *Poetry of the 'Nineties* (1970).

General
Norman Alford, *The Rhymers' Club* (Victoria, B.C., 1980).
Arthur Balfour, *Decadence* (1908).
Thomas Beer, *The Mauve Decade* (1926).
Bernard Bergonzi, *The Turn of a Century* (1973).
Paul Bourget, *Essais de psychologie contemporaine* (2 vols., Paris, 1920).

Jerome Hamilton Buckley, *The Victorian Temper* (1952)
*——*The Triumph of Time* (1967).
Osbert Burdett, *The Beardsley Period* (1925).
*Alfred Edward Carter, *The Idea of Decadence in French Literature 1830–1900* (Toronto, 1958).
J.E. Chamberlin, *Ripe Was the Drowsy Hour* (New York, 1977).
John A.V. Chapple, *Documentary and Imaginative Literature 1880–1920* (1970).
*Barbara Charlesworth, *Dark Passages: the Decadent Consciousness in Victorian Literature* (Madison, 1965).
Austin Clarke, *The Celtic Twilight and the Nineties* (Dublin, 1971).
Rupert Croft-Cooke, *Feasting With Panthers* (1967).
David Daiches, *Some Late Victorian Attitudes* (1969).
Mircea Eliade, *The Myth of the Eternal Return*, trans. Willard R. Trask (New York, 1954).
Henry Havelock Ellis, *Affirmations* (1898)
——*Impressions and Comments* (1914)
——*Views and Reviews* (1932).
*Richard Ellmann, ed., *Edwardians and Late Victorians* (New York, 1959).
Benjamin Ifor Evans, *English Poetry in the Later Nineteenth Century* (2nd edn, 1966).
Albert John Farmer, *Le Mouvement esthétique et 'décadent' en Angleterre (1873–1900)* (Paris, 1931).
Ian Fletcher, ed., *Romantic Mythologies* (1967)
*——*ed., *Decadence and the 1890s* (1979).
William Gaunt, *The Aesthetic Adventure* (1945).
Helmut E. Gerber, 'The Editor's Fence', *English Literature in Transition*, 6 (1963), pp. iv–v.
Tom Gibbons, *Rooms in the Darwin Hotel* (Nedlands, W. Australia, 1973).
Richard Gilman, *Decadence, the Strange Life of an Epithet* (1979).
Rémy de Gourmont, *Decadence and Other Essays on the Culture of Ideas*, trans. W.A. Bradley (1922).
John Gray, *Silverpoints* (1893)
——*Spiritual Poems* (1896).
Graham Hough, *The Last Romantics* (1949).
Walter E. Houghton, *The Victorian Frame of Mind 1830–1870* (Yale, 1957).
John Dixon Hunt, *The Pre-Raphaelite Imagination 1848–1900* (1968).
Joris-Karl Huysmans, *Against Nature*, trans. Robert Baldick (1959).
*Holbrook Jackson, *The Eighteen Nineties* (1913).
Cyril E.M. Joad, *Decadence* (1945).
R.V. Johnson, *Aestheticism* (1969).

Phillippe Jullian, *Dreamers of Decadence: Symbolist Painters of the 1890s*, trans. Robert Baldick (1971).

*Frank Kermode, *Romantic Image* (1957).

Richard Le Gallienne, *English Poems* (1892)
——*Religion of a Literary Man* (1893)
——*Retrospective Reviews* (2 vols., 1896)
——*Robert Louis Stevenson, an Elegy* (1895)
——*The Romantic '90s* (1926).

Edward S. Lauterbach and W. Eugene Davis, *The Transitional Age in British Literature, 1880–1920* (Troy, 1973).

A.G. Lehman, *The Symbolist Aesthetic in France, 1885–1895* (1950).

*John A. Lester, *Journey Through Despair 1880–1914* (Princeton, 1968).

Steven Marcus, *The Other Victorians* (1966).

J. Lewis May, *John Lane and the Nineties* (1936).

John Milner, *Symbolists and Decadents* (1971).

Katherine Lyon Mix, *A Study in Yellow* (1960).

Bernard Muddiman, *The Men of the Nineties* (1920).

*John M. Munro, *The Decadent Poetry of the Eighteen Nineties* (Beirut, 1970).

James G. Nelson, *The Early Nineties: A View from the Bodley Head* (Cambridge, Mass., 1971).

Max Nordau, *Degeneration* (1895)
——*Conventional Lies of Our Civilisation* (1895).

Vincent O'Sullivan, *Opinions* (1959).

Walter Pater, *The Renaissance* (3rd edn, 1888)
——*Marius the Epicurean* (2 vols., 1885).

Robert L. Peters, 'Towards an "Un-Definition" of Decadence as Applied to British Literature of the Nineteenth Century', *Journal of Aesthetics and Art Criticism* XVIII (Dec. 1959), pp. 258–64.

*Jean Pierrot, *The Decadent Imagination: 1880–1900* (Chicago, 1982).

Renato Poggioli, 'Qualis Artifex Pereo! or Barbarism and Decadence', *Harvard Library Bulletin* 13 (1959), pp. 135–59
——*The Theory of the Avant-Garde* (Cambridge, Mass., 1968).

Ezra Pound, *Literary Essays* (1954).

*Mario Praz, *The Romantic Agony* (1923).

E.T. Raymond, *Portraits of the Nineties* (1921).

Brian Reade, *Sexual Heretics* (1970).

Ernest Rhys, *Everyman Remembers* (1931)
——*Letters from Limbo* (1936).

William Rothenstein, *Men and Memories* (2 vols., 1934).

Clyde de L. Ryals, 'Towards a definition of *Decadent* as applied to British Literature in the Nineteenth Century', *Journal of Aesthetics and Art Criticism* XVII (Sept. 1958), pp. 85–92.

Brocard Sewell, *Footnote to the Nineties* (1968)
——ed., *Two Friends* (1963).
George Bernard Shaw, *The Sanity of Art* (1908).
Geoffrey Smerdon and Richard Whittington-Egan, *The Quest of the Golden Boy* (1960).
Timothy d'Arch Smith, *Love in Earnest* (1970).
*Koenraad W. Swart, *The Sense of Decadence in Nineteenth Century France* (The Hague, 1964).
John Russell Taylor, *The Art Nouveau Book in Britain* (rev. edn, 1979).
Ruth Z. Temple, *The Critic's Alchemy* (New Haven, 1953).
——'Truth in Labelling: Pre-Raphaelitism, Aestheticism, Decadence, Fin de Siecle', *English Literature in Transition* 17 (1974), pp. 201–22.
J.R. Tye, *Periodicals of the Nineties: A Checklist* (Oxford, 1974).
Gustave L. Van Roosbroeck, *The Legend of the Decadents* (Columbia, 1927).
Stanley Weintraub, *The Savoy: Nineties Experiment* (1966)
——*The Yellow Book: Quintessence of the Nineties* (New York, 1964).
Cornelius Weygandt, *The Time of Yeats* (1937).
Oscar Wilde, *The Complete Works* (1966).
——*The Letters of Oscar Wilde*, ed. Rupert Hart-Davis (1962).
Edmund Wilson, *Axel's Castle* (1954).
Jean Wilson, 'The "Nineties" Movement in Poetry: Myth or Reality?' *Yearbook of English Studies* I (1971), pp. 160–74.
Yvor Winters, *Primitivism and Decadence* (1937).
Frances Winwar, *Oscar Wilde and the Yellow 'Nineties'* (New York, 1940)

Ernest Dowson
Ernest Dowson, *A Comedy of Masks* (with Arthur Moore, 1893)
——*Dilemmas: Stories and Studies in Sentiment* (1895)
——*Verses* (1896)
——*The Pierrot of the Minute* (1897)
——*Adrian Rome* (with Arthur Moore, 1899)
——*Decorations: in Verse and Prose* (1899).
*Desmond Flower, ed., *The Poetical Works of Ernest Dowson* (1934, 1950, 1967).
*Desmond Flower and Henry Maas, eds., *The Letters of Ernest Dowson* (1967).
Mark Longaker, *Ernest Dowson* (Philadelphia, 1944, 1945 and 1967)
——ed., *The Stories of Ernest Dowson* (Philadelphia, 1947)
——ed., *The Poems of Ernest Dowson* (Philadelphia, 1962).
Victor Plarr, *Ernest Dowson* (1914).
*Jonathan Ramsey, 'Ernest Dowson: an Annotated Bibliography of

Writings about him', *English Literature in Transition* 14 (1971) pp. 17–42.

Arthur Symons, ed., *The Poems of Ernest Dowson* (1905).

Thomas Burnett Swann, *Ernest Dowson* (New York, 1964).

Lionel Johnson

Lionel Johnson, *The Art of Thomas Hardy* (1894)

——*Poems* (1895)

——*Ireland, with Other Poems* (1897).

*Ian Fletcher, ed., *The Complete Poems of Lionel Johnson* (1953, rev. edn, New York, 1981).

David H. Millar, *Lionel Johnson*, unpublished dissertation for Queen's University, Belfast (1947).

*Arthur W. Patrick, *Lionel Johnson (1867–1902) Poète et critique* (Paris, 1939).

Ezra Pound, ed., *Poetical Works of Lionel Johnson* (1915).

Rev. Raymond Roseliep, *Some Letters of Lionel Johnson*, unpublished dissertation for the University of Notre Dame (1954).

Francis, Earl Russell, ed., *Some Winchester Letters of Lionel Johnson* (1919).

Thomas Whittemore, ed., *Post Liminium: Essays and Critical Papers by Lionel Johnson* (1911).

Arthur Symons

Arthur Symons, *The Collected Works* (9 vols. of projected 16?, 1924)

——*An Introduction to the Study of Browning* (1885)

——*Days and Nights* (1889)

——*Silhouettes* (1892, 2nd edn, 1896)

——'The Decadent Movement in Literature', *Harper's New Monthly Magazine* 87 (Nov. 1893), p. 866 ff.

——*London Nights* (1895, 2nd edn, 1897)

——*Studies in Two Literatures* (1897)

——*Images of Good and Evil* (1899)

——*The Symbolist Movement in Literature* (1899)

——*Studies in Prose and Verse* (1904)

——*Studies in Seven Arts* (1906).

Edward Baugh, 'Arthur Symons, Poet: A Centenary Tribute', *REL* VI (1965), p. 3.

Karl Beckson, ed., *The Memoirs of Arthur Symons* (1977).

R.V. Holdsworth, ed., *Arthur Symons: Poetry and Prose* (1974).

*Roger Lhombreaud, *Arthur Symons: a Critical Biography* (1963).

*John M. Munro, *Arthur Symons* (New York, 1969).

*Carol Simpson Stern, 'Arthur Symons: An Annotated Bibliography of Writings About Him', *English Literature in Transition* 17 (1974), pp. 77–133.

W.B. Yeats
W.B. Yeats, *A Vision* (1925, 1937)
——*Collected Poems* (1950)
——*Collected Plays* (1952)
——*Essays and Introductions* (1961)
——*Explorations* (1962)
——*Mythologies* (1962)
*——*Autobiographies* (2nd edn, 1965).
*Peter Allt and Russell K. Alspach, *The Variorum Edition of the Poems of W.B. Yeats* (New York, 1965).
Harold Bloom, *Yeats* (New York, 1970).
*Curtis Bradford, *Yeats at Work* (Illinois, 1965).
Denis Donoghue, *Yeats* (1971)
——ed., *Memoirs* (1972).
Richard Ellmann, *Yeats the Man and the Masks* (1948, 1979)
——*The Identity of Yeats* (1954).
John P. Frayne and Colton Johnson, *Uncollected Prose by W.B. Yeats* (2 vols., 1970 and 1975).
T.R. Henn, *The Lonely Tower* (1950).
Joseph Hone, *W.B. Yeats 1865–1939* (1942, rev. 1965).
A.N. Jeffares, *W.B. Yeats: Man and Poet* (1949)
——*A Commentary on the Collected Poems of W.B. Yeats* (1968).
K.P.S. Jochum, *W.B. Yeats: A Classified Bibliography of Criticism* (Illinois, 1978).
*Edward Malins, *A Preface to Yeats* (1974).
*Thomas Parkinson, *W.B. Yeats, Self-Critic* and *The Later Poetry* (1971).
William H. Pritchard, ed., *W.B. Yeats: a Critical Anthology* (1972).
Balachandra Rajan, *W.B. Yeats* (2nd edn, 1969).
*Jon Stallworthy, *Between The Lines* (1963).
Allan Wade, ed., *The Letters of W.B. Yeats* (1954).

Aubrey Beardsley
Aubrey Beardsley, *A Book of Fifty Drawings* (1897)
——*A Second Book of Fifty Drawings* (1899)
——*The Early Work of Aubrey Beardsley* (1899)
——*The Later Work of Aubrey Beardsley* (1901)
——*Under the Hill and Other Essays in Prose and Verse* (1904)
——*The Story of Venus and Tannhäuser* (1907)
——*The Uncollected Work of Aubrey Beardsley* (1925).
Miriam J. Benkovitz, *Aubrey Beardsley: An Account of His Life* (1981).
Brigid Brophy, *Black and White: a Portrait of Aubrey Beardsley* (1968)
*——*Beardsley and his World* (1976).
*Malcolm Easton, *Aubrey and the Dying Lady* (1972).

**Henry Maas, J.L. Duncan and W.G. Good, eds., *The Letters of Aubrey Beardsley* (1970)

Brian Reade, *Aubrey Beardsley* (1966)

*——*Beardsley* (1967)

——and Frank Dickinson, *Aubrey Beardsley Exhibition at the Victoria and Albert Museum* (1966).

Derek Stanford, *Aubrey Beardsley's Erotic Universe* (1967).

Arthur Symons, *Aubrey Beardsley* (1898).

Stanley Weintraub, *Beardsley: a Biography* (1967, 1972)

——*Aubrey Beardsley, Imp of the Perverse* (1976).

Index